CHELSEA FC

IN THE SWINGING '60s

FOOTBALL'S FIRST ROCK 'N' ROLL CLUB

Greg Tesser

The History Press

Acknowledgements

There are far too many people to thank, but pride-of-place must go to former Chelsea star Alan Hudson for his brilliant foreward. These days, Huddy's skills with the pen match his once-famed artistry with a football.

Another handshake must go to photogapher Jeremy Fletcher, whose iconic photographs are featured widely in the book. I first met Jeremy in 1964, and, even though he now lives in Australia, his support during the production of the book has proved invaluable. Another 'super snapper' to thank is Chelsea fan Terry O'Neill, whose ideas so often bore fruit more than forty years ago. Yet another photographer, Richard Sainsbury of Delmar Studios in Taunton, proved to be a wizard with his scanner. And finally, a special thank you to my wife, Gianna, for her support and her regular supply of tea and sandwiches!

Front cover photo © PA Photos.

First published 2013

The History Press
The Mill, Brimscombe Port
Stroud, Gloucestershire, GL5 2QG
www.thehistorypress.co.uk

© Greg Tesser, 2013

The right of Greg Tesser to be identified as the Author
of this work has been asserted in accordance with the
Copyright, Designs and Patents Act 1988.

British Library Cataloguing in Publication Data.
A catalogue record for this book is available from the British Library.

ISBN 978 0 7524 8626 0

Typesetting and origination by The History Press
Printed in Great Britain

FOREWORD

How the times go flying by. The one thing that I have found is that a lot of the people who will be mentioned in Greg's book will not have the same memories that I hold. Age is our biggest opponent when it comes to something like this, and then there are those who never enjoyed such times like we did at Chelsea.

I first met Greg Tesser when agents were scarce; I remember that George Best had Ken Stanley and I had Ken Adam, all pretty new to the job of handling such players. The only difference with Greg and Peter Osgood was that Greg was not only a massive Chelsea fan, but that his client was his hero. Osgood was exactly what he was to the majority of the Chelsea Shed; the King of Stamford Bridge, just as Charlie Cooke was the prince and I was the upcoming young pretender. My respect for these two players went beyond a love for playing the game.

It was, in those days, magical; just like 'The Logical Song' by Supertramp. But then the magic was lost as the game was streamlined and made more 'logical'. For me, however, it remained magical (and always will) as the 1960s led into the '70s – the last incredible period for our game. The Bosman Ruling, which came into being in 1995, finally allowed freedom of contract, but sadly came along far too late for players of our generation.

And after my first long chat with Greg, this is exactly what he is endeavouring to recapture; if it is not magical then it is ordinary, and today there is far too much of that from English players. The likes of Osgood are now a distant memory, which is one of the reasons I took up writing for a hobby.

I wish Greg endless success with his book, knowing that he will capture those magical times. Once it is in print it is something that can never be taken away from you, even if only one copy is published and one person reads it, and hopefully when reading it that person manages to grab just a little of the glitter and gold of those days; glitter and gold that I'm afraid is missing today.

Alan Hudson
Former Chelsea, Stoke City, Arsenal & England star

PROLOGUE

It's different below in the dressing room before a match. There's no cool beer or King's Road dollies, none of the euphoria of up-top – an excitement, sure, but one that's heavy with anxiety; a religious dedication to the rituals being performed. An implicit notion that a life or two may be changed before the day is out.

The floor, a mass of shin pads, shirts, shorts and socks; tracksuits and towels and bottles of oil; tins of Vaseline and packets of studs; hammers and pliers; laces and boots; scissors; bandages and strips of Elastoplast and tufts of cotton, and small grey balls of spat-out gum.

And, tucked unobtrusively in some quiet corner, sterilising in a stainless steel basin of blue alcohol, the tray of surgical instruments, razor sharp scalpels and evil-looking sutures already threaded with brown stitching gut, awesome tools that ring distant alarm bells in the mind and impose a subtle sobriety on the proceedings.

The air smelling hot and linimenty, and everybody milling round like nervous bulls. White-coated helpers rubbing down muscles and studding boots, while the team manager circulates quietly with last-minute words of encouragement and caution. The room full of naked bodies with massively developed calves and thighs topped with chest cages and arms that look fragile in comparison, bending and stretching and windmilling in well-practised warm-ups. Grown men, whose behaviour in the half-hour or so before the kick-off is a gross caricature of their norm. Extroverts clowning away time, while the introverted retreat to private worlds behind walls of trivia, rituals of boot-lacing and nail-cutting. But the tension is getting through to all – you can be sure. You can tell by the forced laughter that greets even the dullest remarks and by the constant procession to the John.

Yes, this is how it is all right. Your guts like water, your thoughts racing on the edge of hallucination. Alone you sit amidst the jock-strapped torsos pulling jerseys over their heads and bandaging ankles, glad for the times when you trained to exhaustion. And heavy with guilt for all those other times when you did less than you might. There will be a reckoning. You know it. Not today perhaps, not tomorrow either. But you will pay. Remote, you sit in this bustling nervous community making an MGM production of trivial tasks on account you don't want time on your hands.

Yes, this is how it is, that feeling close to vomit just before the 'off'. Your skull is aching like it's ready to burst. The tension is almost tangible, thick in the air, and everything is getting quieter, conversations just above a whisper, but with the referee's buzzer, a sudden babble of voices, each wishing the other well, bodies intertwining in ritual handshaking. Some have a soft moist feel, while others offer only their fingers. And some take a firm masculine grip, perhaps clasping your forearm as well, like it should be, you think, and you feel a bit better for it.

Soon you are lined up at the door, everybody marking time, some jostling neurotically for a particular position, slaves to their superstitions, studs nervously clicking on the floor. But finally the door opens and you are in the tunnel, marking time again, your studs clattering on the concrete and your opponents lined up similarly a couple of yards away. You stand there fidgeting, nowhere to put your eyes, never looking at them, not for any length of time anyway. But you can see your opponents from their waist down and your stomach almost turns at the sight of those massive hairy legs, rock-hard columns of muscle that set you thinking that these geezers can probably go like gazelles. And you think of the irony of it all. Maybe 60,000 excited fans up top that would give anything to be down here in your place.

And you? Right now you wouldn't mind being up there, with the cool beer and the King's Road dollies, immersed in the collective euphoria. Yet you know that when the concrete yields to turf, when your studs cease their chatter, and you start to swing the ball about in those long looping practice passes, it will start to be all right again and the game will take over.

Charlie Cooke, Chelsea's Scotland International winger of the 1960s and early '70s penned this (in collaboration with Greg Tesser) in January 1971 in the Club Secretary's office at Stamford Bridge. It was published on 15 March 1971 in *Vogue*.

ONE

THE BEGINNINGS

At the tender age of seven years and seven months I fell in love. Not some kind of pre-pubescent romance with a girl, but with a football club – Chelsea Football Club.

This was many years before I started to knock back chardonnay or Barolo al fresco with all the aesthetes and 'beautiful people' under a gaudy Martini sunshade at a table of an ultra-modish King's Road eatery in the company of Charlie Cooke, or munch shellfish in his cosy Mini or visit Scottish international Stewart Houston in hospital with the King of Stamford Bridge himself, Peter Osgood.

When I was a boy in the embryonic years of the austere 1950s, we had a housekeeper. Her name was Mrs Brooks, and she was all contentment and geniality and old-fashioned reverence. She was large and she waddled, and she had a husband called Percy, who was a dustman, and she was proud of him and the fact that he wore a bowler hat to work. She always called me 'Master Gregory', and in the manner of some Edwardian nanny, spoilt me rotten. She voted Conservative and was a staunch monarchist. She was the archetypal working-class snob.

She knew nothing of football, or soccer as it was always called at my prep school, an establishment where the masters in charge of sport regarded rugger as the real football. Yet there she was on a dank December day in 1954, handing me a hot drink, as I watched Ted Drake's Chelsea on our 9in 'Ekco' TV, purchased by my father in 1949.

I was reclining languidly, almost ostentatiously, in a 1930s Chesterfield with a cup of tea at my side – Mrs Brooks was an ardent advocate of strong, sweet tea as a cure for all ills – for, following a little bit of vomiting just before breakfast, my mother had decided I was too unwell for the rigours of school.

The BBC were broadcasting the second half of Chelsea's friendly with crack Hungarian outfit Red Banner, captained by the legendary Nandor Hidegkuti; his deep-lying centre-forward play had so tormented England twelve months before at Wembley in the Hungarians' 6–3 demolition of the game's founders.

The result was 2–2 in a contest most notable for some of the poorest penalty kicks ever witnessed at Stamford Bridge, but I didn't mind – I was hooked.

Now, I was born in Hornsey Lane Highgate, just a goal-kick away from Arsenal's home of Highbury; yet despite my North London beginnings, I soon latched on to Chelsea. It was the exploits of Roy Bentley that did it, a Roy of the Rovers-style centre forward who banged in the goals with feet and head, and was the archetypal English sporting hero of those monochrome days of rationing, reserve and stiff upper-lip.

Bentley was about thirty years old, but he looked years older. His roughly chiselled face was lined and his forehead contained deep furrows. But these were special men – men who had survived the Second World War and all its many deaths and deprivations and heartaches.

Even for me, a mere child, the Second World War was still all around us, what with the bombsites we played on, still lit-tered with the detritus of the Blitz, visits to the Food Office on Archway Road with my mother, and the ration books and the gas masks that were tucked away on a shelf in the sitting-room, seemingly waiting for action. I had just missed it. I had been conceived just a few weeks before the guns went silent, but it was still everywhere.

At Stamford Bridge, they were getting excited.Never before had the club, so often the butt of music hall jokes for their lack of success, been League Champions. But by the spring of 1955, when Teddy Boys were ripping up the cinema seats to Bill Haley's 'Rock Around The Clock' and James Dean lookalikes were emerging from suburban front-doors, only champions Wolverhampton Wanderers – or Portsmouth – it seemed, could deprive the Blues of the coveted top-flight title.

By this time I was living in an Art Deco block of flats called Brook Lodge in north-west London, on the junction of Brent Street and the North Circular.

Neither of my two best friends was a Chelsea fan. There was Anthony van Straten, whose father was a leading light in the Edmundo Ros Rumba Band. Anthony was quiet and reserved, and his dance-band-dad mirrored his son; certainly not the archetypal Mayfair musician of the time.

But what a man Edmundo was! Thickset, but extremely stylish, he was the personification of suavity. So much so in fact, that he became a favourite of the Royal Family. In fact, the-then Princess Elizabeth danced in public for the very first time to his band at the fashionable Bagatelle Restaurant. Later he performed regularly at Buckingham Palace.

Despite his extravagant and hedonistic lifestyle, Ros had tremendous staying power, and in 2011 he became a centenarian, only to pass away later that same year.

I think I was about eight when I first encountered Ros. He seemed massive, to such an extent that he rather frightened me. He once asked me a question about football – I can't remember why – and I answered rather sheepishly that I wanted to go to Stamford Bridge to watch Chelsea. He just smiled, and said nothing.

Then there was Geoffrey Levy, whose mother had been a fashion model, and whose father, Leslie, owned La Strada restaurant in Hampstead Garden Suburb in partnership with comedian Charlie Chester (another favourite of the Royal Family, he died in 1997).

Incidentally, Charlie was also a fan of the round ball game, with the iconic 'Wizard of the Dribble', Stanley Matthews, being one of his closest friends. I never managed to discover his favourite football team, but three of his contemporaries, fellow comedians Arthur Askey, Jimmy Jewel and Ben Warris were all committed Chelsea supporters.

Geoffrey broke my arm once. We were re-enacting scenes from the Walt Disney film *Davy Crockett, King of The Wild Frontier* – it was all the rage then – and as we fought out the Battle of the Alamo in Brent Park, my arm suddenly snapped like a twig. It wasn't Geoffrey's fault; the doctor said later it could have happened at any time. It had something to do with calcium deficiency in my young bones.

However, his mother took a different view. She was a strict disciplinarian, and she caned him with a long curved thing she kept in a cupboard. She even thrashed him once in my presence. But Geoffrey was brave, for he never shed a tear. This is how it was back then. Cruel by today's standards, but sixty-odd years ago children knew what to expect and existed within strict parameters. As normal boys we realised that if we transgressed, the outcome would be a painful one!

Anyway, Geoffrey was a dab hand with a cricket bat and a budding footballer, and, just days before my father's thrity-seventh birthday, it was suggested that all three of us make the pilgrimage to Stamford Bridge for the Football League Championship-decider with Wolves.

It was 9 April 1955. The weather was mild; almost balmy, and my head was full of the Bill Haley record 'Crazy Man, Crazy', which my father had bought for me from a record emporium in Hendon. It wasn't a new release, for Haley had hit the charts two years before with this ditty that contained the immortal lines: 'Strauss discovered waltzing, the handyman found the blues, crazy man, crazy, crazy news.'

I kept singing the words out loud, and it must have been really irritating for those around me. Maybe that's why my dad inadvertently sat on the disc, smashing it in two. For as the psychiatrists say, there is no such thing as an accident!

At the eleventh hour, Geoffrey decided he couldn't make it, so it was just Tesser senior and junior. How my father managed to make sure we got seats, I don't know, but he was always a supreme fixer.

My father, Victor, a child of the East End, was born during the dying embers of the First World War. He was what is commonly referred to as a 'self-made man'. He had socialist principles, and in fact had been at the front line when Oswald Moseley's odious Blackshirts had goose-stepped their way into Cable Street, a primarily Jewish area, on 4 October 1936. Known as 'the Battle of Cable Street', it was a day that East Londoners still regard as their own personal victory against Fascism – the day that Oswald Moseley's thugs were driven out of their cosmopolitan domain forever.

Ironically, in later years one of my father's closest friends proved to be the late Clem Mitford (Lord Redesdale), a nephew of Moseley's wife Diana. An elegant, easy-going chap, he later helped me with the launch of my very own football magazine – but more of that later.

Fast-forward nineteen years and by this time my father was a successful businessman, owning a silk screen-printing works in Belsize Park, 'Studio Torron', just a stone's throw away from Hampstead Heath – plus a photographic studio in Dean Street, Soho.

Despite his humble beginnings and rudimentary education, and the fact that his parents – his father from Poland, his mother from Odessa in Ukraine – spoke in Yiddish, my father learned as a young man to cultivate and develop what used to be termed a 'cultured voice'. He was also a serial name-dropper, having at a comparatively early stage in his life somehow managed to befriend actors, aristocrats, politicians and writers.

Both actor Richard Burton and Welsh writer Dylan Thomas – he of *Under Milk Wood* – were his regular drinking companions, mainly at the Cruel Sea, a far from prepossessing pub in Heath Street, Hampstead, where a diverse bunch of bohemians and polymaths would hold court as the alcohol-fuelled voices rose to a crescendo and every ill of society was addressed and cured. They were, by the standards of the 1950s, long-haired young men, many wearing corduroy jackets with leather patches.

It was certainly a far-cry from the likes of Hoxton and Stepney in the East End, but my father's roots were to hold him in good stead when chatting and fraternising with the likes of Rodney Marsh and Bobby Moore. Marsh in particular was proud of his Stepney heritage, and my father and he, despite being of different generations, would revel in comparing nostalgic notes.

So back to the big day itself – 9 April 1955. There were 75,000-plus crammed into Stamford Bridge and many thousands locked out. Flat caps covering Brylcreemed bonces and fags everywhere. Just a shame the game itself was as dour as a Sunday afternoon in January in an English country town, but it didn't matter a jot because Chelsea won 1–0, courtesy of a Peter Sillett penalty. Champions Wolves were but a pale shadow of the side that had advanced so imperiously to the title the previous season.

The 1955 Championship-winning celebration party at that Art Deco monument to good taste, the Dorchester hotel on Park Lane, was indeed a glittering occasion. As former boss Tommy Docherty so aptly put it many years later, 'Chelsea has always been a showbiz club'. On that spring night nearly sixty years ago, the gathered players, wives, girlfriends and club directors and officials danced until the wee small hours to the music of the suave Victor 'Slow-Slow-Quick-Quick-Slow' Sylvester, a diehard Chelsea fan since boyhood.

As an aside to this, many years later I found myself discussing the fortunes of Chelsea during the immediate post-war years with scriptwriter extraordinaire Alan Simpson, he of *Hancock's Half Hour* and *Steptoe and Son* fame.

In a twist of fate that had serious *It's a Wonderful Life* overtones, he told me how if in his youth he hadn't been dealt a particularly dud card, it could well have been Simpson between the sticks during that title-winning season and not the Scottish goalkeeper Bill Robertson.

Simpson's story is one that, in terms of cinematic licence, would be deemed too 'far-fetched'. It all starts on a bleak Boxing Day in 1946. Alan is in goal for crack amateur outfit Dulwich Hamlet at their – by the standards of the time – palatial home of Champion Hill. A senior Chelsea scout was in attendance, his brief being to check on this young up-and-coming 'keeper.

Let Alan himself tell the story: 'My first touch of the ball was to retrieve it from the back of the net. But we did win the game 8–3, and the scout must have been impressed because before I knew it I'd received a letter offering me a trial at Stamford Bridge in June 1947.'

His idol was Blues custodian Vic Woodley, a member of the hellraising team of the 1930s that included the pocket dynamo Hughie Gallacher, known for his size 6 boots, white spats and forty-a-day Woodbines habit, who later tragically committed suicide. Another member was the elegant Scottish international winger, Alex Jackson, who soon immersed himself in the nightlife of London's West End.

'I wanted to be another Vic Woodley,' he admitted to me. 'So, when the opportunity arose to actually play in a game, you can imagine how excited I felt.'

But fate took a hand for the young Simpson in the shape of tuberculosis, a disease that spread its malignant tentacles throughout Western Europe during the aftermath of the Second World War.

Deprived of his Stamford Bridge trial, Alan found himself hospitalised in one form or another for three solid years, during which time he befriended Ray Galton and the legend that became Tony Hancock was created.

So, my Chelsea 'debut' had been and gone; a highly satisfactory one at that. Okay, so the Blues had clinched the Division One crown for the first time, with the lowest number of points ever accrued from 42 matches, but that didn't bother me because by this time I was besotted with the team from Stamford Bridge, and there was still my boyhood idol Jimmy Greaves to come!

TWO

JIMMY GREAVES AND THE NO.28 BUS

Golders Green station, London NW11, circa 1957. It's autumn; the conker season is in full swing and a young boy is waiting by a bus stop, looking resplendent in his pink blazer and cap, both adorned with the black Maltese Cross.

He's waiting for the No.28 bus, and despite his overt prep school uniform and its obvious class associations with the ruffians' game played by gentlemen (otherwise known as rugby), he's soon to be on his way to Stamford Bridge to cheer on Chelsea, and in particular their new seventeen-year-old wunderkind James Peter Greaves.

The first time I saw Jimmy Greaves was on television. It was a youth international involving England and Luxembourg in 1957, and the precocious Greaves and his equally intoxicating Chelsea sidekick winger Peter Brabrook were tormenting the Luxembourg defence in the manner of a cat with an unusually submissive mouse. Commentator Kenneth Wolstenholme – he of 'They think it's all over – well it is now!' – was in raptures.

England netted seven goals with just one in reply. Jimmy helped himself to five of them – a unique star was indeed born.

Later, I regularly used to hop on a bus at Golders Green and make my way to West Hendon to watch the Chelsea youth team in action in the South East Counties League. These were the first occasions that I saw the precocious Greaves in the flesh, and he didn't let me down. When he was around it was always backache time for opposition 'keepers!

So, there I was waiting for my bus. I got on, and the long trek to the Bridge began. West End Lane; Kilburn, and then through the sad streets of Westbourne Grove, where the newly arrived West Indian population had created this wondrous world of speciality shops, selling such food items as capsicums, chilli peppers and plantains.

As we drove through Westbourne Grove into Notting Hill Gate and then Kensington, the atmosphere changed. It was 1950s London again, not this new burgeoning cosmopolitan creation. Twelve months later the peace and tranquillity of this new part of the West Indies was going to be temporarily destroyed by yes, you've guessed it, the odious Oswald Mosley and his Union Movement organisation, founded in 1948, for the ignorant and warped, the bitter and twisted.

Preying on the disaffected youth of the time – mainly ill-educated Teddy Boys – Mosley and his cohorts cultivated a hatred of all human beings who were not white, to such an extent and with so much 'success' that eventually in August 1958, it all boiled over, and racial violence, previously unseen in Britain, took hold for at least a fortnight.

Arriving at Fulham Broadway tube station, my first duty was to buy a programme. Only 6*d* (under 3p nowadays), it was glossy and a good read. Despite being only eleven years old, and despite the fact that I was on my own, and despite the fact that it was a floodlit game, I paid my pennies – six of them, I think – to stand on the cavernous terrace on the halfway line. This was no place for the faint-hearted, as you seemed to spend the full ninety minutes being either buffeted or elbowed, in a constant surge of sweaty humanity shrouded in a fog of tobacco smoke.

Birmingham City visited that autumn evening, and little did I know that I was about to witness football's equivalent to Mozart, in the slight shape of Jimmy Greaves, score one of the most flamboyant goals ever witnessed in London SW6.

Some forty-odd years later I asked Jimmy about this exquisite Birmingham goal – and indeed about his whole Chelsea experience. With modesty itself, and that characteristic little-boy twinkle in his eye, he took me back to that special era when the team epitomised inconsistency (along with often eccentric defending), and Stamford Bridge itself resembled some form of cathedral to post-war austerity with its peeling paint and tired wooden stands and chipped white mugs selling Bovril. It seemed already to be of a bygone age, like an aristocrat who has fallen on hard times.

Unfortunately, this Birmingham goal, despite being an individual effort in which he danced past defender after defender before teasing the 'keeper in the manner of a serial seducer, and then delicately – almost nonchalantly – slotting the ball home, was not one that had remained in Jimmy's memory bank.

As he admitted, some goals he remembered, some he didn't, but one thing he did explain to me was his basic ethos for finding the net.

'I always felt you didn't have to hammer the ball into the net,' he told me. 'After all, all the ball has to do is cross the line, and it's a goal. Too many players these days seem to blast it without picking the spot.'

One encounter that has since gone down in Chelsea folklore was their 6–2 victory over League Champions Wolves in 1958. I was there in the stands, aged twelve-and-a-bit, to witness this humbling of the mighty.

I was feeling pretty upbeat already, as I had just bought Cliff Richard's first single 'Move It', and just couldn't help myself as, *sotto voce*, I hummed along. It was actually the B Side to 'Schoolboy Crush', but it soon whizzed up the charts, and B became A, so to speak. It was the first English rock 'n' roll song, according to John Lennon.

Anyway, let's get back to the grinning Jimmy Greaves, almost purring like the proverbial Cheshire Cat, as he described how the embryonic stars of Chelsea had tormented their battle-hardened opponents on that humid August afternoon at Stamford Bridge in front of over 62,000 joyous supporters. The fact that I was there, cheering on my idol – albeit a drooling schoolboy fan looking out of place in my blazer and pink school cap, like William from *Just William* but without the mishaps and messy fingers – was not lost on this football icon. He made me somehow feel part of it all.

'It was the first time I'd scored five goals in the First Division,' he told me. 'Wolves were the best team in England in those days, and many people said that this was the game that made Billy Wright decide to retire. I think he'd made up his mind before that, but yeah, it was a great day.'

He also became animated when describing how he perfected his skills in the back streets of 1950s austerity England, his whole face lighting up like a beacon.

'We'd just get an old tennis ball out and play in the street,' he explained. 'Playing with a small ball was great. It could be 20-a-side, 30-a-side or even just 2-a-side, and your stomach told you when to finish – you just went in when you were hungry. But you learnt the skills. You certainly weren't having it talked out of you by a coach – you just learnt it all yourself.'

I saw Jimmy's final game for Chelsea on 29 April 1961, and the little man certainly knew how to write the script, scoring all four goals in their 4-3 win over Nottingham Forest. His fourth was his 41st goal of the season, and Chelsea's 98th. Mind you, their defence was porous in the extreme, conceding 100!

Jimmy was off then – to Italy, Milan to be exact. However, the land of pasta and pinot grigio and Sophia Loren wasn't to his taste, and, despite a fatter wallet, the lure of London proved too great. He wanted to return to the Bridge, but Spurs came up with a bigger offer – £99,999 – and so sadly my idol was now in the enemy camp. Also by the age of fifteen, I had 'discovered' James Dean and Jack Kerouac!

Little did I know then that a mere eight years later I would be discussing the merits of Kerouac, Fitzgerald and Hemingway with that footballer with the dancing feet, Charlie Cooke, who, quoting Kerouac himself, 'dug' all things from across the pond.

Despite being entranced by the performance of James Dean in *East of Eden* and wishing I could do a Dean Moriarty and go *On The Road* in America, I remained very much married to the Blues. Relegated to Division Two in 1962, with Tommy Docherty in charge, they regained top-flight status twelve months later in the only way possible for Chelsea, with the sort of Hitchcockian twists and turns and traumas that have been the London club's norm since its inception in 1905.

THREE

SNOWDRIFTS AND TOMMY'S STOMACH

Boxing Day 1962, and the first flakes are being blown crazily in the biting easterly wind. Chelsea are at Luton. Despite the arctic conditions, and with a frost as sharp as flint, the game goes ahead.

Docherty's Chelsea boys are riding high at the summit of Division Two. It is a young side, with Barry Bridges, he of the cheetah-like speed, and penalty-area predator Bobby Tambling the shining lights.

The Blues prevail 2–0 at Luton and all is sweetness and light. A quick return to the top division as champions is a surely a given. But dear old Mother Nature had other ideas.

'The snow will continue in London and the South East for several hours and then turn to rain,' said the BBC Home Service Announcer just prior to the Boxing Day News. But unfortunately the Meteorological Office was way off beam with this forecast. Not only did the white stuff continue to fall from the sky; far from 'turning to rain', it regrouped and found a new lease of life. Two days of solid snow was enough to bring London to a standstill. Maybe it wasn't quite a white Christmas, but never before had so much white been seen on the Feast of Stephen!

Now, having endured a winter which had so far thrown up snow in November and the last of the great London pea-souper fogs in December, complete with sub-zero temperatures and a bone-chilling hoar frost, little did the population of Greater London realise what was to come, in the huge white shape of a blizzard possessed of so much anger and viciousness and violence that even a mundane activity such as opening a front door became a task of Herculean proportions.

It was 29 December and the wind moaned like a soul in torment as the snow cascaded down crazily. It was Saturday night, not far off the witching hour, and I was at a family party, watching David Frost and his pals on the box in *That Was The Week That Was*. A few minutes after the programme came to a halt, guests started to leave, but we were unable to open our front door as snowdrifts as tall as the average child had formed themselves into grotesquely shaped igloos.

Chelsea were top-dogs at Christmas, but the big freeze not only pulled the plug on virtually all competitive football for months, it also put a big white dampener on the promotion aspirations of Docherty's charges.

Despite taking his squad to Malta for some sunshine and match practice, Docherty's young team seemed edgy and lacking in confidence when they eventually returned to competitive League football. In a contest that some-how managed to survive the conditions at Swansea on 9 February 1963, they went down 2–0 and looked a shadow of the pre-Freeze outfit.

At first the Swansea result was regarded as a minor aber-ration, but with continuity lost thanks to the arctic conditions, whenever Chelsea did manage to play, they somehow con-trived to lose. As loss followed loss, the confidence, which with such a young team was based on the innate swagger of youth itself, evaporated to be replaced by jangling nerves and uncertainty. Certainly desperation was becoming the order of the day down at the Bridge, as long-term victory was turning into short-term defeat.

Come 11 May 1963, it looked all over for Docherty's young bucks. It seemed that only a home victory over top-of-the-heap Stoke City, Sir Stanley Matthews and all, could keep their promotion aspirations alive. Defeat, and all the pre-Christmas euphoria would dissolve into one massive squelchy debacle amidst the springtime slush.

On that spring afternoon 66,000 were packed into Stamford Bridge. Stoke's line-up included veterans Jimmy McIlroy, Jackie Mudie and the forty-eight-year-old Matthews. Seventeen-year-old Chelsea defender Ronnie Harris, in the days before he was christened 'Chopper', was briefed to mark the iconic Matthews. At one stage, the great man was poleaxed by the tough teenager, and despite his gentlemanly image, Sir Stan made his feelings known with a litany of ripe words.

A 1–0 defeat and Chelsea's dreams seemed dashed. Only victory away at Sunderland – Roker Road and all – would realise Docherty's dream, but this seemed about as unlikely as a Labour General Election victory. But as John Profumo's affair with Christine Keeler had hijacked the fortunes of the Tory party, so Tommy Harmer's groin – or his 'third leg' as Sunderland skipper Stan Anderson described it – put paid to their advance to the top division.

I actually spoke to Harmer on two occasions; once, when as a teenage fan in the stands I watched Chelsea take on Wimbledon one afternoon in the early 1960s at Stamford Bridge in the London Challenge Cup, and then much later, a year or two after I had teamed-up with Peter Osgood, and the Wizard was wowing them down the King's Road.

As a callow youth I sat next to the little waif that was the impish Harmer. I plucked up the courage and asked him about his 'fluke goal' at Sunderland.

'It went in off my groin,' he said, 'I didn't really know much about it.'

Later – much later, when I was full of the joys of spring 'doing deals' for Peter Osgood – a journalist friend introduced me to Tommy at a game. He was just as polite as he had been seven or eight years before and once more the fluke Sunderland goal came into the conversation. 'It was just one of those things,' he admitted.

A little later, Chelsea pillaged Portsmouth 7–0 at the Bridge in front of 57,000 supporters high on rapture and relief, and there was a pitch invasion (a friendly one, no coming-together of drunken fans and over-enthusiastic stewards);

and boss Docherty announced to the crowd that 'promotion to Division One would be worth £100,000 to the club'.

So, the mini Ice Age had ended; 1963 was to become 1964, and the country was soon to rock to a social change that altered British society. However, it was an urban thing, and away from Carnaby Street and the Cavern Club, life was just an extension of the 1950s. People still 'knew their place', and law and order and respect for authority were king. Murder was still a hanging offence; children were regularly beaten at schools; abortion was punishable by incarceration and being gay risked confinement in one of Her Majesty's prisons.

Harold Wilson's Labour Party won the 1964 General Election by a squeak, with a mere four seats separating the overall majority. The Conservative Party, rocked by scandal, was at the crossroads. The grandees within the party had a dilemma – change or be damned; and since those early days of The Beatles and The Rolling Stones, it has been ever thus.

As for Chelsea FC, one match in 1964 stands out above all others – the FA Cup third round replay at Stamford Bridge against Tottenham Hotspur. Some forty years later I asked Jimmy Greaves about this iconic encounter, but surprisingly his memory was hazy – in fact, he said he didn't remember it at all. Jokingly, he quipped, 'I was probably pissed at the time!'

The first contest ended in stalemate: 1–1 with Terry Dyson opening the scoring for Spurs. The second game was a headline writer's dream.

All-ticket affairs were (apart from the FA Cup Final and England v Scotland battles that is) non-existent. But for a variety of reasons, this Cup tie captured the imagination of the London public to such a surreal extent that traffic on the Fulham Road became gridlocked as more and more people attempted to pay at the gate. Chaos reigned supreme!

Exactly 70,123 packed into the decrepit old lady that was Stamford Bridge circa 1964. A host of season ticket holders, most notably Tory Transport Minister Ernest Marples, were denied access. Mr Marples, the man behind both the M1 Motorway and Premium Bonds, was, understandably, more than just a wee bit peeved.

The game itself was a real one-off. It was a strange sight; the 'yoof' of blue-shirted Chelsea starlets trying to knock the elder statesmen of North London off their elevated perch. The Blues, inspired by Terry Venables – 'Docherty's Diamonds', as they were called – buzzed around Spurs like a swarm of blue bees on speed. There was only one team in it.

Despite missing a penalty, Venables had a great night, and it came as no surprise when little Bert Murray found the net. Bobby Tambling added a second, and the cheers were heard all the way down the King's Road to Sloane Square and beyond.

I got to know Terry later when acting as Rodney Marsh's agent; in fact I did a few journo things with him. I also attended a benefit dinner he had organised (I'd given him a cheque for £25 whilst reclining in Marsh's brand-new Lotus Europa) in aid of Queens Park Rangers central defender Frank Sibley, who was forced to retire at the tender age of twenty-three because of a serious knee injury.

As the food disappeared and more and more champagne flowed, I mentioned the 1964 Cup-tie. His eyes lit up as he became more and more animated, and he told me it was one of those matches that remained in the memory forever. I am sure by this time my speech had become slurred and as thick as school custard, and I probably had one of those idiotic smiles on my face, but he answered my questions seriously, yet at the same time his eyes laughed – he had a real touch of the showbiz about him.

It was 1964 and the Chelsea *v.* Spurs epic was indeed a landmark game. For years, the 'End of The World Is Nigh'-merchants had been predicting that the decline in football attendances would continue at an alarming rate, but here was an example of football capturing the public's imagination; in many ways it was a sign of how London was beginning to swing and become the chic capital of the world.

Chelsea finished the season in fifth spot, seven points adrift of champions Liverpool. As fans, we knew we were on the cusp of something big – something momentous in the club's chequered history. It could take a few years, but the Bridge was fast becoming the buzzword in London's football circles. And the Soho waiters, those connoisseurs of all things Chelsea football, were often seen leaving their posts in droves to cheer on Docherty's men – they knew the 'days of wine and roses' were not far away.

As for me, I was about to enter the labyrinths of Soho, the Blues and rock 'n' roll, and Andrew Loog Oldham, the man known as the fifth Rolling Stone, who wore green make-up – in short, the land of the artful dodgers and fornicators and fixers who frequented Tin Pan Alley.

FOUR

THE YARDIFYING YARDBIRDS AND NOT FORGETTING CHELSEA

In 1964 there was more blues music being played in Kingston and Surbiton than Chicago.

So, as an eighteen-year-old, giving a 'V-sign' to any thoughts of Oxford or Cambridge – they wanted me but I didn't want them! – I bought a pair of expensive Chelsea boots to go with my Italian shades; made sure I had my soft packet of Disque Bleu fags neatly tucked into my Lord John jacket; put on my solid gold ID bracelet, making sure it hung limply – almost apologetically – on my wrist à la Jerry Lee Lewis, and announced to my father that I wanted to be 'another Andrew Loog Oldham'.

Oldham was all flamboyance and Hollywood kitsch; you could say he orchestrated his own presence. He drove round London in a shiny American limousine – a Caddy or some such – making calls on his car phone. On his well-defined, almost beaky nose were green-tinted spectacles. He had what became known as 'attitude'. It was all an act, of course, and he knew it was all an act, but he revelled in it; the job of hauling in huge quantities of the folding stuff was for him like some massive game of Monopoly.

Andrew – I never imagined anyone addressing him as Andy – was a narcissistic hustler. In 1963, aged just nineteen, he had helped publicise Bob Dylan's first UK tour and had also assisted The Beatles' manager Brian Epstein. Then in the spring of '63 his whole life changed when he saw a group sing blues and rock.

Now this group (we didn't call them bands then) had already built-up a Home Counties following, thanks to the efforts of a wild Georgian (the birthplace of the odious Joseph Stalin), with a Swiss passport named Giorgio Gomelsky. However, no contract had been signed and when the cocky young Oldham turned up and spieled, the group put pen to paper and The Rolling Stones were born.

Our family business, Studio Torron, had first seen the light of day back when London was recovering from the Blitz – 1942 to be exact. It was a company specialising in the art of silk-screen printing – cinema posters, government posters and the like.

It thrived, and my father soon had a clientele list of interesting and often outlandish characters. He built up a rapport with film director Roman Polanski, and in so doing produced dynamic posters for two of Polankski's acclaimed movies, *Knife in the Water* (1962) and *Repulsion* (1965).

Later in the '60s, he embarked on the idea of producing pennants – small triangular posters – of headline pop acts including Peter and Gordon and (most notably) The Rolling Stones. And so he met Andrew Oldham and his business partner Peter Meaden, and so did I.

Talking of Meaden, despite his untimely death at the age of thirty-six, his influence remains to this day. Another exhibitionist and hustler, he is often given the title 'The Mod Father' or 'Mod God' by modern rock-culture historians.

Probably his biggest claim to fame was discovering The Who. He changed the band's name to The High Numbers, and they released a record, 'I'm The Face', aimed at their Mod fans. The disc bombed, with most of the copies being bought by Meaden himself. He later lost control of the group, and teamed up with Oldham. The High Numbers reverted to The Who, and the rest, as they say, is history!

Meaden never struck me as a contented man, and sadly, in 1978, he died of a barbiturate overdose.

Anyway, my father got on really well with these two people, and when I was introduced to Oldham, I literally shook with excitement.

It was at our house in Hampstead, and Andrew and Peter sat reclining languidly in the sitting room smoking cigars. I attempted to do the same, but forgetting to snip off the end, I failed miserably. I even tried to get a flame via the electric fire. Boy did I feel a fool! However, thankfully Andrew was more than interested in my record collection, which was pretty way-out, made up as it was by a whole clutch of LPs sent to me by my Aunt Trudie from America.

To say The Rolling Stones' manager was interested in these records would be an understatement. However, he never seemed to display any emotion in his waxwork-like face, which at times resembled Mr Sardonicus in that cult William Castle horror film of the '60s of the same name – frozen in the manner of a Botox OD.

Two Lavern Baker albums particularly fascinated him, as he scrutinised them in the manner of a pathologist examining a body found in suspicious circumstances, and he asked me if I'd lend them to him. I agreed, but never saw them again. How he utilised them, I'm not sure, but rest assured he would have done.

Having endured my 'audition' with Andrew Oldham, I set about aping him. But I was, and still am, a romantic, and I found this hard to achieve, for his brand of wheeling-and-dealing did not come naturally to me. So, any outgoing cockiness or overconfidence on my part was one big overblown charade. However, I remained undaunted, and set about 'finding' a rock group of my very own. My Chelsea boots were at long last doing some walking!

I got to know Pete Bardens through a guy called Dave Ambrose. Bardens was the leader of The Cheynes, a progressive band appearing regularly on the under card at The Marquee in Soho's Wardour Street. A nervous, shy man, Bardens was not an easy man to approach, but despite his diffidence, he did indicate a modicum of interest in my becoming their publicity manager. So I jumped into a black cab and made my way to that unapologetic haven of hedonism to see them perform live.

John Mayall's Bluesbreakers topped the bill that spring evening in 1964, playing their unique brand of blues.

The Marquee was by no means packed, but it was full enough, and that particular aroma of cigarette smoke and sweaty bodies, mixed with a fragrance of whisky and coke, so evocative of 1960s clubs, gave it a special ambience.

The Cheynes were good – maybe not sensational – but they looked disaffected and rebellious enough to be emblematic of this cultural change; this youth-based rejection of values that had remained entrenched in British society since the Depression years of the 1930s.

I did my best, but essentially Bardens was a loner, a man who wore the total rejection of all things commercial on his sleeve – very similar in character to Chelsea footballer Charlie Cooke. He was certainly not driven by money. A bit later Bardens must have changed, as indeed seemingly did Cooke.

Having left The Cheynes, Peter Bardens went on to perform with some of rock music's most iconic performers, including Van Morrison in Them and Rod Stewart, Peter Green and Mick Fleetwood in Shotgun Express. He sadly died in January 2002, aged fifty-six.

Anyway, I did a little bit of PR for The Cheynes, but realising there was no future in this I somehow wangled a job in 'the British Tin Pan Alley'.

Bob Baker was tall and blond. He wore pinstripe suits, and somewhat bizarrely, Chelsea boots. He had been a whiz-kid with Warner Bros, but the lure of the burgeoning British music scene proved too strong, so there he was in the spring of 1964, heading a PR organisation at No. 7 Denmark Street called Press Presentations. This was a new company, but several of its clients were potential headliners, with Georgie Fame, Screaming Lord Sutch and The Savages, The Yardbirds and Zoot Money's Big Roll Band, the prime potential money-spinners.

Now, Denmark Street circa 1964 was not only a cosmopolitan place, with its close proximity to the drinking dens and fleshpots of Soho; it was also the hub of the British pop music industry, known as 'the British Tin Pan Alley' (there already being a Tin Pan Alley in New York) – a microcosm of the changing landscape of British culture.

Having rejected university, and failed rather miserably to emulate Andrew Loog Oldham, I had no choice but to swallow my pride and get a job – but what a job it proved to be!

Bob Baker was regarded as a highly effective wheeler-and-dealer at Warner Bros, and there was no doubt he was ambitious, almost obsessively so. However, his aspirations – even to me, a rookie eighteen-year-old – seemed sometimes to verge on the fantastical.

My father had 'done deals' with him, and following his persuasive tongue, the enigmatic Baker agreed to take me on as his number two. He had the experience, but my youth gave me a huge advantage over him. He was stuck rigidly in the 1950s, whereas I was part of this new generation – a generation that was doing its utmost to bring colour to a monochrome London – a London that was finding a new identity as bands all over the West End played the blues and reinvented rock 'n' roll.

It is a Monday morning in late March 1964. The time is 9 a.m. The location is La Gioconda, an Italian café on Denmark Street, specialising in the all-day breakfast many years before such a culinary creation was known to the British public.

Now, the 'Gio' was, to young eyes, a wondrous place. To your left could be George Harrison tucking into egg on toast, while at the same time behind you, Eric Clapton or John Lennon or the-then unknown David Bowie were filling up on beans and strong coffee.

At a table, tackling a huge plate of baked beans sit three people, one, a wide-eyed eighteen-year-old – the other two, more cynical men in suits. The younger of the threesome is told he would soon be meeting some of the company's more illustrious clients – the musicians and their managers. Little then did this teenager appreciate what was in store for him; the gangsters, the dances till dawn, the drugs and the drink and the whole madcap stuff that were to dominate his life for several years, not forgetting trying to find time to make for Fulham Broadway and Stamford Bridge to cheer on Chelsea.

Having acquainted himself with his office and met the secretary Ursula, a young lady with the voice of Wendy Richard and the face of Sandie Shaw, he embarks upon a series of meetings with his boss, Bob Baker. Lucky Strike gaspers are smoked incessantly as ideas are thrown around. As the air gradually becomes thick with tobacco smoke, the youngster listens as the older man spouts loads of meaningless words about exposure and promotion and PR and publicity. In the boy's opinion all this is old hat – it has absolutely nothing to do with what is going on in the country, or more specifically, what is happening in London.

As his eyes glaze over, he falls into a reverie, but reality returns when Bob Baker exclaims: 'Greg, do you have a formal suit you can wear?'

Baffled and bemused by his question, I replied, rather sarcastically, that I did, and then, in the manner of a schoolboy, speaking to a particularly strict teacher, I said, almost *sotto voce*, 'But why do you ask?', just missing was the word 'Sir'.

His argument was that, despite my youth and self-professed 'hipster' attitudes, I had to remain 'above the artists' in terms of persona. To cut a long story short, I acquiesced and turned up the next day wearing a Cecil Gee creation, complete with pristine white Oxford shirt and burnished black brogues.

Coffees and teas at La Gioconda often resembled mini-board meetings, and it was there that I first discovered that Baker was just using Press Presentations as a stepping-stone to 'greater things'. The other thing I soon realised was that he was ultra-professional, but only in terms of dealing with erratic and often thuggish rock managers and acting as a suave maître d' at high-level press receptions. When it came to ideas he was, in my book, out of touch.

Anyway, after these preliminary exchanges, which I must admit I found somewhat deflating and tedious, it was time for me to be introduced to the various agents, managers and star names that kept the company's kitty happy.

The first time I met Giorgio Gomelsky, I thought I was in the presence of Grigori Rasputin, the mad mystic who had dominated the lives of the ill-fated Russian Royal Family, the Romanovs. His hair was greasy and wild, and he waved his hands around like some demented tic-tac man at the Derby. He had this habit of staring at you, and if some-thing, no matter how outlandish, appealed to his aesthetic sense, he shouted 'knockout!'

Born in the old Soviet Republic of Georgia, his early life saw the family travel extensively throughout Europe, eventu-ally settling in Switzerland in the 1940s, which explained why by 1964 he had managed to get hold of a Swiss passport. He drove his Ferrari or Maserati or whatever it was like the wind – in fact his skill with the steering wheel was witnessed to good effect in the Mille Miglia, Italy's answer to the Le Mans 24-hour endurance race.

Giorgio was manager and general all-round guru of The Yardbirds. His eye for talent was masterly, but this innate talent was negated by a complete lack of any normal busi-ness practice.

Here was a man who had discovered The Rolling Stones – he was the group's first manager before the hustler that was Andrew Loog Oldham came sauntering in to 'pinch' them – and who later turned The Yardbirds into London's number one cult band. And if that wasn't enough he launched the career of the enigmatic and ethereal beauty Julie Driscoll – 'The Face'. He was also a mass of contra-dictions, one minute waxing lyrical about art and the blues and the next minute arguing with Eric Clapton on the direc-tion the band should take, with Clapton being the purist and Giorgio wearing his 'we need to become more commercial to make money' hat.

Maureen Cleave interviewed all the great and good of British pop culture in the 1960s. Her page in the *London Evening Standard* became a must-read for any one embroiled in the mushrooming rock scene. She spoke with what used to be called a 'cut glass accent', was elegant to the point of perfection, and cultivated a close relation-ship with The Beatles. In fact it was during the interview with John Lennon that he came out with those famous or infamous – depending on your viewpoint – words in March 1966: 'Christianity will go. It will vanish and shrink. I needn't argue with that; I'm right and I will be proved right.

We're more popular than Jesus now; I don't know which will go first – rock 'n' roll or Christianity. Jesus was all right but his disciples were thick and ordinary. It's them twisting it that ruins it for me.'

So, when it came to The Yardbirds being interviewed by Cleave, Giorgio Gomelsky – always a man to demand that he be the centre of attention – did his utmost to curb his more extravagant instincts.

Cleave was class, but as a young man with little experience of columnist headliners, she struck me as snooty and frankly up herself. 'Are you in the group too?' she asked me rather dismissively. 'No,' I replied sheepishly. 'I'm with their publicity people.'

A wave of the hand dismissed me from the scene, and the interview began. Her attitude made me all the more determined to fight my corner. 'I bet she wouldn't treat Andrew Oldham like that,' I said to myself.

My first organised media interview session was over, and I felt deflated. Cultural revolution was in the air, but none of this seemed to permeate through to the people with whom I was working. And my next 'assignment', a meeting with Georgie Fame's manager Rik Gunnell, only reinforced this general feeling of being let down.

Even as a teenager, I was no shrinking violet, but Gunnell frightened me. He exuded gangster from every pore, and even his smile was creepy. Georgie Fame once described him as 'a loveable villain', but in my book there was nothing remotely 'loveable' about him!

In stature Gunnell was broad – he had boxed as an amateur in his youth – and he always donned tinted spectacles, which only added to his Hollywood gangster hard man image. Born in Germany, he and his British father (who feared internment if war was declared) settled in London in 1937.

After a series of dead-end jobs in the early 1950s, which included that of a bouncer at the Studio 51 jazz club, specialising in the modish bebop sound of Charlie Parker, he opened his own club, the 2-Way, headlining such diverse home grown talents as Johnny Dankworth and George Melly.

His second excursion into club ownership, the Blue Room, was a financial failure. Typically, he skipped the scene, later to reappear telling all and sundry that he'd been living in Paris, 'The City of Light', hustling around and promoting low-level fights.

Later he bought the Flamingo Club in Wardour Street; at first glance it seemed to be just another seedy-looking Soho venue, but in reality it was a citadel – a temple at which, every weekend, worshippers would arrive en masse to pray and affirm their belief in this new religion of unadulterated 'having a good time – for tomorrow will never come'.

It was at the Flamingo that Georgie Fame (with his Blue Flames) morphed from utility backing bloke for Billy Fury to coolness and cult. His jazz-inspired blues, with serious Mose Allison overtones, entranced the cosmopolitan crowd that flocked to Gunnell's club. Here was a heady mixture of Mods and gangsters and pimps and prostitutes and American servicemen; where black faces were as common as white, and any thoughts of colour were washed away in this swathe of sweat and smoke. Fame later recalled his early days at the Flamingo: 'There were only a handful of hip young white people that used to go to the club. When I first went there as a punter I was scared. Once I started to play there, it was no problem.'

Friday nights were dance 'til dawn nights. At 6 a.m. the Mods and cool dudes would meander slowly out of the club, all bleary-eyed and zoned-out, having had their fix of Georgie Fame, or the other Gunnell headliner, Zoot Money and his Big Roll Band.

I first met Georgie Fame face-to-face in a pub on Old Compton Street with an EMI publicity bod in attendance. I was nervous and a bit tongue-tied, but managed to get on pretty well with the cool Lancastrian, who didn't say very much.

Much later, I organised all the PR folderol for Georgie's twenty-first birthday party, held at Rik Gunnell's Gerrard Street office in Chinatown. It was 12 June 1964, and the sun shone and Soho glistened like some vibrant lipstick worn by a voluptuous vamp on the prowl.

Chris Farlowe was there and Elkie Brooks added a touch of authentic female glamour. There was a cake and I had made sure the press and all the in-snappers were there in force. It went extremely well, and despite always feeling uneasy in Gunnell's company – his stare was enough to give you the heebie-jeebies – I found myself chatting to Georgie's uncle. He was a lovely little chap, all gnarled and folksy. He seemed incredibly old – almost wizened in fact – and he had this thin fag permanently glued to his top lip. In build there was something of the Wilfrid Brambell (in his father Steptoe role) about him.

Now Fame's real name was Clive Powell, so his uncle, who was a miner by the way, obviously spoke of 'Clive this' and 'Clive that'. He asked me how much Clive made on average each week. I told him – I cannot remember the actual figure I gave – and his sparse eyebrows were raised as he said to me in his thin Lancashire accent: 'That's more than you get for a whole year down the pits.'

Now I was getting a bit restless, what with Bob Baker disappearing all over the place, so when I learned that he had this fantasy of opening some kind of cool nightclub for kids in Colchester, roping in a load of media people and getting them to fork out the folding stuff as well, I thought it was about time I became recognised as these bands' publicity manager. But I needed something that would make them all sit up. And it was then that Lord Ted Willis made a speech in the House of Lords.

Ted Willis was a dedicated Labour Party man and a Spurs supporter. He had been ennobled just twelve months before, thanks in part to the pulling of strings by pragmatic party leader Harold Wilson. A talented writer of film scripts and TV plays, he is best remembered as the creator of *Dixon of Dock Green*, undoubtedly the most successful BBC series of the 1950s and early '60s. Starring the evergreen Jack Warner, it portrayed the London copper as a thoroughly decent bloke, brimful of homespun philosophy and genuine compassion. A bit wishy-washy for some, it was usurped in the early 1960s by the earthier *Z Cars*.

At the Palace of Westminster, politicians of all hues continued to gripe about the moral lassitude of modern youth. Their world essentially remained as it had in the 1930s – one of extreme conformity and deference. London was beginning to swing, but in their opinion, this 'new music' was but an extension of a dangerous hedonistic lifestyle; they neither appreciated nor understood.

One spring day in 1964, Lord Willis stood up and started to speak – it may well have been his maiden speech. During this oration, he launched an attack on pop culture, rubbishing the music of The Beatles and The Rolling Stones, describing it as 'candyfloss culture'. To paraphrase George Orwell from his classic fable *Animal Farm*, 'Classical music good, pop music bad'.

Later back in Soho, I bought an *Evening Standard* from the toothless newspaper seller on the corner of Tottenham Court Road and Charing Cross Road. Lighting a Lucky Strike, I inhaled deeply, and as I did so, my eyes were drawn like a magnet to the Ted Willis speech. It was then that this outrageous idea came to me. Talking to myself like some demented drunk, I said: 'Why not take The Yardbirds to Willis' house and get them to play the blues on his lawn!'

Dashing back Usain Bolt-style to Denmark Street, I got Giorgio Gomelsky on the blower and sounded him out. 'Knock out! Knock out!' he boomed. As always when excited by something, his response was always over-the-top. I could see him in my mind's eye, waving his hands around with his fingers pointing in several directions at once, in the manner of someone suffering from Saint Vitus Dance.

Now I have to be honest, luck was on my side with this stunt. My father, and indeed my mother, had been pally with Willis for donkey's years. They were all young political animals together in the 1930s, demonstrating against General Franco in Spain as well as actively supporting the International Brigade (that gallant mixture of idealistic humanity, including the likes of Ernest Hemingway and George Orwell that travelled to Spain to fight the Fascist Franco and his troops). So knowing where Willis lived was no problem. All that remained was for me to bombard every single national paper with my 'story' and hopefully reap the rewards - in the words of C.C. Baxter in the movie *The Apartment* – publicity-wise.

It was a balmy Whitsun Bank Holiday, and the Mods and Rockers were getting restless on Brighton Beach. Meanwhile, down in the leafy stockbroker belt of Chislehurst in Kent (the home these days of rapper and West Ham fan Dizzee Rascal), a horde of men and some women arrived at the Willis house, many armed with cameras. My father was there, of course – his friendship with Willis was to prove invaluable. In fact he had chauffeured Gomelsky (with me sitting nervously on the back seat) in his brand-new Bond Equipe to the Willis residence.

Throughout the journey to the Kent border, Gomelsky griped and groaned about the quality of my father's driving. All he kept saying was 'incredible, incredible'. To say my father was (no pun intended) driven to distraction was an understatement!

Lord Ted's daughter Sally answered the door, looking somewhat nonplussed. As for Willis, at first he wasn't at all happy. Sally, then in her early teens, remembers the day well.

'I thought it was going to be the usual very boring day, and suddenly there was this knock at the door. Dad wanted to turn everyone away, as he felt it was just a stunt – which we all knew it was – but I begged him to let the band and their entourage in.'

Willis then saw my father, and smiling ruefully, he said something like, 'you rascal, you'. My father smiled back, finding it somewhat difficult hiding his embarrassment.

Sally then showed the band where to plug in, and without the semblance of a sound balance check, they bashed out the blues, and in so doing woke up much of the neighbourhood. These people weren't happy, and with more than a touch of irony considering Lord Ted's TV creation, several of their number threatened to call the police!

'The group played several songs,' said Sally. 'Then a neighbour actually did telephone the police, but when they turned up, and realised it was my father, and that he had created *Dixon of Dock Green*, they allowed it to continue for a little while before it had to stop.'

Despite being reserved and withdrawn, Eric Clapton was the only member of the band to ask for a grand tour of the Willis abode. Lady Willis was his guide, and a visit to the bedchamber gave her the opportunity in years to come to boast that she 'had had Eric Clapton in my bedroom'.

Okay, so Lord Ted was irritated at first, but he soon recovered his smiling demeanour – after all, he was more than adept at publicity himself – and he even seemed to start to enjoy himself. He certainly lapped up all the compliments paid to him by Giorgio Gomelsky, and they got on like a couple of soulmates. He went on to say to Giorgio that he hadn't realised how good this form of music could be – you could say 'the Candyfloss culture' merchants had won hands down.

The next day, the national newspapers were full of Lord Ted Willis and The Yardbirds. Apart from The Beatles, no group – not even Andrew Oldham's The Rolling Stones – had garnered so much countrywide exposure in one hit. The *Daily Mirror* in particular went overboard for the story – photos, the lot. Even the Conservative *Daily Telegraph* found room, complete with photo. Mind you, the paper's sub-editor had transformed the band's name into 'The Yardsticks'!

By this time, my forays down the Fulham Road to watch 'Docherty's Diamonds' were few-and-far-between. The FA Cup replay victory over Spurs in early January '64 was the highlight, with the 2–1 loss to Huddersfield in the next round a real low ebb, but by the spring Chelsea were bidding for a Fairs Cup spot. A 1–0 win over Everton saw them finish in a very satisfactory 5th slot, just 7 points shy of champions Liverpool.

Sleep was in short supply, as I seemed to be living in a parallel universe of hyper people dashing hither and thither, often going nowhere fast, without contemplation or rest. Even my trips to the Bridge were not as life enhancing as they had once been. Life was all about The Flamingo, The Marquee and conflabs with Giorgio Gomelsky, Rik Gunnell and other 1960s pop culture luminaries.

There was also renewed contact with Andrew Oldham. Now, Oldham was a Chelsea fan, and by a quirky set of circumstances I not only visited his pad (Ivor Court, in Gloucester Place near Baker Street), but I also renewed a friendship with an old family friend, Stanley Moore.

Stanley was a solicitor, specialising in assisting what he termed 'society's underdogs'. There was definitely a touch of the Horace Rumpole about him. He had a set of chambers in Smithfield, all musty smell and Victorian furniture. You half-expected to see a row of clerks perched at high desks in wing collars, writing in huge leather-bound ledgers with quill pens. Somehow the ambience of the place didn't quite match Stanley's persona, which was all about NOW and progress and rebellion and ridding the country of what he regarded as bigoted, old-fashioned values.

He was also a fanatical Chelsea supporter and season-ticket holder for many years. He died on 1 May 1992, aged seventy-seven, and his ashes were scattered on his beloved Stamford Bridge turf. His father ran a watering hole in Soho, the Old Coffee House, which was regularly frequented by the Chelsea stars of the pre-war era.

His son, Stephen, is an actor often seen treading the boards at the National Theatre. Now aged seventy-five, he has had an eclectic career, with roles in such hits as *Rock Follies*. However, to some people he is best known as the long-suffering father of Harry Enfield's brilliant TV comic creation Kevin. Like his father, he is a confirmed True Blue.

'I've supported Chelsea since the '50s,' he once told me. 'Charlie Cooke is my own personal number one player, but I also remember watching in awe as Jimmy Greaves banged in the goals.

'I don't get to Stamford Bridge much these days because of my theatre commitments, but when I did go regularly, that star of British film, John Mills, used to sit very near me. Michael Crawford, who is a real Blues devotee, lives upstairs from me.'

The Puppets were a group managed by the enigmatic Joe Meek, but we looked after their publicity. They had not yet achieved the success in the charts compared to other members of Meek's stable, but they had already built up a considerable reputation backing such rock superstars as Billy Fury, Brenda Lee, and the 'Be-Bop-A-Lula' man Gene Vincent.

Now, preventing cupboard skeletons from hitting the press was, in those more strait-laced days, one of the prime briefs of any self-respecting PR man. These days, whether or not a singer is gay (or 'queer' as we would have said), or has or has not fathered kids all over the place wouldn't matter one iota. But in '64, it was imperative to keep this stuff away from prying press people.

Anyway, this Puppets band member called me and told me that a paternity suit was out against him; could I help. I immediately contacted Stanley Moore – the case was just up his street – and handed the whole mess over to him. Needless to say, Stanley, who always relished a good fight, won the day. The Puppets were happy and I was happy, as indeed were the main men at Press Presentations, including the guy who actually owned the joint, leading showbiz agent Terry King.

Exactly why the members of the Puppets were all staying at Oldham's flat, I never did discover, and having to act as some kind of chaperone for these Lancashire lads was certainly a novel experience for an eighteen-year-old. Another 'novel experience' was meeting their guru, Joe Meek.

Meek was a legend. He lived like a hermit, and many people believed and still believe passionately that he was a genius. His home was a flat on the Holloway Road. Despite producing some of the most iconic pop records of the late 1950s and early '60s, he had a reputation for frugality. In fact, his lifestyle was that of someone counting pennies on a daily basis. He often recorded his artists in his bathroom or in his kitchen – in fact anywhere where he felt the sound would be more original. My memory of him is that he spoke little and that he had brooding eyes and a face locked into permanent sadness.

His biggest smash was in 1962 with The Tornados' 'Telstar' – the first US number one by a British band. Britain's answer to James Dean, John Leyton – he was even mobbed more than once by teenagers thinking the *Rebel Without a Cause* icon 'had returned from the dead' – was another one of his artists, with 'Johnny Remember Me' hitting the UK number one spot in 1961. And even by 1964 when the whole scene was dominated by the likes of The Beatles (in Meek's words 'just another bunch of noise, copying other people's music') and The Rolling Stones, he was still having hits, with The Honeycombe's 'Have I The Right?' topping the British charts.

It was surreal in the extreme; this whole Meek set-up in just a few badly furnished rooms above a leather goods shop. I once saw him smile; it came out of the blue and, somewhat rudely, I stared at him, noticing his hair and its homage to the 1950s and the Teddy Boy for the first time. Andrew Oldham once said of him, 'He looks like a real mean-queen Teddy Boy and his eyes were riveting.'

Later, his depression and paranoia (exacerbated by drug use), plus the pressures of being a homosexual in a society which still imprisoned gay men, led to a complete nervous breakdown. And on 3 February 1967, he killed his landlady Violet Shenton and then himself with a single-barrelled shotgun.

Three gay men – The Beatles manager Brian Epstein, Joe Meek and playwright Joe Orton – all died in 1967, and all in tragic circumstances. Ironically, by 1 August 1967 the Labour Government had repealed the 1885 Act, decriminalising homosexuality and allowing gay relationships, removing forever the once ever-present threat of blackmail.

One particular artist that Meek recorded, but who never made it into the charts despite a huge cult following, was Screaming Lord Sutch. At Press Presentations we were handed the brief of publicising the launch of his pirate radio station, 'Radio Sutch'.

So, having pointed the media crew in the right direction, we all congregated by the Thames. There he was, David Sutch, arriving in an ostentatious American automobile, all chrome and fins and bad taste. Photos were taken of Sutch with his band, The Savages, hanging precariously from the mast of a flimsy-looking craft. Later Sutch and his cronies set up shop on a Second World War army fort on the splendidly named Shivering Sands in the Thames Estuary – boy did it look creepy!

'Radio Sutch' eventually became 'Radio City', and the Screaming Lord soon lost interest in the whole madcap scheme, selling it to his manager Reg Calvert for about £5,000.

On 20 June 1966, the whole thing took a dramatic and tragic turn when Major Oliver Smedley, an erstwhile business colleague of Calvert, organised a band of men to take control of Shivering Sands. Later, that same day, Calvert turned up at Smedley's house, and in a frenetic scuffle, Smedley shot and killed Calvert. Smedley was charged with murder, but he claimed it was self-defence, and was subsequently acquitted. The following year, the station made its final broadcast.

Talking of pirate radio stations brings to mind a 'Radio Caroline' party in Mayfair. The Rolling Stones' manager Andrew Loog Oldham was there, as was his discovery Marianne Faithfull, whom he described later as 'an angel with big tits'. It was there that I was introduced to one-time Elvis double and now hit performer P.J. Proby. Caroline was the premier Pirate, and their parties, laid on by station owner Ronan O'Rahilly, were real happening events.

Now, having laced down a few too many drinks of dubious content, I suddenly realised that for some reason my wallet was empty. Where my money had gone was a mystery. Now, in those days, credit cards were limited to a few ultra-rich Americans and the odd tycoon or three this side of the pond. Remember, this is a world without debit cards or ATMs; it seemed I was stuffed.

It was now the wee small hours, and things were beginning to really hot up. I asked around for a lift, but everyone who was leaving was going to some out-of-London place such as Richmond or Kingston or Twickenham or just around the corner to some pad in Chelsea. They didn't really care about little old me. So I just left this salubrious Mayfair penthouse, and trudged all the way back to North West London and the green swathes of Hampstead.

It took me hours, and it was well past dawn when I eventually turned the key in my front door. But no sleep for me! I showered, fuelled up on a nice greasy spoon-like fry-up and lashings of coffee, and prepared myself for yet another trip to Stamford Bridge. You see, despite being overwhelmed by the star-studded Caroline party, watching Chelsea was still a priority. The game itself, by the way, was nothing to write home about, but the Blues did manage to eke out a 1–0 victory over Burnley.

FIVE

MORE SOHO ADVENTURES AND CHELSEA'S TREBLE-CHASE

St Anne's Court, by the side of Foyle's Bookshop.It was then a dingy alleyway, reeking of all things Charles Dickens; however, I found it an ideal shortcut into the heart of Soho.

Little delis with drab-looking faded fascias; even drabber doorways offering you Italian lessons on the second floor; these were everywhere in '60s Soho. It was all about sound and smell and night, and after midnight in particular when tongues loosened and responsibility evaporated in a sea of pungent booze and swirling cigarette smoke and that sweet, almost sickly, aroma of marijuana. Now it's too clean, too sanitised. Back then it was a dream world – a heady mixture of continental Europe and the USA. And the heart of this 'dream world' was now my base.

Having won over Gomelsky with my Lord Ted Willis coup, I was now operating on my own as a publicity manager. Much to the chagrin of the powers that be at Press Presentations, I had made the big decision to go out and fend for myself, taking the likes of Georgie Fame, Zoot Money and The Yardbirds with me.

One of Giorgio Gomelsky's newest recruits was Gary Farr & The T Bones. Having wowed them in Brighton, Giorgio was hell bent on exposing them to the blues aficionados at The Marquee – all those young hipsters in their Mod suits who dug anything that sounded like John Lee Hooker or Muddy Waters or Sonny Boy Williamson.

Gary Farr, who sadly died in 1994, was a striking character, with a mop of beautiful blond hair. He was the son of boxing legend and Welsh hero Tommy Farr, who on 30 August 1937 fought Joe Louis at the Yankee Stadium in New York for the World Heavyweight title.

'The Tonypandy Terror' as he was known took champion Louis the full distance of 15 rounds, and the majority of the 50,000 fans were of the opinion that the Welshman had outgunned the seemingly unbeatable American, but referee Arthur Donovan had other ideas and awarded the fight to the American. There was a chorus of boos following the decision, and some seven years later the beleaguered ref actually apologised in print for his mistake.

Farr did something no other boxer managed to achieve; he lived with the legend that was Louis. Later, life dealt Farr some cruel blows, which led to bankruptcy. He did have somewhat of a revival in the 1940s as a singer – in fact he made several recordings with the legendary George Formby – but by 1964 he displayed all the characteristics of man embittered by life's dirty tricks.

As a young PR operator, I wanted to really tap into this father/son relationship, so I gave Tommy a ring. Before I could plead my case, he told me to 'F*** off!'

I even got a freelance journalist I knew, Ian Gilchrist (he'd once shared a flat with Mick Jagger and the other Stones in Edith Grove) to give it a go. But the answer was the same, only this time with even more vehemence and even more expletives.

Tommy seemed to hate everything about Gary's lifestyle, but even though he failed to co-operate we did manage to exploit the relationship to good PR effect; cynical maybe, but Gomelsky liked it.

One incident really stands out. It was 11 June 1964 and an eighteen-year-old Harvey Goldsmith, he of Live Aid and so much more, had put on a show at the Brighton Dome. The headliners were The Animals, The Yardbirds and The Cheynes.

Now, as it happened, the gig was a success, but it was no thanks to The Animals. The Brighton Mods were there in force, and just a few minutes before the start of the show, Giorgio Gomelsky stood like a statue on the stage to announce that The Animals would not be appearing as a whole because two members of the band had been involved in a car accident. The fans accepted this lame excuse, but we all knew the real reason: a couple of them had got well and truly smashed. Not in a car crash, but by numerous bottles of booze.

Later we sampled the delights of one of Brighton's many excellent Italian restaurants, and after copious amounts of Barolo or chianti, Giorgio managed to convince me that Gary Farr and his T-Bones would be the 'next big thing', so a contract was drawn up on the back of a paper napkin for me to sign. The fact that it was a paltry £5 per week didn't seem to matter to me, as the bonhomie created by the booze made life seem just right.

We then made our way back to Gomelsky's apartment in Lexham Gardens. Giorgio was on fire, all his Mille Miglia background erupting as he climbed into his Ferrari or Maserati or whatever it was – no doubt fuelled by the wine – and we made it back to London W8 in just over 29 minutes!

Georgie Fame's birthday party, which as I have already noted was held on 12 June, was more an orchestrated press reception than anything else, but press receptions were my business. One other such event stood out, which involved the 'Fab Four' themselves, The Beatles.

On 3 June, Ringo Starr collapsed with tonsillitis and was ferried to hospital. It was the eve of the group's big Australasian tour. A class drummer was needed and fast, which is where I came in. Jimmie Nicol was Fame's drummer. He was experienced, having cut his rock 'n' roll teeth back in 1957 at the 2i's Coffee Bar in Old Compton Street. But despite both Beatles manager Brian Epstein and George Martin being adamant that the group needed a replacement drummer, it proved a difficult job convincing George Harrison in particular. He was all for cancelling the tour, but eventually everything was ironed out, and Rik Gunnell, who was as sharp as flint, knew that there was loads of publicity mileage for his man with this.

Jimmie was unveiled at EMI's headquarters in Manchester Square, and my brief was to make sure that the press were sweet-talked and pointed in the direction of Georgie Fame. Boy, it was a daunting task for a callow youth, but Bob Baker loved thrusting these googlies at me, probably hoping I'd be bamboozled and hit my wicket, but I managed to pull it off.

So everyone was happy. Gunnell grinned like some self-satisfied Buddha and I even managed to say 'how do you do?' to John Lennon. The Beatles got a load of print, as indeed did Georgie Fame and The Blue Flames. Mentally I was exhausted, but it was another hurdle crossed, albeit with the odd slip or two.

Another obstacle was Larry Page. During the 1950s he had strutted his stuff as a British rocker complete with massive spectacles. Known then as Larry Page The Teenage Rage, his teenage rebellion seemed all spent out by the time the Mods were rocking at the Marquee; in fact to my eighteen-year-old eyes he looked as conventional and as typical an example of corporate man you could ever meet – all smiles and insincerity and cut-throat ambition.

His is a story of ambition coupled with overt dedication. Initially it is a tale very much of the monochrome 1950s, but he soon realised that his talents lay not as a rocker, but more in terms of promotion.

Born Leonard Davies just round the corner from the massive EMI factory in Hayes, Middlesex, it was almost mapped out for him that upon leaving school, he would end up working for the international record conglomerate like so many of his contemporaries.

However, the teenage Leonard, enthralled with the new sensation Elvis Presley, had ambitions of his own to be a rock singer; he managed to get an audition with EMI, which he passed with flying colours. A record followed, and despite this new-found fame, he continued to work at the EMI factory.

Having been dubbed 'The Teenage Rage' by *Sunday Mirror* showbiz columnist Jack Bentley, the precocious youngster did his utmost to live up to the name with a variety of publicity stunts. These included a whirlwind romance and marriage to a teenage fan, and appearing on stage with blue-rinsed hair, which was actually the result of an accident following some overeager work by a TV make-up department. His ridiculously large glasses also added to his aura of unconventionality.

Another record followed, which in the words of Page himself '… was the biggest load of crap you ever heard'. His record producer had come up with the idea of the song, which he had told Page would never be released in Britain 'because it's terrible'. Needless to say it wasn't a hit. It is also worth noting that the song was Buddy Holly's 'That'll Be The Day'!

Fast forward a few years; this is where I came in. By 1964 Larry was a rock manager and promoter, and one of his charges was a group called The Pickwicks. To be honest, they were nothing to write home about – in fact they were lousy. Dressed as Dickensian dandies, or to use the Victorian vernacular, 'Mashers', their version of 'Apple Blossom Time' was released at about the same time as the musical 'Pickwick', starring Harry Secombe, was packing them in in London's West End.

The obvious is very often the only way. So, it came as no surprise that Page wanted his band to be photographed on the stage of the Saville Theatre in Shaftesbury Avenue with ex-Goon Secombe. The necessary phone calls were made, and I arranged for our own snapper Julian Hann to be on site to take as many photos as Secombe would put up with.

It all went down a treat with the print media, and Larry was as happy as a lamb! A bonus for me was a visit to the theatre to see the show, in the company of Larry and a lady. Later Julian Hann (his stage name at the time) or Jeremy Fletcher, to give him his real identity, joined me for a gratis dinner at The Pickwick Club in Great Newport Street in Leicester Square, all paid for by the grateful Page, where we sampled such delights as 'Mrs Bardell's fruit pie'. Having consumed a cellar-full of best claret, we climbed into Jeremy's Maigret-style Citroen and he drove me somewhat erratically back to Hampstead Way – talk about footloose and fancy-free!

Jeremy was (and indeed is, as he is still going strong) a photographer of talent, but apart from his obvious skill with a camera, here was, amongst all the back-stabbers and sell-their-grandmother-for-a-few bob merchants, a thoroughly decent bloke.

His colourful and interesting father, Ronald, a man so famous during the 1950s that an irreverent reference to him during the course of radio show could result in a tumult of guffaws.

It was during an episode of *The Goon Show* in 1955 – 'The Greenslade Story' – which purported to tell of announcer Wallace Greenslade's defection to a better-paid job, that John Snagge, whose eccentric Boat Race commentaries became legend, intoned in the manner of a newsreader announcing the death of a monarch over the music of 'The Last Post': 'So this, then, is the end of the once great BBC announcing staff. Where are they now, that noble band? Andrew Timothy – missing. Alvar Liddell – went down with his lift. And, finally, Ronald Fletcher – gone to the dogs.' The last was an in-joke reference to Fletcher's well-known gambling habit.

Having joined the BBC after the Second World War, his rise up the BBC newsreader ladder was meteoric. By 1947, his was the voice on the Home Service that announced the engagement of Princess Elizabeth to Philip Mountbatten.

A Wodehouseian character, during the 1950s he reached a wider audience with his witty appearances on Bernard Braden's shows *Breakfast With Braden* and *Bedtime With Braden.*

The 1960s saw him branch out into television with shows like *Twice a Fortnight* and *Braden's Week.*

Then in 1975, John Lloyd and Nigel Rees selected him to read the quotations on the long-running Radio 4 programme *Quote, Unquote,* which he did for 200 shows before ill health forced him to retire in 1994. He died in 1996, and Rees described his voice as having a 'suggestion of an earlier, more carefree age'.

Now, please remember that I was young and full of myself, and thought I was God's gift to women; to my eyes the 'Teenage Rage' was ugly. But his ugliness didn't seem to put off the girls, as accompanying him to the theatre was his sexy girlfriend/secretary. She was really friendly and had a smile that lit up her whole face. There was a reference in the show to the female bosom, which she seemed to like and she laughed and smiled at me. I was captivated!

I must admit I didn't find Larry easy to relate to. I remember that he insisted that I wore a particular type of suit. It is amazing to think that some years later he was the man who not only signed The Kinks (they later had a serious legal wrangle, but that's another story) but also managed The Troggs, who in 1966 reached number two in the UK charts with the classic 'Wild Thing' (in America it did one better).

Six years later, Page was the producer behind the Chelsea song 'Blue Is The Colour', released to celebrate the club reaching the 1972 League Cup Final. Surprisingly, they lost 2–1 to 'the old men' of Stoke City, in a final that in so many ways encapsulated the dying embers of that flamboyant side lit up by the likes of Cooke, Hudson and Osgood et al. The disc proved popular with the record-buying public, reaching number five in the charts in March 1972.

The Ted Willis stunt had allowed me more freedom of expression. It also gave me confidence to confront the many middle-aged wheeler-dealers, who were often the bane of my life. The time had come to move on, and I did, to a new office all of my very own: above a strip club in Old Compton Street. I was now on my own – GT Publicity was born.

I was pretty gung-ho as far as rent was concerned, and after visiting just a handful of estate agents, I found just the right premises in the heart of Soho. Climbing the stairs and doing your best to avoid popping in for a quick eyeful in the strip club, you came to a mini-suite with one office on its own. There was also a large area adjacent to it that was ideal as a reception. No deposit was required, no credit or identity checks – it was all so easy in those days.

My next task was to buy some suitable furniture, another simple task. I just walked into a West End store specialising in modernist office paraphernalia, chose what I wanted, handed over a cheque (no guarantee card or identity check required) and delivery was made the following day – several days before my cheque had actually cleared!

GT Publicity had a small, but exciting list of clients: The Yardbirds, Georgie Fame & The Blue Flames, Gary Farr & The T-Bones and Zoot Money's Big Roll Band.

Zoot Money's personal manager, Bob Hind, had the adjacent office. Later, Libby, his – well I never quite worked out what she was – joined us as receptionist/secretary, working in tandem with the Sandie Shaw-look-alike Ursula.

I didn't really like Libby. And as for Bob Hind, well he seemed dodgy, to say the least. He was also meant to be an architect, but what he actually designed, remained one of those unsolved mysteries.

He had a fawning gofer – a sort of tall version of Oscar Wilde's Bosie with cockney overtones. I cannot remember his name, but he was very blonde. I thought maybe Bob was queer, as we termed it then. But then I rationalised. I pointed out to myself that a guy who was forever waxing lyrical over female breasts couldn't be gay. Then I thought maybe all this bosom-thing was just show.

Bob kept prattling on about his life preserver. I hadn't a clue what he meant. Initially, I thought he was talking about sweets – you know those things you bought on the way home from school when you were a kid. Only later did I realise that he was referring to the long leather stick he carried, purchased from a leading gentlemen's emporium in St James's, to protect himself against any potential assailants. As I have said, the word 'dodgy' oozed from every pore of his body.

He fancied himself big time, as a sort of amalgam of James Bond and Simon Templar. What spoilt this image was his thin high-pitched Thames Estuary accent. He always wore tweeds, but gentry he was not.

I have already mentioned the strip club downstairs. It was by no means the worst place of its type – in fact by the Soho standards of the day it was pretty neat and tidy. It was owned by a Maltese chap, who despite a smile that generated contentment, also had a haunted look around the eyes, caused no doubt by the fact that he was in hoc to the Mafia. He was forever asking me to be his guest at one of the shows, and I'd be lying if I said I never succumbed.

Deep in the bowels of the building was a clip joint. You know the sort of thing, rubbishy booze or 'champagne' that was really apple juice costing a small fortune, a sit-down at one of the tables with a voluptuous hostess, and then paid-for sex later.

It is important to remember that these were the days when various Mafia offshoots ruled so much of Soho's night-life, and one morning when I arrived early at my new office I witnessed the fruits of their labours. Outside our premises were a whole load of police cars and guys in less-than-clean trench coats. Later, some newspaper hacks turned up, dressed like the plainclothes men, but all with fags stuck to their lips. The clip joint had been firebombed. The only cock-tail served that night was courtesy of Mr Molotov!

As for Zoot Money, he was proving to be a wow at the Flamingo. It was now my job to promote his first record: a disc with the unattractive title of 'The Uncle Willie'. An idea was mooted that we should produce a load of pound notes to promote the disc, but this caused us more headaches as legal objections were made to Zoot having his fizzog on a banknote – so they had to be withdrawn. The record was not a hit, even though I managed to get it played on the BBC Light Programme's *Housewives' Choice* show by posting off literally hundreds of postcards with fictitious names and addresses. Believe it nor not, the name that was chosen by the presenter – it could have been Kenneth Horne at the time, he of *Round the Horne* fame – was probably my most unlikely, Gregory Turnstile!

Frankly, I found the Rick Gunnell/Bob Hind axis bad for my nerves, and with former associate Bob Baker decamping to East Anglia to develop his fantasy of some kind of youth-themed nightclub, I found that more and more I was living in the pocket of the unpredictable and unreliable, yet more humane frame of Giorgio Gomelsky. The gangsters and the geezers were not for me, so I moved out, leaving Hind and Libby and the blonde gofer to their own devices as I moved into an office with Giorgio in the National Jazz Federation premises overlooking Soho Square.

It was a tight-knit unit in Soho Square, with Bob Hind and his crew being replaced by Gomelsky's number two Hamish Grimes and The Yardbirds' beautiful fan club secretary

Julie Driscoll, who reminded me at first glance of a younger version of Julie Christie. There was a touch of irony attached to this, as the woman-obsessed Hamish had cut his photographic teeth on Hampstead Heath by taking some striking snaps of Ms Christie herself.

I remember having an argument with Hamish. I was extremely touchy in those days. Julie was in the office at the time, and she took my side. Later, Hamish, who was a real character, but could also be extremely crude and irritating, said to me: 'Would you like to poke Julie?'

Taken aback, I replied rather sheepishly and stupidly, 'Yes, of course.'

Never in a million years did I imagine that this same Julie Driscoll, sitting at a desk in a rather ramshackle office would morph into *the* Julie Driscoll – 'This Wheel's On Fire' with Brian Auger and all that.

Her first foray into the 'Beat Scene', as it was christened by the tabloids, was in 1965 when she became a founding member of the original supergroup, The Steampacket, formed by Long John Baldry. Its other members included Rod Stewart and Brian Auger.

'This Wheel's On Fire' made it to number five in the charts in 1968, and some twenty-odd years later Julie's rendition (with Adrian Edmondson) reached an even wider audience as the theme music to the hit TV comedy show *Absolutely Fabulous*, starring Jennifer Saunders and Joanna Lumley (yet another showbiz Chelsea fan by the way).

Hamish was a real jack-of-all-trades in Giorgio's organisation. He was an accomplished photographer and a talented artist – he designed all the adverts and posters and record covers – as well on occasions acting as a more than adequate master of ceremonies.

Mind you, as I have already said, he could easily get under your skin, and it certainly wasn't difficult to lose your rag when talking to him. I remember one particular occasion – it was all so petty – when we started chatting about the whole concept of publicity when he said something, probably tongue-in-cheek, that upset me. I went on a bit of a rant, but Julie – who was a really nice quiet girl – stuck up for me, and this was enough to shut Hamish up!

****

The autumn of '64 saw the precocious Chelsea outfit play a brand of football that had the finicky fans at the Bridge smiling broadly and rubbing their hands as the puppet master Venables and the elegant Scotsman George Graham (it was said he used Vaseline on his eyebrows) and the rest collected victory after victory as they surged to the top of the First Division table.

Several games stand out; most notably the 3–1 away success at Arsenal on 26 September and the 5–1 home drubbing of Everton on 14 November, with Graham grabbing a couple of goals. Seven days later he did one better, netting a hat-trick as the Chelsea plundered Birmingham City 6–1.

However, there is one game – played nineteen days before Christmas in front of a paltry attendance of just under 8,000 – that will remain forever in the scrapbook of my brain. It was the debut of a seventeen-year-old from Windsor, who a mere four years or so later, would turn my life on its head. His name was Peter Leslie Osgood. It was a League Cup quarter-final replay against lowly Workington of the Third Division.

In the first encounter at their place, Docherty's championship aspirants had somehow managed to struggle to a 2–2 draw. The replay was a pretty tame affair, but the contest was lit up on a dank, dismal December evening by the young Osgood's poaching prowess, as he put away both his side's goals in their somewhat laborious advance to the semi-finals.

Being Chelsea, of course, it all imploded in the spring as internal division and ongoing schisms and fall-outs with manager Docherty saw their dream of an unprecedented treble crumble.

Four games remained and a first title since 1955 was very much on the cards as Docherty's Diamonds remained top of the tree. But having drawn 2–2 with West Bromwich

Albion at the Bridge on Good Friday, and then gone down 2–0 to Liverpool at Anfield two days later, it was imperative that they accrued points from the next two away games, at Burnley and Blackpool respectively.

Docherty's plan was to spend a relaxing few days in that very English seaside enclave of Blackpool. But eight of the manager's blue-eyed boys had other ideas, breaking the imposed curfew by going out on the town. The manager was not at all happy; in fact he was livid. So he sent home the Naughty Eight: Terry Venables, George Graham, Barry Bridges, John Hollins, Eddie McCreadie, Bert Murray, Marvin Hinton and Joe Fascione – and filled his side with untried reserves for the Burnley battle on 24 April 1965. Needless to say, it resulted in a 6–2 humbling; just two of Docherty's 'innocents', Ron Harris and the late Peter Houseman, were on target.

Their final game two days later at Blackpool saw them go down 3–2, so any thoughts of the title had evaporated. However, the season itself had already plummeted to its lowest ebb on 27 March when, despite being hot favourites, Chelsea had flopped 2–0 to Liverpool in the FA Cup semi-final at Villa Park. There was one crumb of comfort in the shape of a 3–2 aggregate win over Leicester City in the League Cup Final, Chelsea's first major trophy for ten years. But in truth, April was all about anti-climax!

Now more than ever, Chelsea Football Club was in my veins. Still making the daily tube trip to Soho and the madcap world of blues and rock, the glamour of it all was beginning to slowly but surely pall. Football was taking over, so I said to myself, 'how about launching a one-off magazine?'

I had somehow managed to store away a bit of dosh, despite the slothful nature of both Gunnell and Gomelsky in paying their monthly bills, and in late March I 'created' *Penalty* magazine.

It cost 1/6*d* (under 8p), and to say it was Chelsea-centric would be an understatement. Apart from a full-page team photo, and a 'low-down', complete with potted biographies of the whole squad, my 'Match of the Month' was their 2–1 home victory over Arsenal played at Stamford Bridge on 6 February.

The sub-heading to this report was 'GRAHAM OUTSHINES THEM ALL', and the first paragraph read: 'George Graham, Chelsea's bargain buy from Aston Villa, again proved what a deadly scorer he can be. His two goals were impeccable in their execution, and his whole performance was almost a soccer education in itself.'

Later, I went on to write under the *nom de plume* of 'Ronald Hall', 'this, of course, meant Chelsea were top of the league. "We are top of the League," chanted the Chelsea throng. The crowd cheered almost continuously from that moment on to the final whistle, happy in the knowledge that Chelsea were indeed top of the League.'

Not yet nineteen, I was now doing my utmost to balance rock PR with football. I remember one occasion at the HMV shop in Oxford Street. I had arranged for The Yardbirds to make a personal appearance, meet a few fans (mainly girls), sign a few autographs and generally to show themselves to be nice friendly approachable chaps.

During this (in my view) pretty boring experience, I got chatting to Eric Clapton. He was a bit clam-like, but I did manage to ask about his music preferences. I threw a few blues names at him coupled with the odd rocker or two – Jerry Lee Lewis was one – and he dismissed all these revered names with just two words: 'Bob Dylan'.

Having endured Chelsea's fall of grace that spring, and spent a whole load of lolly on the launch of *Penalty*, I found myself at a crossroads. Did I continue to flog my guts out trying to plug The Yardbirds et al in the press, or should I diversify full time into football?

It was then that I received an offer of a job. Tito Burns was a large man. He was broad and possessed a luxuriant black moustache that dominated his whole face. He was friendly, polite and probably the most celebrated agent and impresario in Britain.

Born in the East End to Jewish/Polish parents, he left school at fifteen years old. Jazz was his first love, and by

1947 his group the Tito Burns Septet was performing the new-fangled bebop on BBC radio. Burns himself was a more than proficient accordionist, and two years later his outfit was touring the country and recording numerous records with the likes of Johnny Dankworth.

A seminal year, 1955, that saw the birth of million-selling rock records, and Burns, who was always a realist, saw the light and disbanded his group. He knew his brand of music was well and truly passé; from now on, the money would be where the rock 'n' roll music blared.

In 1959 he replaced Franklyn Boyd as Cliff Richard's manager. A little later he discovered and signed up Dusty Springfield, who had broken free from The Springfields; he was fast building up an array of outstanding talent.

Then, completely out of the blue, one afternoon in 1965 he gave me a ring. 'I want to see you,' he said. 'This is important, so how about tomorrow afternoon.'

I asked him what it was about, but he was adamant that we needed to chat about it in person, so I agreed to be at his office in Vere Street off Oxford Street at 3 p.m. next day.

Arriving at his office in my best bib and tucker, I was confronted by this larger-than-life individual who oozed suavity from every pore.

'I would very much like you to join us,' he announced.

I was about to ask him something when one of his many phones rang.

'Put her through,' he said.

There followed a very detailed and personal chat with Dusty Springfield during which it became evident that she was a lesbian. Tito said the right things to her, which seemed to placate the singer, and the conversation ended on the usual pleasantries.

Looking very serious, Tito spoke to me in hushed tones. 'Please forget everything you have just heard,' he said, the permanent smile still lighting up his large face. 'Please don't repeat any of it to anyone,' he emphasised. 'Dusty needed to speak to me urgently from America.' He remained overtly matey, but I got the picture.

Placing the receiver back on to its cradle, his smile became even more animated.

'Yes, I'd like you to work for us,' he reiterated. 'When would you be able to start?'

I thanked him profusely for the offer, said I would think about it, and took my leave with a handshake and a wave.

Needless to say, I declined. A mistake? Maybe. But if I had said yes, I would not have had the pleasure of being a small part of that great Chelsea side of the late 1960s and early '70s that swaggered to two major trophies in as many years.

By now, my PR work for Giorgio Gomelsky was beginning to take a back seat, and having failed to reach a wide audience with *Penalty*, I decided to launch a completely different type of football magazine – one catering for the still buoyant world of the amateur game. So, in December 1965, *The Amateur Footballer* was born.

My idea was to sell the copies en masse through the clubs. Our old family friend Clem Mitford (Lord Redesdale) wrote an effusive intro for the first issue, and in a short space of time my world was no longer dominated by pretentious aesthetes and doubtful dealers, but by amateur football club committee types and secretaries and enthusiastic programme editors – from the sublime to the ridiculous you could say!

SIX

CHELSEA 'ALONE IN EUROPE' AND 'THEY THINK IT'S ALL OVER' AND ALL THAT

I was nineteen in 1965, and nothing appealed to me more than a Friday night at the Marquee, pilled up on purple hearts, dressed to kill in my finest, followed by marvelling at the new Stamford Bridge wunderkind Peter Osgood on Saturday.

Having made his mark the previous campaign with two goals on his debut, he returned to first-team competitive action on 22 September 1965 for the first leg of Chelsea's home Inter-Cities Fairs Cup first round tie with Roma; what a fraught and tempestuous affair that turned out to be.

Known as 'The Battle of The Bridge', the contest was notable for Terry Venables' hat-trick; one of his goals was a cheeky free-kick that bamboozled the Italian defenders as he and Eddie McCreadie pretended to argue about who should take it.

One of the highlights for me was sitting next to a young man who was an Aryan clone of Jesus Christ; the look on his sensitive face when someone – I don't know who – put a match to blue touch paper of some kind of rocket that almost singed his silky-looking though straggly beard, was one of sheer fear.

The match itself had a surreal quality about it. It was bad-tempered, with the players all seemingly adopting a ratty persona. Chelsea won 4–1, McCreadie was sent off, and between the posts for Roma that night was the father of future Chelsea goalkeeper Carlo Cudicini.

Following the Roma clash, Ossie really hit the headlines with seven goals, including one at Burnley that saw him gracefully slalom some sixty yards past bemused defender after bemused defender before slotting the ball home. Burnley goalkeeper, Scottish international Adam Blacklaw, proclaimed the youngster's effort 'the best goal I have ever seen'.

Come April and the nineteen-year-old was selected in Alf Ramsey's provisional World Cup squad of 40, and even though he failed to make the final 22, everyone, whether pundit or supporter, was convinced that he was destined to mature into one of the game's authentic all-time greats.

T.S. Eliot wrote in his magnum opus *The Waste Land*: 'April is the cruellest month.' Certainly as far as the players and fans of Chelsea were concerned, 23 April was a real downer.

Sheffield Wednesday were the opponents in their FA Cup semi-final at the mud heap that was Villa Park, and if the press favoured Chelsea twelve months earlier against Liverpool, then they were the proverbial banker against what was on paper a moderate Sheffield Wednesday outfit.

But once more they failed to reach their first-ever Wembley final, putting on a performance that was mediocre in the extreme, made even worse by the fact that one of Wednesday's goals was put away by former Blue, Jim McCalliog, who signed for the Yorkshire club in October 1965 for £37,500 – a record fee for a teenager at the time.

Their advance to the semi-final stage was a saga in itself. Having struggled to deal with Third Division Shewsbury (3–2) in round four, they were drawn at home to Third Division table-toppers Hull City in the quarter-finals.

The game was notable for several reasons, one of which was that Chelsea became the first club to produce a programme with colour photographs. As for the game itself, the Blues cruised into pipe and slippers time by taking a 2–0 advantage, but home complacency brought the Yorkshire visitors back into the affair, and they purloined two goals to take the tie to a replay.

Fixture chaos ensued; on Monday Docherty's charges had a Fairs Cup second leg match up with TSV 1860 München, with their Hull replay scheduled for Thursday, and Leeds United away the following Monday! Modern managers and pros would be moaning and groaning about such a fixture congestion.

A 2–2 draw in Munich on 15 March meant Chelsea needed a victory to progress to the semi-finals (away goals counting double was not an issue in those days). With so much on their plate, it was understandable that the Chelsea boys were more than just a wee bit edgy. In a game in which the result was all that mattered, Ossie was on target to poach the only goal, yet again displaying coolness and expertise well beyond his years. The Shed chants of 'Osgood Is Good' were at full blast that dramatic night.

Thursday 31 March was General Election Day. Two years of Labour Prime Minister Harold Wilson's government had seen the atmosphere in the country grow from depression and doubt to one of optimism. Labour were odds-on to retain power, but by how many seats?

BBC TV's Election Night extravaganza was hosted by the peerless professional Cliff Michelmore, whose first job that momentous night for the Labour Party was to announce: 'I have my first result for you: Hull City 1–3 Chelsea in the FA Cup quarter-final replay.'

Over 45,000 packed Boothferry Park to see two goals from Bobby Tambling and one from George Graham ease Chelsea into their second successive FA Cup semi-final.

The 2–0 Sheffield Wednesday defeat was a major dent, and Barcelona, their opponents for the Fairs Cup semi, were not the force they are today. Docherty knew that if his team played to their potential, a first European final was more than just a remote possibility.

A 2–0 defeat at the Camp Nou on 27 April in front of 70,000 screaming Catalans was indeed a struggle, but confidence remained high for the second leg.

11 May 1966, my twentieth birthday, was a wet old day. It rained and it rained with all the intensity of an angry autumn day. I was perched in Chelsea's new stand, sitting next to

a sartorially elegant Barcelona fan on one side and England cricket legend Jim Laker, the man who took 19 wickets with his lethal off-spin in the Fourth Test against Australia at Old Trafford in 1956 on the other. The encounter aped the Roma game in so many ways. To say it was a stormy affair would be an understatement.

However, the early portents were for a boring 0–0 draw, without incident and lacking in the finer arts. Then, late in the first period, Barca's Eladio Silvestre decided to take a wild swing at the home side's bundle of energy John Hollins, and he was not unsurprisingly given his marching orders. This moment of madness swung the match in Chelsea's favour, and despite the obdurate Uruguayan Julio Cesar Benitez, the Catalan club's defence eventually cracked in the 71st minute, when Gallego somehow managed to deflect Bobby Tambling's header into his own net.

The equaliser was even more of a mess; with goalkeeper Manuel Reina, the father of Liverpool's Pepe, parrying Peter Houseman's speculative effort into his own goal. In the dying minutes, a Ron Harris effort found the net, but much to the chagrin of the home fans, the goal was ruled out for offside.

So, following a coin toss, which went in the favour of the visitors, there was to be a play-off two weeks later at the Camp Nou.

The headline on the back page of the following day's *Daily Mail* was a real screamer: 'CHELSEA ALONE IN EUROPE'.

The play-off was an embarrassment for Docherty's men, as they were torn apart 5–0. In fact the most notable aspect of the whole event was that the tussle was shown on big screens at Stamford Bridge, with a programme and all the add-ons of a typical match day.

As a dyed-in-the-wool Blues fan, I took full advantage of this piece of innovation, settling into much the same position in the new stand as for the second leg. It was all very depressing – definitely a game too far for the Stamford Bridge youngsters.

The commentator chosen for this 'Big Screen Bash' was Simon Smith, who died in 2001 aged eighty-six. A jaunty East

Ender, boxing was really his game. In fact he became the first British commentator to cover a World Heavyweight title bout when he commentated on the fight involving Muhammad Ali (then called Cassius Clay) and Henry Cooper. Ali liked Smith a lot, often referring to him as 'my man from the BBC'.

So, it was all over, a season that at one stage looked like producing a remarkable quadruple, but fizzling out as spring turned into summer. Football now closed its shutters, packed the suncream and went on its hols, but only for a few weeks, as on 11 July, the FIFA World Cup – the biggest sporting spectacle since the 1948 Olympics – was to make its debut on these shores.

Talking of balls, I was attempting to juggle a few, with my *The Amateur Footballer* magazine and rock PR now joined by my nod to management as I signed on a cockney group called The Ricochets.

The Ricochets were good, the boys in the band combining earthy rock with tinges of the blues mixed in with 1950s' doo-wop. We actually cut one disc, 'Well', which had been on the B-side of The Olympics' 1958 hit 'Western Movies', a record that had charted at number twelve in the UK, and reached number eight in the Billboard Hot 100 in the USA.

But soon I was to wave goodbye to sex, drugs and rock 'n' roll, and wrap myself completely in the then conserva-tive environment that was association football. I didn't know it then, but just a few years down the line and this conservatism would all but disappear as the worlds of football and rock col-lided, thanks almost entirely to one man: George Best.

'World Cup Willie' was the official mascot of the 1966 World Cup; there was also a song of the same name recorded by the King of Skiffle, Lonnie Donegan. It hardly seemed an appropriate match, but the population of England didn't seem to mind as the tight-lipped Alf Ramsey, who some years before – much to the bemusement of both press and public alike – had predicted World Cup success for the hosts, continued to spout optimism as the England side developed into a hard-to-beat unit. Ramsey possessed two players who would have graced even the most arty of Brazilian sides in

Bobby Moore and Bobby Charlton; and in Gordon Banks, England had the finest goalkeeper on the planet.

I am a privileged person. I have seen an England captain lift the World Cup in the flesh. I saw every single one of England's games. For this, I didn't have to go online and wait for hours to get my transaction confirmed, worried all the time that some gangster or money-launderer or terrorist would grab my credit card details or even my whole identity. No, I simply turned up on the day with a few shillings in my palm and paid at the gate – simple!

England's World Cup adventure began badly, with a tedious, goalless draw with the ultra-physical Uruguayans. Undaunted, boss Ramsey took his squad to Pinewood Studios to have a 'butchers' at Sean Connery in Bond action. The ploy obviously worked, for in their next game, with Bobby Charlton running the show, they prevailed 2–0 over Mexico.

The third game against a weak French team was a 2–0 stroll, but Jimmy Greaves, never a favourite with the manager, was injured and took no further part in the tournament.

'Cometh the hour, cometh the man'. In this case it was Geoff Hurst, who replaced the goal-greedy Greaves, and proceeded to grab the headlines with his headed winner in a battle that lived up to its name.

The opposition, Argentina, were rightly considered one of the tournament favourites. They played a brand of football that was as alien to Ramsey as the Bolshoi Ballet, but their Achilles heel was temperament – they had turned being temperamental into a fine art.

Their captain, Antonio Rattin, was a midfielder of the hard school. The expression 'he takes no prisoners' could have been written for him. He had this arrogant, dismissive air about him, and the general impression he gave was that he was always likely to combust, and combust he did.

The main cause of his and his colleagues' ire was German referee Rudolf Kreitlein, who having endured a torrid time from the South Americans, eventually decided he had had enough by dismissing Rattin from the field for 'violence of the tongue', despite the fact that he spoke no Spanish!

This decision sparked a sequence of events unprecedented in modern football, with Rattin, believing the harassed official was displaying extreme bias in favour of the home nation, refusing point-blank to leave the pitch.

It was at this stage the entire Argentine eleven threatened to walk off the field. Eventually, the enraged Rattin made his way to the dressing rooms, but not before he had overtly sat down on the red carpet, which had been laid exclusively for the Queen. Two policemen were then needed to escort him off, but he was not yet done. As he left, he wrinkled a British pennant.

Ironically, this whole episode proved to be a landmark, as the behaviour of Rattin and his team undoubtedly led to the introduction of yellow and red cards.

Down to 10 men, the Argentinians lost any impetus gained during the early stages, and it was left to replacement Hurst to head England into a semi-final with Portugal, Eusébio and all.

Unbeknown to 99.9 per cent of Blues supporters, Portugal's epic 5–3 victory over North Korea in the quarter-finals had a Chelsea flavour about it. Lifelong Chelsea fan Stanley Moore, who possessed a grin as wide as former US President Richard Nixon's, but with 100 times more sincerity attached to it, is seen in *Goal!*, the movie of the World Cup, beaming as North Korea's unknowns tore into a 3–0 lead. The reason for this was simplicity itself; his Korean wife was the team's official ambassador for the tournament.

England just needed victory over Portugal to be in their first final, and as I have already said, I was there. West Germany, who had ousted the Soviets in their semi-final, were the opponents. Life not being at all politically correct back in '66, it was the Battle of Britain all over again – the Second World War revisited – our revenge for the Blitz.

On the morning of the great day, 30 July, I awoke early, an event in itself. Friday nights at the Flamingo or the Marquee were exhausting affairs, liberally laced with pills and sex. But I was twenty and I could take it. A friend and I picked up two tickets for a fiver from a consumptive-looking tout, puffing away merrily on a roll-up, outside Wembley.

We found our places in the cavernous terraces and for a few minutes just stood in silence, soaking up the atmosphere. Standing near us were some Germans who spoke excellent English. They were overtly polite and wished England all the best. They were inhaling large cigars. To our right were some vociferous Everton fans. They weren't so friendly.

These Evertonians baffled the Germans, with their non-stop jeering aimed at Liverpool's Roger Hunt every time he touched the ball. Hunt rhymed with 'the C word', and this was used to noisy effect. The Germans were incredulous, wondering why they were rubbishing their own player. Explanations of the intense Merseyside rivalry somehow failed to satisfy them.

The score was 2–1, with seconds left on the clock. The Germans, who seemed down-and-out, found a second wind and managed, I know not how, to conjure an equaliser. Extra-time, and yet another 'Lucky Strike' was lit – it tasted foul. Dry mouth, dry throat, heart thumping – this was not good.

A Hurst shot thundered against the crossbar; 'Was it a goal?' I screamed. No one, not even the officials, seemed to know. Then suddenly the diminutive linesman from the Soviet Union, Tofiq Bahramov – he was actually from Azerbaijan, but the press labelled him Russian – signalled to referee Gottfried Dienst from Switzerland. Following a conference, which to the majority of the nearly 100,000 present seemed of interminable length, Dienst – almost begrudgingly – gave the goal. The German players were not happy, and our German friends looked like they needed a Valium or three. Then it was 4–2: the Hurst hat-trick. People on the pitch... I won't go on.

Bahramov's legacy is what dreams are made of. The Azerbaijan national stadium is named after him, and when England travelled to Azerbaijan for a World Cup qualifier in 2006, a statue of him was unveiled making him the only referee to have a stadium named after him. Unfortunately Bahramov was not there to see it, as he died in 1993, aged sixty-eight.

One of the German fans handed me a cigar. Boy, it was bitter. By this time I had a mouth like a plumber's handkerchief, but who cared. England were World Champions. There were no Chelsea players on view that day, but I didn't care. It was in many ways the beginning of an era. An era during which English and British football shone as it had never shone before. It wasn't yet the new rock 'n' roll, but we were on the cusp.

Manager Alf Ramsey was the right man for the occasion, but many people suggested then, and more have suggested since, that his inflexible rigidity held back the game in this country. Certainly much later, in the early 1970s, the German midfield general Gunther Netzer made Ramsey's England team resemble a collection of journeymen. Ramsey was a good manager, of this there is no doubt, but he could have achieved true greatness if he had studied the social situation of the 1960s and adapted accordingly. Flair never appealed to him, so the likes of Alan Hudson, Rodney Marsh and Peter Osgood were never considered integral members of his exclusive club. Would George Best have made it into Ramsey's first eleven if the über-talented Irishman had been English? That is the question.

SEVEN

A FIRST FINAL FOR THE BLUES AND OSSIE'S NIGHTMARE

Three weeks later, the England boys were back doing their day job. The game of the day on Saturday 20 August was undoubtedly West Ham's home London derby with Chelsea.

The three Hammers heroes, hat-trick man Geoff Hurst, skipper Bobby Moore and midfield artist Martin Peters (Alf Ramsey once said he was fifteen years ahead of his time) received a rapturous reception from home and away fans alike. It was carnival time down in the East End. 'I'm forever blowing bubbles' was being sung as never before.

I made the long journey by underground from Golders Green to the wonderfully atmospheric Boleyn Ground, and arrived some half-an-hour or so before kick-off. One memory I have of the whole occasion, apart from the quality of football itself, was the amount of young men with transistor radios glued to their ears listening to commentary of the final cricket Test Match at the Oval between England and the West Indies – something that in these football-obsessed days would be about as likely as the current Chelsea team taking a pay cut!

Some of Chelsea's play that hot August afternoon was as exciting as anything you could ever wish to see on a football field. Charlie Cooke was magical and mesmerising; Peter Osgood was all élan, elegance and movement, and there was John Hollins running his socks off; the harrier and hustler-in-chief. The game flowed like some sporting version of vintage Dom Perignon.

West Ham lost the game 1–2, but in a way, despite the piz-zazz of the football from the visitors from the King's Road, it was all a bit unfair. After all, three of the Hammers – Moore, Hurst and Peters – had been put through the mental and physical mill just three weeks before in a World Cup final, whereas all the Chelsea players were fighting fit.

Chelsea opened the new campaign with an unbeaten run of twelve games. Then on 5 October in a third round League Cup-tie, the tide turned in dramatic fashion when their Mozart of the football field, Peter Osgood, broke his leg fol-lowing a tackle with Emlyn Hughes.

Ossie's injury understandably knocked the stuffing out of Docherty's team. Later that same month, the manager signed big target man Tony Hateley from Aston Villa for a club record fee of £100,000 as a replacement for Osgood. But Hately was no Osgood, and the purchase was not a sen-sible one – it smacked of panic.

In many respects, the sparkling Chelsea side of the 1960s (and in particular the later version that captured the FA Cup and the UEFA European Cup Winners' Cup) was a forerunner of the more modern version. The Cookes and the Osgoods thrived because of the quick passing and movement coupled with off-the-cuff dribbles and feints, whereas Hateley was a long-ball merchant. For him, the nectar of the gods was a perfect cross into the penalty box where he could rise and head home – he really was a truly magnificent header of a ball. On the ground, however, he was average to say the least. Interestingly enough, Docherty, the man who bought him once said that Hateley's passes 'ought to be labelled to whom it may concern'!

His final goals tally – a paltry 6 from 27 appearances – was indeed a poor return. But there was one goal that at the time was an historic one for the Stamford Bridge club.

It was Saturday 29 April 1967. The place was Villa Park in Birmingham, and Chelsea, whose form had deteriorated since Osgood's traumatic leg break, were definitely second favourites in their FA Cup semi-final with Leeds United.

I was there with both Stanley and Stephen Moore. I had travelled the country with Stanley throughout this epic FA Cup run, beginning with a January visit courtesy of British Railways to Huddersfield Town's old ground on Leeds Road: a 2–1 victory there. In early February we drove the comparatively short distance to a bleak Brighton where, some two hours before battle commenced, we sampled some Italian-style haute cuisine in a restaurant where the owner, who was a friend of the ebullient solicitor, was so Italian it wasn't true. But having said that, he was also a Chelsea fan, and methinks he played the part of the British idea of your typical Roman.

Following an unpromising 1–1 draw at the old Goldstone Ground (after which *Daily Express* sportswriter supreme Desmond Hackett wrote that if Chelsea won the Cup 'I would eat my hat'), the Blues had blasted Brighton 4–0 in their rematch. Hackett was such a household name in those days that the cockney rhyming word for a jacket became known as a Desmond, even though he himself was a Lancastrian by birth.

He was possibly the last man in Britain to don a brown bowler, and he was forever threatening to consume it if his forecasts proved inaccurate.

Round 5 on 11 March, and a comparative cruise at the Bridge: 2–0 against an oh-so-average Sheffield United.

The other club in Sheffield, Wednesday, were the opponents in the last eight. A dour affair looked to be heading for a replay when, with thousands of supporters making for the exits, up popped Tommy Baldwin to nick victory in the dying seconds. And so to Villa Park and a semi-final that was as controversial as it was dramatic.

Sitting just a few feet away from us were *The Likely Lads* stars James Bolam and confirmed Blue, Rodney Bewes. This was some nine years before their well-documented fall-out – they haven't spoken since – but back then they were as inseparable as any best mates could be. In its halcyon years, *The Likely Lads* and its early 1970s sequel *Whatever Happened to the Likely Lads?* attracted an audience of 27 million.

Some years later Ian La Frenais, one half of the Dick Clement/Ian La Frenais writing team, responsible for not only the *Likely Lads* series but also such classics as *Porridge* and *Auf Wiedersehen Pet*, would meet up with other showbiz personalities at Alvaro's in Chelsea for a pre-match lunch before joining the throng at Stamford Bridge to urge on Ossie and co., but more of this anon.

Anyway, back to the game itself: it is fair to say that controversy and debate raged unabated for weeks, indeed months, about one decision in particular made by referee Ken Burns. A respected official, Burns stuck to the letter of the law, but in retrospect his decision to deny Leeds substitute Peter Lorimer an equalising goal was incorrect, certainly from a moral standpoint.

Chelsea had taken the lead just sixty seconds before the interval, when Charlie Cooke waltzed past both Billy Bremner and Rod Belfitt before sending in a perfect cross for the much-maligned Hateley to head powerfully into the net, leaving Leeds 'keeper Gary Sprake grasping at thin air.

The Lorimer 'goal that never was' came literally seconds from the end, but just a few minutes prior to that, Leeds' England international full-back Terry Cooper had a goal ruled out for offside – another debatable decision.

Then, with Chelsea fans almost audibly counting down the clock, a free-kick was awarded to Leeds on the edge of the Blues box. Johnny Giles rolled the ball to Lorimer, who let fly with a venomous effort that eluded the defensive wall to find the net. Lorimer was understandably ecstatic, but Burns had other ideas. He maintained that the Chelsea wall had not been the required ten yards when the kick was taken, so it would have to be retaken. Cue vehement protest from the Leeds boys, but to no avail – Chelsea had made it to their first-ever Wembley FA Cup final.

As we left Villa Park, and despite the fact that none of us was wearing a Chelsea rosette or sporting a royal blue scarf, one mean-looking, very irate Leeds fan dashed towards me, fists outstretched in the manner of an early Victorian prize-fighter. If it hadn't been for the efforts of both Stanley and Stephen Moore – they were both built like rugby forwards – I could well have suffered a black eye or worse!

Even boss Docherty admitted afterwards that, 'I would have had no complaints if the goal had counted'. But as Chelsea fans through-and-through, the two Moores and I didn't really give a fig for what was right or wrong. We were going to Wembley Stadium – 'The Venue of Legends' – for a meeting with old London foes Tottenham Hotspur on Saturday 20 May, a mere nine days after I had achieved the age of majority, and I tell you that was some wild party.

My twenty-first birthday – 11 May 1967: I had a party in my father's luxury flat in Maida Vale. It doesn't sound much, but with Kaftans and cannabis the norm, champagne on tap and a load of folk groups including the legendary Bert Jansch and John Renbourn – later to achieve worldwide plaudits with their group Pentangle – the night was just like one long ever-lasting drink-fuelled gig. It woke the neighbours, however, and the police turned up in force to bark at us and order us to be quiet and even threaten us with arrest.

There was even more din when Scottish Communist and legendary drinker Bruce Dunnett, the man responsible for headlining the two musicians at The Horseshoe pub in Tottenham Court Road, reached that stage of inebriation in which every visible thing in life resembles a work in oils by an iconic French impressionist. He was noisy, and in the manner of a Scottish Giorgio Gomelsky he was classically crazy and delightfully demented.

He was, in most respects, Jansch and Renbourn's manager. He also looked after some archetypal folk groups, one of which was fronted by this unbelievably attractive Scottish girl – a sort of hip Moira Anderson. They were a real hit at my birthday bash, complete with bagpipes that would wake the dead from their everlasting slumbers.

She and I soon built up a definite rapport (it was more than just a dash of flirting) and only a few minutes after I had inadvertently hit Enfield footballer Laurie Churchill just under the right eye with an errant champagne cork, we were indulging in what *Carry On* films describe as 'a bit of the other'.

Churchill was an interesting character. He had just the one lung, and despite his gangly build and gauche movements, he was a winger of natural flair. At the time he was an integral member of the Enfield side that had just captured the FA Amateur Cup in a replay at Maine Road Manchester. Later he was to sign for Chelsea.

That Enfield Cup success was achieved with a team of 'professional' performers playing to their full potential in a game for amateurs. Managed by the articulate and highly intelligent former Hendon goal-snatcher Tommy Lawrence, they were odds-on favourites to overcome little Skelmersdale United in the final at Wembley on 22 April, but failed to live up to their lofty reputation and were lucky to get away with a 0–0 draw; 75,000 highly vocal fans were in attendance.

Skelmersdale probably deserved to win, thanks to winger Steve Heighway. He was unique, having put a full-time professional football career on hold in order to obtain a degree in economics and politics at Warwick University (he went on to sign for Liverpool in 1970). If it hadn't been for Enfield 'keeper Ian Wolstenholme's penalty save in the dying embers of extra time, the Cup would have gone north.

The replay, seven days later, was a totally different affair. Played at Manchester City's ground Maine Road in front of 55,000 spectators, Enfield upped their game, and with two goals from Ray Hill and one from John Connell, outplayed their opponents in every department.

These two games were, of course, given extensive coverage in my *The Amateur Footballer* magazine, and as the circulation continued to improve apace, I found that my biggest headache was getting club officials to cough up the money they owed me from bigger and bigger sales. Talk about blood out of a stone time!

FA Cup Final Day – 20 May 1967: It was cool and gave no hint of the summer to come. It was not yet the Summer of Love, but embryonic hippies were abroad on the King's Road, and the youth of Great Britain were already into peace protests and the like. 'Legalise Pot' was soon to become the mantra of this new intellectual young man and woman. Jack Kerouac sowed the seed, and Bob Dylan was transplanting the seedlings.

I had somehow managed to obtain a ticket, but the day itself began badly for me. Overindulgence on the booze had given me the most excruciating stomach pains on the Friday, and by Saturday morning I was struggling. Unwisely I chose an alcohol-based medicine, namely Moët et Chandon champers. Initially this made me feel somewhat better, although by the time I climbed into Stanley Moore's car, I was feeling like death warmed up.

From a Chelsea perspective, the final itself was a nonevent. Spurs went 2–0 up thanks to Jimmy Robertson and Frank Saul, and all Docherty's troops could muster was a late consolation from Bobby Tambling. How the Blues missed the precocious talents of Peter Osgood!

My day reached a real nadir when, after leaving Wembley, I could not locate Stanley's motor. After what seemed like hours of torment – by this time I was in pain and feeling thoroughly depressed – I found it. Stanley wasn't happy, but we made it up and he drove me home. Little did I know then that three years later I would be witnessing Chelsea's first-ever FA Cup final triumph, when as Peter Osgood's agent and business partner, we would be riding the crest of a very lucrative wave. But on 20 May 1967 I was just a walking zombie of out-and-out misery.

Having sold loads of copies of *The The Amateur Footballer* at Wembley Stadium both before and after the Amateur Cup Final, I now thought it was time that I treated myself to a short holiday, as the magazine would not be published again until August.

However, my association with Enfield FC was strong, so strong that when I was invited to join them on their end-of-season trip to Sweden, I jumped at the chance.

We travelled to Gothenburg by boat – or is it ship, I've never really discovered the correct terminology – from Tilbury. I shared a cabin with the Enfield reserve goalkeeper, and the few days spent on this travelling hotel in many ways resembled a surreal dream, with various indiscreet liaisons with young Scandinavian women and copious amounts of alcohol being consumed.

The Enfield FC committee on the trip, grey middle-aged men with ill-fitting suits, sat together most of the time talking in hushed tones as they downed their whiskies. You could see from their expressions that they were envious. Their lives as young men had been spent in wartime London. Their youth was all about survival and confronting head-on death and destruction. We baby boomers, all born during or in the weeks immediately after the War, had money in our pockets and new sexual freedoms that were barred to our elders and betters.

Arriving in Gothenburg, we were transported to a magnificent complex a few miles outside the city, home to the Soviet Union squad for the 1958 World Cup in Sweden, the World Cup that transformed a young teenager nicknamed Pelé into a household name.

We spent the first night glued to the box, cheering on Celtic ('The Lisbon Lions') as they became the first British team, and indeed the first non-Latin outfit to lift the European Cup. It was a great night for football, as the ultra-defensive tactics of the Italians – the 'Catenaccio' system – was brought to book by a Celtic eleven intent upon attacking. As manager Jock Stein so aptly put it: 'we did it by playing football; pure, beautiful, inventive football. There was not a negative thought in our heads.'

Apart from lazy hazy days spent in rooms occupied by the legendary Soviet goalie Lev Yashin and his mates, we also had a prestigious game organised at the world-famous Ullevi Stadium, the venue of several World Cup contests in '58, including Sweden's semi-final win over West Germany, against a Swedish League XI.

Many of the Enfield players were, shall we say, a wee bit the worse for wear come kick-off, and manager Tommy Lawrence approached me to enquire how I felt about being, if necessary, a substitute. I can see it now, me waving a fag in his face, hands shaking from too much beer and whisky and schnapps, nodding as I tentatively agreed to his request.

The game was played in just the right spirit, and I did manage to get on for a few seconds – whether I touched the ball or not was certainly open to debate. Enfield lost the match, but simply putting a foot on the famous Ullevi turf was enough to make any football-obsessed twenty-one-year-old as euphoric as a hippy on magic mushrooms.

I later sold a story of the trip to *Soccer Star* magazine, Britain's biggest-selling football weekly, edited by the legendary Jack Rollin. My fee was half-a-guinea, 10/6 (about 53p in today's monetary values).

Tommy Docherty was a character. Like all 'characters', he could be loveable and unpredictable at the same time. He took over at Stamford Bridge when the club was in dire straits. About to be relegated to the second tier, life looked bleak for London's quirkiest football club, but his foresight quickly turned doom into delight, thanks to a policy of encouraging young talent plus shrewd bargain basement buys.

Unfortunately Docherty's erratic behaviour often alienated the likes of George Graham and Terry Venables, and when he began a major work of surgery on the spine of the squad, the atmosphere at the club noticeably changed – and not for the better.

The player who was his pride and joy was undoubtedly Peter Osgood. Docherty turned down various bids from the likes of Roma and Real Madrid – the latter making a formal offer of £100,000 – proclaiming, 'We wouldn't dream of selling Osgood any more than Brazil would sell Pelé!'

Ossie himself later told me more than once that Docherty was 'a real mentor' and that he loved the man.

However, events during an end-of-season tour to Bermuda, which remain shadowy even to this day, resulted in an FA suspension for the 'Doc' plus a fine of £700. Add to this a record of a measly 2 victories from 13 matches, during which they conceded 29 goals, and it was obvious that Tommy's days were numbered. Some have compared the André Villas-Boas situation in 2012 to that of Docherty during the autumn of '67: The leading lights at the Bridge – Cole, Lampard and Terry, to name a few – seemingly wanted AVB out, and forty-six years ago, many experts maintained and continue to maintain that some of Chelsea's young bucks, seeing the writing on the wall, craved a change at the top. The man they wanted was Dave Sexton, and within hours of Docherty's departure, the quietly spoken East Ender took charge.

It was 7 October 1967 and a Chelsea squad low on confidence following a series of defeats, most notably 5–1 at Newcastle and 6–2 at Southampton, took on Leeds at Elland Road. It was an embarrassing afternoon for all those wearing blue as 40,000-plus fans witnessed a slaughter with a rampant Leeds finding the net on no less than seven occasions without reply.

The Fulham Road had become a forlorn place, and despite Osgood's return to regular first-team action following his broken leg, he was patently not the dynamic performer he had been prior to his clash with Emlyn Hughes. He told me later that it was essentially psychological, which was understandable considering the seriousness of his injury.

Under new boss Sexton, Chelsea's form improved markedly, and a final league placing of 6th was a more than satisfactory outcome, qualifying them for the Fairs Cup. Even though Osgood's prowess as a finisher of flair and finesse did not as yet match the sublime years pre-broken leg, he still managed to top the Blues' scoring charts with 17 goals.

The season of 1968–69 was another curate's egg of a campaign. Sexton had moved Peter Osgood permanently into midfield. The No. 4 shirt didn't somehow seem right for the elegant ex-striker, and it would be fair to say that his career had lurched into a kind of limbo. As he told me later it was all about confidence, and his had reached such a low ebb that the club doctor prescribed him tranquillisers to help him cope with this ongoing anxiety.

A final First Division placing of 5th was not a bad return, but just like the previous campaign, Chelsea choked in the FA Cup quarter-finals. Their Fairs Cup adventure was short-lived. Greenock Morton in round one were easy foe, but at the next stage DWS Amsterdam proved a surprisingly tough nut to crack, and following two 0–0 stalemates,

Sexton's men were eliminated on that most undemocratic of rules – the toss of a coin!

Now, while Chelsea were going through this period of consolidation and then improvement – albeit not of the headline-making variety – I was finding myself once more embroiled in the world of rock.

The Amateur Footballer was continuing to thrive, but the whole '60s scene (what *Time* magazine referred to in 1966 as 'Swinging London') was fast taking over my life again, this time in the shape of full-colour posters of current stars, marketed by our family company Star Posters Ltd.

Breaking away from the likes of Jimi Hendrix, Frank Zappa and Mick Jagger – by this time Andrew Oldham had ceased being The Stones' manager, with the shrewd Jagger having bought out his contract – our company changed direction.

And as the 1960s were ever so slowly beginning to turn from idealism and hope into unfulfilled dreams and despair, Oldham became mired in a culture of drugs, and with it, mental and physical degradation. Only much later was he able to resurrect his career and life, thanks in part to his dedication to the much-maligned Church of Scientology. It was then that I decided, on the back of England's World Cup success-story and the new pop-style adulation of footballers that we should diverge from our previous approach and 'go into footballers'. What I meant by this was actually one player in particular – and his name was George Best.

There were literally loads of pictures and posters and other more outlandish knick-knacks available of Best on the market – most if not all published on a 'pirate' basis by companies that never came to an agreement with the player or his agent. As such, the player received zilch in terms of royalties, which led to obvious discontent. I believed our product should be an official George Best enterprise, so my first port of call was Besty's agent, the Huddersfield-based Ken Stanley.

Stanley had been a table tennis player of some distinction, and as a football agent he had already made a name for himself with his astute and honest representation of 'The King' of Old Trafford, Denis Law.

Our concept was totally different to the standard posed posters of the day – footballers with forced cheesy smiles looking uncomfortable in their football togs with boot-clad foot over ball. What I had in mind was a 'rock-style' product. Gone would be the football shirt and shorts, and in would come a King's Road shirt, designer-stubble and a James Dean-style moody glance at the camera.

Negotiations with Stanley were short, sweet and to the point – 6*d* (under 3p) for every poster sold, royalty cheques to be submitted on a monthly basis. Ken was happy; George was happy; we were happy.

Taking a photo of George presented no problem, as so many trendy 1960s snappers were queuing up to shoot his photogenic fizzog. Terry O'Neill, with whom we had had several dealings, was an option, but instead we chose a couple of guys working out of an Art Deco block of flats in West Hampstead.

Mission accomplished, but would the public take to this unique concept? The answer was a massive yes, as the posters literally flew off the shelves of shops and stores all over the country. Then there was the mail-order side, helped considerably by advertising in not only that must-have of every teenaged football fan, *Shoot* magazine, but also via our burgeoning mail-order operation, which was boosted enormously by the co-operation we received from the Manchester United Supporters' Club.

Thousands were sold in double-quick time. 10,000 became 20,000. Soon it was 40,000 – would it never stop? Rubbing our hands together at this undoubted coup some months later, I said to my father: 'Do you realise we've now topped 50,000?'

Having shouted this figure to the rooftops, I then said to Tesser senior: 'How about doing a whole series of pop-style football posters?' Without seeming to consider my proposition, he agreed. And it was this decision that led me to meet the King of Stamford Bridge, Peter Osgood, and embark on a wildly exciting journey of success and failure, coupled with more than a tinge of irresponsibility and madness.

EIGHT

I TELL OSSIE ABOUT ERIC CLAPTON

I made a list – I love making lists – of the nine most likely players to match Best in terms of teenage fan worship. Number
one was obviously England's 'Golden Boy', World Cup-winning
captain Bobby Moore. Not far behind, in my estimation, was
the Stamford Bridge embryonic superstar, Peter Osgood.

Meeting Moore and his lovely wife, Tina, elegantly draped
and with hair of burnished gold, at their spacious house in
Chigwell, Essex was a pleasure. Despite all the trappings
of comparative wealth, I found Moore to be an easy-going,
unassuming man. In fact, a little later I interviewed him for
World Soccer magazine, and found him both articulate and
honest. But like most of us, Bobby was flattered by praise.
I don't mean by this that he was in any way inward-looking or
on an ego-trip, but when my shrewd – some would say cynical – father suggested to him that sales of his poster would
easily emulate those of Best's, he readily agreed.

The photo used for the poster was a head-and-shoulders
job that had an almost ethereal quality about it. He looked
impressive – just like a Hollywood star.

Now you have to understand that my father, who was the
senior partner in our Star Posters operation, was a salesman
of almost frightening expertise and out-and-out guile, plus a
smooth velvety voice that seduced even the most sceptical
of potential customers to part with his or her hard-earned lolly.

Bobby Moore was not a vain man, but he was human. So,
having convinced Bobby that sales of his poster would match

those of Best's, it was then comparatively easy to soft-tongue the England captain with the words: 'With your contacts you could sell loads – how about your buying 25,000?'

At that time, Moore owned Bobby Moore Sportswear Ltd, a retail and souvenir emporium outside West Ham United's ground at Upton Park. He also had a partnership in Harrison-Moore, an upmarket purveyor of suede and leather coats based in the East End. Using these outlets would, my father maintained, shift the posters in double-quick time. Bobby was easily sold on the idea, and before you could say 'World Cup Winners', the deal was done.

I was unhappy with this deal. I felt my father had taken advantage of Moore's gullibility, and had used flattery for his own personal gain. I tried to disassociate myself from the whole episode, but unfortunately in the closed world of professional football, matters can easily become distorted or misreported. The fact that the name 'Tesser' was an unusual one didn't help either, so later when I was in the throes of adding Chelsea whiz-kid Alan Hudson to my stable, 'Huddy' decided to sign a contract with Ken Adam, the former editor of *Jimmy Hill's Football Weekly* who had morphed into a wheeler-dealer agent. The reason given to me was that 'I had conned Bobby Moore!'

Despite my protestations to one Chelsea player in particular, and despite my 'success' in promoting Peter Osgood, Hudson never became one of 'my players'. Ironically, many years later – during the mid-1990s – I did actually arrange a few things for him, but that's another story.

Moore's World Cup-winning colleagues Geoff Hurst and Martin Peters were on my 'special list', and meeting Peters' agent Jack Turner proved very fruitful for me. In many ways it was my first foray into the relatively new world of sports agents.

Jack was a real salt-of-the-earth character. He was East End down to his bootlaces, and as straight as a dye. He was passionate in an almost pre-war, very English way. He and my father got on well – my dad's East End roots were always a big plus – and to cut a long story short, Jack suggested

I become Martin Peters' 'literary agent'. I jumped at the opportunity, but remained determined that this would just be a launch pad for bigger and better things in the future.

But there was one player that I was convinced would give George Best a run for his money in the celebrity stakes, and it wasn't Moore; it was, of course, Peter Osgood.

Getting hold of Ossie via the football club was not the big deal it would be these days. Having left a message with the club secretary I waited with baited breath for Peter to return my call, which he did some twenty-four hours later. I explained what it was all about, the royalty cheques and all that, and soon we were back in West Hampstead for the photo shoot that was to change my life (and without sounding too full of myself, also changed the life of the twenty-one-year-old soccer starlet).

Despite being essentially a 'country boy', Ossie clearly enjoyed the photo session and the whole Swinging London/hip David Bailey atmosphere that was generated in this West Hampstead apartment. He was obviously relaxed and lapped up the purring noises that emanated from the two snappers.

Once it was all over, and I had confirmed how much money could be accrued from the sales of his poster, I deftly managed to slip the word agent into the conversation. I then went on to mention in passing that I had been publicity manager of The Yardbirds and Georgie Fame, threw in that in promoting The Yardbirds, I had also publicised Eric Clapton, and without any more tugging from me, Peter said: 'Would you like to be my agent on a trial basis?''

My eyes lit up when he uttered those words, and my next step was to suggest a meeting. He lived out in Windsor, so it was decided I would meet him and his wife Rosemary (they had married at the tender age of seventeen) at their house. We could have something to eat – Rose cooked a mean steak I was told – and we could plan our campaign.

It was 1968, and the students had taken to the chic boulevards of Paris, marching to the beat of a middle-aged existentialist author and pseudo-Marxist Jean-Paul Sartre. Youth was a powerful weapon in 1968, powerful enough indeed to dislodge the old-order government of President de Gaulle.

In London, Tariq Ali was leading a march in the environs of Grosvenor Square, demonstrating against the Vietnam War. It turned ugly, but it was yet another example of youth engaging itself with serious political and international issues.

Also in London, the Marylebone Cricket Club was under massive pressure not to include Cape Town-born Basil D'Oliveira in its cricket squad for the tour of South Africa. Eventually, hoping to avoid incident, the MCC called off the tour – no engagement with what was morally reprehensible, just bucketloads of hypocrisy.

On the football front, England lost 1–0 at the semi-final stage of the European Championships in Italy to Yugoslavia, before going on to claim third place with a 2–0 success over the Soviet Union.

Back to my meeting with the Osgoods: it was a relaxed affair, with an excellent meal (yes, it was steak prepared to perfection by Rose), topped up with ice-cold lager, and it went down a treat. His wife was small in stature and almost cuddly. She was homely and sweet and so unassuming. I liked her, and I think she liked me. She was the same age as Ossie, but despite her apparent lack of sophistication, there was something different about her. On the surface she was the typical mother/wife figure so prevalent in 1950s British households, but in my view there was more to her than just that. One thing that could be said about her: she knew exactly how to behave, which is more than can be said of the wags of these more celebrity-centric and materialistic times.

Peter explained that he had already formed a company, Peter Osgood Ltd, and that maybe it would be advisable to use this as a proper business vehicle for our project. Peter and his wife were the sole directors, and my name was added within a matter of days.

I arranged for some classy headed paper to be printed. For some reason best known to myself, I chose an insipid yellow, but it was tasteful and it was trendy and very King's Road.

Next stop was Lloyds Bank on Fulham Broadway. The manager rolled out the red carpet, not for me of course, but for 'The Wizard of Os' – the star of the show. The manager, a spare man of indeterminate age in a demob-style suit and a wispy undernourished moustache, possessed a smile that was grotesquely cheesy. When he moved his pencil-thin lips upwards, some strands of his moustache became entangled in his mouth. He was also forever blowing his nose from a large white handkerchief that he kept secreted in his right sleeve.

He revelled in the paperwork, handing sheets to us like some magician producing the proverbial rabbit from a hat. He was, he said, a Chelsea fan. Whether he was or not, or was just cashing in on the whole King's Road thing, I couldn't quite work out; but it made him happy, so who was I to be dismissive of him?

This branch of Lloyds on the Fulham Road was typical of how banks used to be before the barrow boys and hustlers and spivs took over the reins of these conservative institutions and ran them like some kind of glorified Cash-and-Carry, depositing great chunks of the population's cash down the lavatory pan in the process.

Having said our goodbyes to what seemed like the entire staff, and drawn a few quid as, Ossie put it, 'for our general expenses', we made our way to a greasy spoon for a cup of tea and a wad and another chat about our future plans.

The 1968–69 season was not one of Peter's happiest periods as a player: he had been shifted to the midfield by manager Sexton where, in my view, he was like a duck out of water; subsequently much of his natural inborn talent appeared to be repressed and completely stifled. Prior to his broken leg he played the game in a cavalier, off-the-cuff manner that was both refreshing and overtly un-English. Now, he was performing more like a cog in a not-so-well-oiled machine.

I was no Freudian psychiatrist, but for me it was all about confidence, or should I say, the lack of it. Like all great artists – and in sporting terms Osgood was a great artist – he needed ladles of flattery and reassurance to get him back on the right track and to begin drinking from that full glass once more.

Later he told me that the medics at Stamford Bridge had prescribed him some form of tranquilliser. This was the era of such things. Valium, Librium and God-knows-what-else were being dished out to people like Smarties. These 'happy pills' became the norm for so many people that their lives started to take on an almost surreal guise, like some chemical-induced nirvana that would then burn itself out to such an extent that those very same anxieties and doubts and devils would eventually return in an even more virulent form.

Thankfully this chemical hangover wasn't affecting Ossie at all; he had already stopped swallowing the tiny pills. What he needed now was another form of fix: a regular ego-massage from me!

Thankfully Ossie lapped up my boyish enthusiasm like a cat with the cream. He was fully aware from the outset that I was a mad Blues fan, and he also knew that, like Jimmy Greaves during my boyhood, he was my number one sportsman. This was, as they say, a 'marriage made in heaven'.

Having made a plan, I now started to get things moving by making a clutch of phone calls. As I said time after time to Osgood, I can push his name here there and everywhere, but he has to start performing on the pitch. I didn't actually say any of this in such a brusque, harsh tone – it was done with a more silky tongue, in the manner of a therapist. But Ossie got the point.

Peter was born and raised in Windsor, and the nearest industrial centre to the famous castle town is, of course, Slough. During the embryonic years of my existence, in the late 1940s and early '50s, we used to go on Sunday afternoon trips to the country in the summer in my father's 1939 Standard Flying 12. Berkshire, Buckinghamshire and Hertfordshire were our regular destinations, and very often we would have tea in Slough.

In those days, to a boy of three or four or five, the town possessed a country feel to it, but maybe this was just 'rose coloured spectacles' because back in 1937, Sir John Betjeman, in his ten-stanza poem 'Slough' had, shall we say, been less than complimentary about the place: 'Come, friendly bombs, and fall on Slough! It isn't fit for humans now. There isn't grass to graze a cow. Swarm over, Death!'

In 2006, on the centenary of his birth, his daughter, Candida Lycett-Green apologised for the poem, stating her father 'regretted having ever written it'. So, despite my early impressions of the place, even by the late 1930s, it had already begun its decline from market town to 'building and office site'.

And as the 1950s became the 1960s, more and more internationally famous companies decamped to this area of Berkshire, so conveniently close to the environs of London itself.

We therefore craved a company that would exploit the Chelsea man's fast-growing status as a national celebrity, but at the same time utilise it subtly from a local perspective. And we found the right man in Tom Pink, a hard-working Ford agent, who, despite his name, was Chelsea Blue from his collar-and-tie down to his socks and polished black brogues.

The idea was to plaster Peter Osgood's face all over Slough, Windsor and adjoining towns promoting Ford cars, but in particular Pink's thriving dealership in Slough. For this, we received a monthly retainer. Also, every time someone popped in to see Pink and ended up buying a motor after using Ossie's name, a substantial bonus would be paid.

I told Peter I would pay him the dosh each and every month in cash, making it a nice little tax-free income; in the words of Arthur Daley it was 'a nice little earner'. A few months down the line, in 1970, during his time on World Cup duty in Mexico, I journeyed to Windsor via minicab armed with my Ford pound notes and handed the envelope containing the oncers to Ossie's wife, Rosemary. She really appeared to appreciate my visits, and as it was summer, we always spent an hour or two in her garden drinking tea and eating biscuits and cake. She was, as I have already said, really homely, and I think she thought I was 'a bit of a gent'.

As for Pink, well, he was what you would call the archetypal salesman. They are a breed, these people: matching estate agents in their blandness and patter. Unfortunately, once or twice he got on my nerves and I remember one occasion in particular when his whole attitude to life got right up my nose. He had phoned me to discuss a particular aspect of Ossie's Ford promotion, and after the usual insincere pleasantries, I lost my rag. Now, to be fair to the pugnacious Pink, I was living a very strange existence in those days; an existence that, had it carried on, would have tested my sanity to its extreme limits.

It was now the back-end of the so-called 'Swinging '60s'. All hope of Wilson's 'white hot technology' ethos was fast dissipating into just another balls-up by just another government. Rock stars were dying like flies as the drink and the drugs became serious and were no longer just a small part of this cultural and social revolution. Adopting this arrogant agent persona – a whippersnapper who took no prisoners and had essentially transferred all that was Andrew Loog Oldham into a football version of the man – meant that I was playing a part that was not truly me. So, to counteract this feeling of betraying my innate principles, I swallowed all kinds of pills.

At the time of our Ford promotion, 'my pill' was an iniquitous white tablet called Mandrax or 'Mandy' to many addicts, some of whom later used it as a substitute for heroin. Now Mandrax could make a person feel like he was king of the world. It could, in the manner of LSD, make the colours come to life. But on the other side of the coin, it could also make a person stammer and stutter and feel incredibly lethargic, and when mixed with alcohol, it was a recipe for a bad trip. Too many 'Mandies' and you were potentially an undertaker's client.

So, back to this phone call with poor old Pink. I was having a particularly 'bad Mandrax day', and midway through our phone conversation I let him have it. Of course, he didn't know a jot about my pill-popping, and just put it down to my being an arrogant, pushy young bastard. C'est la vie!

Ossie loved the Ford deal, but from my standpoint it was just a start. I kept telling him that my goal was to make him London's version of George Best. And of course, he had one major advantage over George and that was, that unlike Best, Peter was playing for a team based around the most iconic and hip thoroughfare in Europe – if not the world – the King's Road.

The early months of 1969 were all about setting the scene for Osgood's resurgence. I learnt a great deal during my rock 'n' roll period, the most important thing being that in order to promote something or somebody, the best way was to 'flood the media', or beat them into submission; not an easy task back in the days when even a fax machine was a thing of fantasy, to be found only in the works of science fiction writers such as Ray Bradbury.

My one instrument was the phone, and when a journalist colleague told me about *Striker* magazine and its editor, a real whiz-kid of a guy called Tony Power, I immediately went out and bought a copy.

Striker was a mixture of comic and football mag, and its obvious aspiration was to poach thousands of readers from *Shoot*, already the established paper in this comparatively new, and some would say, milieu for morons. This criticism was levelled at these publications by middle-aged journos and writers who simply did not get the new brand of culture in football that was beginning to take hold. *Charles Buchan's Football Monthly* had led the way for nigh-on a generation with pretty dull, dry material, and then along came these brash newcomers full of comic strips and colour and columns by the stars, and with them the game changed forever.

The main columnist in *Striker* was the elegant and naturally talented Manchester City and England midfielder Colin Bell. There was no doubt that Bell was a great player, but he was not really a '60s' man. Peter Osgood, however, was a product of the age, and 'selling' him to editor Tony Power was the proverbial piece of cake, for Tony, despite all his overt business acumen, was very much a young man of the era – and to top it all he was as Chelsea as I was!

So, *Striker* now had two 'star columnists', and as Ossie's 'ghost', it was up to me to make his column not only appealing to kids, but at the same time endeavour to add that extra morsel of spice to it; in other words, to reflect the Chelsea star's natural flamboyance and flair.

Power was what many people would term a poseur. He dressed foppishly, often sporting a bow tie. He had an RAF fighter pilot's moustache, and I liked him. In fact we got on so well that we seemed to spend literally hours having lunch, often at Gerry's Club in Soho, a drinking den and haunt of layabouts and luvvies – comedian Tony Hancock was a member – owned by actor Gerald Campion, who in the 1950s had become an early and unlikely TV star, thanks to his brilliant performances as Billy Bunter.

He would also invite me to various 'events'. One such was a charity do at which the VIP guest was Jimmy Savile. Now, Tony knew Savile, albeit only as a nodding acquaintance, but he was pushy (although not aggressively so), as he was always so friendly and polite. Tony was one of those people who wore a permanent smile of contentment. Whether he was or not I never quite discovered. Anyway, up to Savile he goes and starts chatting to the blond-haired DJ about the North and the South and Chelsea and Leeds. It was obvious that Savile was not completely out of his depth when it came to cultural differences, but it was also blatantly obvious that he was not a deep-thinker.

Savile was from Leeds. Waving one of his ostentatious cigars in my face, he said that the animosity between the two teams was a 'North/South cultural thing'. His whole manner was insincere, and it was crystal clear from the outset that he didn't really want to talk to us.

By this time Tony, who enjoyed the odd chardonnay or three, was at his most ebullient. It was obvious to all that Savile, who didn't drink, craved to get back to all the fawners and kowtowers, the people who sat at his feet purring at his every inane word and sentence.

Ossie was as pleased as a child on Christmas morning with the column. Often we would chat on the phone to thrash out a few ideas that he had, but on other occasions when he was tied-up doing what he did best – playing for Chelsea – I just pretended to be him and imagined what he would say. Anyway, it worked like a dream. Tony, despite his incessant enthusiasm and over-the-top persona, was also a realist. He told me that sales were up and that much of this was down to the Osgood page.

We would occasionally visit Stamford Bridge together, and it was during one of these trips that Tony saw first-hand how the world of showbiz had adopted Chelsea FC as its own.

Tony loved life, and he loved women, and much later when the company publishing *Striker* was bought out, he swapped football for topless females and the world of soft porn publishing in the shape of *Men Only* magazine.

Men Only at the end of the 1960s and into the very early years of the '70s was, by modern standards, harmless fun. It was packed with all kinds of articles, some actually well-written. In most people's eyes it was like a second-class *Playboy*. Only the likes of that puritanical disciple of chastity, Mary Whitehouse, could object to it. Its nudity was genteel and frankly lacking in sexual allure, and its popularity was on the wane, as Britain's answer to *Playboy* – *Penthouse* – started to capture this booming market.

In 1970, Tony commissioned me to write an article for one of their glossy special editions, 'Men At Arms'. Called 'Playing the Game', it was a light-hearted look at the way sport had changed over the years and how it was now being promoted. Within the intro to the piece, I was described as 'business and promotional manager for some of the country's top footballers'.

Now as far as the current generation of football fans is concerned, the game only started to exist in 1992, with the advent of the Premier League and all the Sky TV megabucks sloshing about aboard some kind of ongoing gravy train. Also in media terms, the world of celebrity and soccer only formed a marriage in the 1990s and beyond. The world of Chelsea FC in the 1960s and '70s, and its vast array of star supporters, seems to have been conveniently forgotten.

In fact Peter Osgood summed it all up for me some sixteen years ago when he said: 'I suppose many people will think we lived it up à la Hollywood, all champagne fountains and all-night parties. When the vice-chairman, Dickie Attenborough, brought Steve McQueen to our dressing room, it was the proudest moment of my life. In those days, everyone who was anyone was a Blues nut: Leonard Rossiter, John Cleese, Michael Caine, even Henry Kissinger. Life is so much different now – stars watching their favourite football team is not such a novelty.'

And certainly in my *Men Only* article, I highlighted how football had and was still changing culturally: 'Now footballers own boutiques and drive flashy sports cars and wear kipper ties decorated with red flowers and grow elegant beards or moustaches.'

Sportsmanship in the modern game has disappeared, write the scribes. Well, take a look at what I penned over forty years ago in the same piece: 'After all, what is professional sport, but a world where young men are kicked, hit and occasionally spat at. It has no relationship with the old ideals of sportsmanship. Today it is essentially an extension of war. We cannot drop nuclear bombs so we play international soccer and bite and spit.'

This 'special' was the final production of *Men Only* in its original form; soon it was to change – some would say for the worse – as Tony Power became a highly-paid employee of the King of Soho himself, Paul Raymond, following the purchase of the title for £10,000.

Under Raymond's more raunchy direction, *Men Only* threw any thoughts of quality magazine writing out the window, as its pages became more and more visually sexually explicit. As editor, Tony promoted this new-look production with relish, and even that collector of babes, Hugh Hefner, suddenly realised he had a fight on his hands. For years, and in particular during the 1950s and early '60s Hefner had fought the cause of more sexual freedoms, but now thanks to Power and Raymond, poor old Hugh's *Playboy* was looking old hat as the *Men Only* brand of pin-up evolved each month into out-and-out pornography.

Raymond was a rich man. During the austere, black-and-white years of the 1950s, he had cleverly tapped into the world of erotica by flouting the censorship laws that still dominated British society. Women could appear nude, but could not move. The'Windmill Theatre ('We never close') had been the provider of visual titillation since the 1930s with its 'tasteful' tableau of nudes, but Raymond realised that the public (well the men anyway!) craved more. So, in a quiet Soho alleyway – Walker's Court – he opened a club, Raymond's Revuebar. It being a club, it gave him carte blanche to put on a show which could defy the archaic censorship regulations, without breaking the law.

The heyday of the club was undoubtedly the 1960s, when a whole host of stars visited the club. I remember one late-night at this 'symbol of sin' in particular, when looking round I noticed not dirty old men in dirty macs, but well-heeled people of both sexes, including actors Peter Sellers and John Mills (a Chelsea fan by the way) and rugby aficionado Stanley Baker. Singer Alma Cogan and Britain's blond bombshell Diana Dors were other regular poppers-in, as was Judy Garland. There was no doubt that this temple to bosoms was the place to be.

Tony Power introduced me to Paul Raymond. He smiled a great deal and was polite, but I must say I found him difficult to relate to. He certainly didn't seem to me to be Tony's cup of tea, but he was obviously paying the former editor of *Striker* a wad of cash, so I guess Tony just adapted.

Ossie met Tony a few times, and like me, he enjoyed his company and his general bonhomie. Certainly during his tenure as *Striker* editor he proved himself to be a close ally and did much to help bolster the PR side of the Chelsea man, no more so than in August 1970 when he came to announce the Striker of the Year Award. There was obviously going to be only one winner, and his name was Peter Osgood. To say that we fixed the result would be harsh, but let us say we 'massaged' the votes a wee bit – just a case of two Blues fans sticking together!

The match chosen for the presentation was the 1970 Charity Shield. In those days the season curtain raiser was not a Wembley event, and on a hot August afternoon FA Cup holders Chelsea played host to League Champions Everton at Stamford Bridge.

Everton dominated the encounter, with Alan Ball, sporting a natty pair of white boots, in sparkling form. Alan Hudson remembers it well: 'You have got to remember that I was still recovering from all my ankle problems. I was also zonked mentally because my injury problems meant that I had not only missed out on our FA Cup success, but also had to cry off from any England involvement in Mexico.

'Frankly I spent much of the afternoon just limping about – in many ways it was all a bit of a nightmare. In my opinion I shouldn't have played, particularly as the Charity Shield is not just a prestige pre-season affair, it's a very important game, and a real pointer to the season ahead.

'Parading the Cup to our fans before the game was nice, but as far as the game itself was concerned, they simply played us off the park. The 2–1 score in their favour certainly didn't flatter them. The star of the show was undoubtedly Alan Ball – he ripped us apart. To be frank, they looked fitter than us. Bally played a blinder, and you couldn't help noticing him in his fancy cut-away white boots – it was a real football education watching him!'

It was just like one big party down the Fulham Road prior to kick-off. To many fans, the game didn't matter one iota, it was just an extension of the FA Cup-winning knees-up. Tony Power, realising the publicity potential of the fixture, had arranged for leading radio and TV DJ Ed 'Stewpot' Stewart to present Ossie with his Striker of the Year Award before kick-off. Never missing a trick, Tony had lined up Ed, knowing full well the Radio One star was a diehard Toffee.

Despite his and his side's low-key display, Ossie enjoyed the afternoon. 'I remember the heat, but I suppose having been out in Mexico for the World Cup, I should have been used to it. I didn't have many opportunities to score. But I do remember one in particular. I was put through, I can't remember by who, and let fly with my left foot. But unfortunately their keeper Gordon West made a fantastic save. I think Westy dined out for some months on that particular save! Hutch (Ian Hutchinson) played well, and it was fitting he should score our goal.'

Having left *Striker* to become Paul Raymond's blue-eyed boy, the magazine was eventually swallowed up via various (to me) baffling buy-outs, so its main rival (in fact its only rival), *Shoot*, had the market all to itself once more. Following the amalgamations and mergers and general reorganisation, the 'new' company launched a serious weekly football newspaper called *Inside Football*, which was edited by a gentle bohemian character called Bob Dawbarn, who initially, until its demise, had also edited the comic-style *Striker*.

The eventual changes of ownership within the organisation that controlled *Striker*, Morgan Grampian, were both confusing and convoluted, but the upshot was that Banner Press became the publishers, later transmogrifying into Spotlite Publications.

Now, Tony Power forewarned me about all these chops and changes, following his decision to join up with Raymond. 'You'll love the new editor,' he told me with a grin. 'He's like an ageing hippy.'

After meeting Bob, I got back to Tony and joked that he 'looked just like Charles Manson!'

There was no doubt that Bob, who died aged seventy-two some twelve years ago, was a genuine legend. Public-school educated (at Merchant Taylors), he was one of the original members of the Mick Mulligan jazz band, playing trombone. Its vocalist was another legend in the shape of George Melly.

However, Bob's ambition was to be a journalist, and after a period as a court reporter (his shorthand speed had to be seen to be believed), he joined the *Melody Maker* in the mid-1950s. It was at 'MM' that he created a gossip column, 'The Raver', in which all his natural satirical instincts came to the fore.

This column soon established itself as a must-read for all the high and not-so-high-flyers in the jazz and burgeoning rock scene. His annual 'Old Dawbarn's Almanac' was another innovative look at the music scene; its publication was eagerly awaited by readers, but often dreaded by the purveyors of popular music.

Stories abounded about Dawbarn, none of which were apocryphal. The most famous undoubtedly was in 1962 when a then unknown Bob Dylan ambled up, without warning, to the *Melody Maker* offices, and there was Bob embroiled in deadline day panic, confronting this American folk singer. As far as he was concerned, the number one priority was press day; so much to the chagrin of the young Dylan, he had him ejected!

Like several members of the cast of *Inside Football*, sartorially Bob was a wreck. In fact during his 'MM' years, there was an appeal for the 'Buy Bob Dawbarn a New Raincoat Fund'. There was no doubt that the whole essence of *Striker* was a foreign land to him, but with *Inside Football*, he could express himself intellectually. So when in early March 1972 *Striker* was given the push by its owners and amalgamated with the more intellectually driven and upmarket *Inside Football*, Dawbarn was undoubtedly delighted. The demise of *Striker* also coincided with the apparent demise of that flamboyant Chelsea side of Cooke, Osgood and Hudson. By then, the game was changing; indeed it was about to enter a dark age of negativity, hooliganism and falling attendances.

Perhaps surprisingly, considering his 'arty' persona, Bob was an authentic football fanatic. During the1960s he had regularly turned out for the *Melody Maker* soccer team, lining up with the likes of Ray and Dave Davies of The Kinks and actor Tom Courtenay.

As for Tony Power, we drifted apart. In fact we met just a couple of times later during the 1970s, the last being when I was endeavouring to sell him a story for *Men Only* about the erotic antics of Joyce McKinney, the Mormon beauty queen!

I was told that by this time the twin devils of cocaine and booze had taken hold of his whole being and way of life, and according to his former assistant editor John Barraclough, he was 'suffering from a dose of the clap'. Tony Power's descent into depression and drugs encapsulated the era for so many people in so many ways; fun, hedonism, and innovation followed by the realisation of age as bodies and minds burnt out. Idealism was replaced by cynicism and then desperation, as untouchable youth lost its lustre forever.

NINE

1969-70 -
OSSIE HITS THE HIGHSPOTS
AND SHAMATEURISM IS EXPOSED

What a momentous season it turned out to be! But the early portents were not good, with just one victory garnered from the first nine games, and that was a scrappy 1–0 home success over a struggling Ipswich Town at Stamford Bridge, thanks to an Ian Hutchinson goal.

In many ways, the whole campaign really only came alive on 27 September when a crowd of over 46,000 saw Ossie and the boys outsmart Arsenal 3–0. This win was the start of a run of just two defeats from sixteen starts, one black day being at Elland Road in front of more than 57,000 fans where the old foe, Don Revie's Leeds United, banged in five goals with just two in reply. An unbeaten period of nine games followed, and then perversely another 5–2 score in favour of the opposition when, on 28 March, eventual champions Everton 'did a Leeds' at Goodison Park. But these bare facts tell just a soupçon of the whole story, and that story was all about the FA Cup.

There has probably never been an FA Cup quite like it. It all began quietly enough with Birmingham City being dumped at the Bridge 3–0. It then got more than a bit edgy in round four with Burnley proving to be obdurate opposition. A home 2–2 draw and Turf Moor on a bleak January evening loomed for the replay. It was 1–1 after 90 minutes, but Chelsea found a second wind in extra time to advance 3–1.

As far as Osgood was concerned, the autumn of 1969 saw both his confidence and his form improve almost weekly. By December, my trips to his home in Windsor increased, and often he would drive me around the Berkshire countryside looking for a pub in his wife's small Hillman Imp, listening to his car radio, which just a few weeks later always seemed to be playing the Edison Lighthouse number one 'Love Grows' – 'Oh, but love grows where my Rosemary goes'. Ossie loved to sing those words, in obvious homage to his wife. Of course, the mind does play tricks as the disc wasn't released until January 1970, but I'll always associate that particular song with the great man. I can see him now, dressed in sweater and slacks, and telling me he must become more up-to-date by buying some 'proper gear', asking me about boutiques and shops and the like, joining in with Edison Lighthouse between sentences.

Having established a business-like, and in many ways friendly rapport with Tom Pink at Ford – after a sluggish beginning the money was starting to increase monthly – it was now imperative to build on this with other commercial deals.

By this time *The Amateur Footballer* magazine was prospering so much, both in terms of circulation and public exposure in the press, that I was finding it difficult to cope with both the business and editorial side of this now-established enterprise with my new role as football agent and business partner to Peter Osgood – there were simply not enough hours in the day!

Also, having lifted the lid on 'shamateurism' in the amateur game some months before, I was now fully involved in exposing the hypocrisy of a situation in which amateur footballers could 'earn' more than their professional counterparts in the lower leagues.

I had already made reference in the magazine to amateur players moving from club to club, dropping hints that somewhere in this maze of club disloyalty the old pounds and pennies sign was somewhere in the background. Then in the autumn of '69, I really let fly, this time using television and

the highly acclaimed sports journalist Ian Wooldridge to highlight the growing epidemic of 'boot money'.

Wooldridge hosted a Sunday afternoon half-hour show on
London Weekend TV, *Sports Arena*, which preceded the football highlights package *The Big Match*, hosted by Jimmy Hill.

The show was in a sense the moral mouthpiece of sport,
concentrating on wrongs that should be righted as well as
some of the more positive aspects of a whole raft of sports.
On this particular September afternoon, half the programme
was in essence a mini-documentary delving into the dark
world of amateur football and illegal payments.

I had put this shamateurism story to one of the show's pro-
ducers, Tony McCarthy. After some subtle persuasion, he gave
my idea the thumbs-up. So now it was simply a matter of finding some officials and players willing, to 'blow the gaffe' on film.

My next task was to write the script. Actually finding
people prepared to appear on TV and denounce the whole
system proved to be comparatively easy. At the same time
I upped the coverage in *The Amateur Footballer*, and in order
to try to get some form of balance, I phoned FA secretary
Denis Follows. To say that our conversation was a non-event
would be an understatement. He knew amateur players en
masse were being paid; I knew they were being paid; in fact
everyone in the game knew players were receiving money,
but throughout our tense and at times bitter conversation, he
struck rigidly to the status quo and vehemently denied it all!

The scene was then set for the filming – there was no
video in 1969 – and club officials and players seemed, somewhat surprisingly, only too keen to tell all. As far as the players
were concerned, the only proviso was that some demanded
that their faces should be hidden: all very cloak-and-dagger!

The show caused a stir in the FA corridors of power,
but overall the response from the people that mattered,
the honest and dedicated football club secretaries and the
like, was positive. Rob Hughes – later to become *The Times*
football correspondent and currently writing about the game
for the *International Herald Tribune* – was the inquisitor
in chief, and he asked me a few very pertinent questions,

during which I replied that when contacting the Football Association I had encountered 'a brick wall'.

Later, in *The Amateur Footballer*, I wrote a feature, 'Is The Shamateurism Nut About To Be Cracked?' on the whole episode, and it is interesting to read some of the reaction. For example, Tilbury secretary Geoff Paisley stated it was about time something was done, and he quoted from an article appearing in *The Amateur Footballer* written by that doyen of football writers David Miller, a man whose words graced the pages for many years of both the *Daily Express* and the *Daily Telegraph*.

Miller had written: 'It is several months since the publication of the 'Chester Report, yet it seems that there is no move afoot to rationalise the situation in senior amateur football, where all but a handful of clubs are professional in everything but name. Abuse continues, but nothing is done.

'Half the trouble is that many of the FA Council, who are responsible for implementing any changes, have connections either now or in the past, with the very clubs who break the rules, or with the leagues in which they play. In effect officials must therefore legislate against themselves, which is unlikely.'

Paisley commented: 'I enjoyed the programme, and I would certainly like to see the FA take some action, but I honestly doubt it. The great pity was that no FA officials would appear to be interviewed.'

Well I had tried, but my requests fell on deaf ears. I think one of the main reasons for this was that, unlike the situation today, youth was not courted by seemingly every aspect of society. The grey men in the higher echelons of the FA regarded the likes of me, young, long-haired and – by their standards – unconventionally attired, with extreme suspicion. I was seen as a young troublemaker.

Another club official, Bishop's Stortford treasurer Bob Turner made the point that 'without doubt the *Sports Arena* programme laid everything on a plate.'

The whole 'Boot Money' saga certainly ruffled a few feathers in high places, but it took a further three years before the FA decided to abolish the distinction between amateur and professional. Definitely a case of better late than never!

I 'created' another coup for the magazine early in 1970 by asking Peter Osgood to write an article extolling the virtues of the amateur game. Headlined 'WELL DONE SUTTON!' he complimented Sutton United on reaching the FA Cup fourth round, but was more interested in outlining his opinions on one of the leading amateur protagonists of the day.

'I remember very distinctly being marked by Enfield's experienced centre-half Alf D'Arcy,' he wrote, 'in a friendly fixture at Stamford Bridge against the British Olympic team. He certainly gave me a rough ride that day, and I must say that I was tremendously surprised by not only his tough tackling, but also his all-round skill. I am sure he could have made the grade if he had decided to become a professional.'

As for Sutton, Osgood was impressed with the calibre of the Surrey club's squad: 'They certainly have some fine players – Ted Powell, Micky Mellows and Larry Pritchard to name just three. I have always thought highly of Mellows' ability as a striker. He is just the type of forward I admire – always there at the right time to snap up chances, similar in fact to our own Tommy Baldwin.'

Utilising Ossie's natural use of words for a whole range of articles was proving not only successful, but also profitable. I beat magazine editors into submission with incessant phone calls and a whole raft of different ideas, attempting at all times to concentrate on the way football was transcending sport and morphing into a vital part of the entertainment – the new rock 'n' roll, in fact.

The rock-style soccer posters were selling well, and the various photographic sessions were like an open door for me in my quest to increase my client list. The West Ham guys, Hurst, Moore and Peters, were already signed to an agent, but the likes of Chelsea's mercurial winger Charlie Cooke and QPR talisman Rodney Marsh (what an ideal member of that Chelsea team he would have made – all flash and flounce) were available.

Charlie Cooke lived out Richmond way near the Thames. He was a friendly guy, but somewhat introverted. His wife Edith was also friendly, and as warm as toast. Charlie enjoyed being snapped, but it was obvious from the outset that as a general rule he disliked publicity for publicity's sake.

There was, to my mind, something of the James Dean about him. Here was a man who was obviously a serious thinker. On the whole, professional sportsmen were and are very eager to embrace opportunity where money is concerned, but not Charlie – not back in 1969 anyway.

The photo session was a success, and I soon built up a rapport with the enigmatic Scotsman. I mentioned my association with Peter Osgood and how I had agreed to be his agent. He immediately indicated a real disdain for agents and all that they represented, but despite his jaundiced view, he seemed quite prepared for me to promote his name, although not without his input. For example he made it clear to me from the outset that ghosted columns and the like were a big no-no as far as he was concerned – where possible he wanted to put pen to paper himself.

I realised from the off that at all times I had to handle Charlie with kid gloves, and the fact that we got on like a house on fire made my task a great deal easier. However, Ossie was my number one priority and as the 1969-'70 season developed and his potency in front of goal increased with almost every contest, the business of 'selling' his name, a hard graft at first, became that much easier. What helped, of course, was the celebrity sideshow of Stamford Bridge – the film and TV stars regularly attending games, and the post-match social side in the so-called 'Long Bar' or 'Tea Room', as it was sometimes referred to.

As a boy, I had ambitions to be an actor. At the age of thirteen, living the 'Luvvie Dream' appealed to me so much that my father managed to fiddle me on to the books of an agency called Corona. Based in Chiswick, West London, they looked after the budding careers of such wannabes as Francesca Annis, Richard O'Sullivan and Dennis Waterman (the latter two both staunch Chelsea supporters, by the way).

I was soon on a film set at Elstree Studios working as an extra in *The Young Ones*, starring Cliff Richard and Robert Morley. During the filming I became matey with a young actor called Joey White, brother of *Cathy Come Home* star Carol, who later, like so many stars of that momentous era, gravitated to the Fulham Road and the football shrine of Stamford Bridge.

So, it seemed appropriate that some nine years later – 1969 to exact, I should be strolling towards the car park at Stamford Bridge, chatting to club vice-chairman Richard (now Lord) Attenborough.

He was somewhat shorter than I had imagined, but he was classically dapper and stylish, and I have to say I felt somewhat intimidated. For here I was, aged just twenty-three, in the presence of true greatness. Charisma is an almost impossible thing to quantify, but when you encounter it, believe me, you know it. George Best had it, in bagfuls. Many years later I was introduced to Prime Minister John Major at a football exhibition – 'just call me John', he said – well, he didn't have it, yet when I interviewed Tony Blair it was apparent that here was somebody whose pores oozed it. And Richard Attenborough, despite his modest persona, was an overtly special person.

It is true that during my Soho days I had met and become close to a wide variety of rock people, but many of them were not yet the megastars they were to become. Organising a press reception for The Beatles in 1964 was an obvious high point, but my interaction with John Lennon and Paul McCartney had been very matter-of-fact – just common pleasantries and the odd 'thank you' or three.

Attenborough's voice was soft in the extreme – so very English and strangely reassuring. There was also an endearing twinkle in his eye; when he smiled, his compassion and sincerity and genuine niceness really shone through like a shaft of sunlight on miserable November day. In fact his whole face appeared to generate all that was fine and good and somehow respectable.

I must say that having encountered some truly 'dodgy geezers' during my time as publicity manager of Georgie Fame, Zoot Money and The Yardbirds, his whole demeanour was a refreshing novelty. It highlighted the fact that to be top of your profession did not necessarily mean that it was a prerequisite that you had to trample on those around you to achieve this goal.

It was one of those autumn days when the crispness in the air coupled with a light breeze seems to act as a tonic from Mother Nature. The fact that the Blues had just prevailed 2–0 over West Bromwich Albion, with goals from Charlie Cooke and Peter Osgood, only heightened my already hyper senses (no doubt exaggerated tenfold by the popping of a white pill or two). It had not been a vintage Chelsea display, but there was still something about it that smacked of class – that special *je ne sais quoi* you get from seeing a Jacobi or an Olivier – or indeed an Attenborough – perform on stage and screen.

As we walked, we talked, or, more accurately, I just listened. Having explained my role as Peter Osgood's agent and business partner – he displayed particular interest in how I intended promoting the striker, and paid me various compliments on what I had already achieved – he then proceeded to wax lyrical about the inbuilt talents of 'the King of Stamford Bridge' – his balance, his poise and his innate ability of being able to somehow fashion a goal out of absolutely nothing.

We must have sauntered along the tarmac leading to the car park that Saturday afternoon, and despite being in awe of such an icon of the British cinema, I simply could not resist asking him how his love for all things Blue and Chelsea had first surfaced.

He explained to me that he had first started cheering them on from the terraces during the war, in 1942. Then in 1947, when starring in the film *Brighton Rock* (based on Graham Greene's acclaimed novel), he was told he must lose some weight, so he managed to train with the team, and in so doing, got to know everyone at the club, and in particular Chelsea's then-record signing, centre-forward Tommy Lawton, who became a great friend.

He then went on to recount how he used to go to the Bridge with those two titans of the cinema and theatre, John Mills and Laurence Olivier.

This was indeed a far cry from the days of cloth caps and roll-your-own fags and acrid Bovril in cracked white discoloured cups.

As he climbed into his car, he sketched a wave with a flourish, and then he was gone.

Richard Attenborough's name cropped up in unlikely fashion during a conversation I had on Boxing Day 1970, when I found myself drinking what appeared to be pints, if not litres, of violently strong black coffee from soup bowls with stage and screen actor Donald Sinden, looking resplendent in silk dressing gown and pyjamas, in the kitchen of his home in Hampstead Garden Suburb. I am sure I was probably boring him rigid about Chelsea and Peter Osgood and the whole King's Road cultural scene, for Sinden was certainly no follower of the beautiful game. But, to be fair to him, he made all the right noises when I attempted to explain to him my job as a football agent and PR guru.

'How very interesting,' he boomed – his voice boomed throughout our surreal conversation. 'Please tell me more.'

So tell him I did, with all the arrogance of youth and all the sincerity and seriousness of someone in his twenties in 1970, a year in which the spirit of the 1960s continued to live on, until the reality check of the Ted Heath government and the Three-Day Week and the civil unrest hit.

And when it came to Richard Attenborough and his Chelsea addiction, Sinden stopped for a moment, laid down his huge bowl of coffee and stared at me in disbelief. You see, for the layman, actors and aristocrats and society hairdressers and other what would now be termed A-listers, supporting a particular football club in 1960s England was looked upon as quirky, if not downright odd.

'Have another cup of coffee,' boomed Sinden, his face now expressing genuine interest. And I did. And I lit yet another Lucky Strike. And I spieled on and on about football and fashion and, above all, Chelsea FC. I think by then the eyes of the great thespian were just beginning to glaze over, but also by then I was fully wound up like some ongoing tape machine, so I just sipped coffee and smoked and spoke until even I realised I had outstayed my welcome.

Some weeks later I apologised most profusely to Sinden about my bad manners, and I must say he was most gracious: 'you are just young and enthusiastic, dear boy,' he boomed.

Ossie's goal against West Bromwich was a seed: a promise of what was to come. His goals flowed in the League: two at Ipswich in November and four on 27 December 1969 in the 5–1 demolition of Crystal Palace at Selhurst Park. He was now the most talked-about goalscorer in the country, and as Chelsea hurdled up the table, so more and more media pressure was brought to bear on England manager Alf Ramsey to include him in his England squad. Ossie had become the darling of the tabloids.

Meanwhile, as manager Dave Sexton's men continued to captivate press and public alike with their brand of cavalier, devil-may-care football, more and more celebrities could be seen at the Bridge on match days. As Peter Osgood said to me much later: 'nobody likes watching guys play like robots, and we certainly didn't!'

Alan Hudson was fulsome in his praise of two of his colleagues from that pulsating period: 'Os and Charlie Cooke were geniuses, and there was this constant buzz-thing at the club.

'Everybody (in those days) was trying to change society. I guess it was unique, and most of us at the Bridge at the time – in other words, the players – knew something big, something special, was going to happen. A fantastic bond was built up between players and fans; as I say, it was unique.

'Okay, so we earned good money in those days, but we still met and spoke to our supporters in pubs in and around the ground. Yes, it was a glamorous time, and in many ways our lifestyle in the 1960s and '70s is being aped by the Premier League boys, but in a much, much bigger way.

'In any branch of showbiz, there are poseurs, and football is just the same. I suppose the likes of Os and me had to deal with more hangers-on than was good for us, but we never grew apart from the genuine fans, the real football people.

'However, comparisons between different eras are not only difficult, they serve no real purpose. In 1969 and 1970 life was more easy-going; you were in many ways allowed to express yourself with more freedom – the free-thinker, free-spirit syndrome.'

The word glamour is defined in the *Oxford English Dictionary* as 'alluring or exciting beauty or charm'. And a visit to the 'Long Bar' for a cuppa or something stronger post-match was witness to that. Without knowing it, you could strike up a conversation with, for example, that zany comedian Marty Feldman, who would later be elevated to Hollywood star status by Mel Brooks and his movie *Young Frankenstein.*

Now, in the mid-to-late 1960s Feldman lived above me in Wellesley Court, a late Art Deco block flats in Maida Vale. Many a night's sleep in the block became almost impossible, as raucous sounds emanated from Marty's apartment. 'Did you hear the noise?' was the question the day after. And the answer was always the same: 'Oh, it was just one of Marty's parties!'

His breakthrough as a scriptwriter came in collaboration with Barry Took, courtesy of such TV classics as ITV's *The Army Game* and *Bootsie and Snudge* as well as *Round the Horne* for BBC Radio.

In many ways it was *The Compartment*, a short TV play written in 1962 by Alf Garnett creator, Johnny Speight, in which he co-starred with another Chelsea fan, Michael Caine, that brought Feldman to the fore as a consumate comedy actor.

Feldman loved Chelsea. He had the most incredible eyes. They resembled large olives, and when he was excited or trying to emphasise a particular point, it seemed they had a life of their own. 'Would they pop out?' I kept asking myself when I stood near him.

He was a passionate fan, and meeting him for the first time in the company of Peter Osgood, I don't know who was more star-struck, Feldman or Osgood himself!

I always remember one short sentence he uttered in my presence. It had been another typical show from Ossie, all grace, guts and goals plus natural organic energy. 'I wish I had Peter Osgood's talents,' he said wistfully. Some irony there, I thought.

In this day-and-age, 'celebrity-spotting' at London restaurants is a must for any readers of *Tatler*. Certainly a trip to Alvaro's restaurant in 1969 would have had the most ardent celeb-watcher in ecstasies of delight.

Picture the scene: it's match day at Stamford Bridge, and Alvaro's is buzzing. Looking round, any diner could not fail to notice one table in particular, packed with a whole host of national and international stars, tucking in to haute cuisine, sipping fine wines and all straining at the leash to venture forth to the Holy Grail on the Fulham Road and roar on Ossie and his pals.

'All the faces were there,' photographer-to-the-stars and Blues diehard Terry O'Neill would later recount to me. 'Even some people who were not natural fans such as Tommy Steele came along. As did Ian La Frenais.'

The man who organised many of these glitzy celebrity nosh-ups was Mayfair man-about-town tailor, Doug Hayward, described by Terry O'Neill as 'the Buddha of Mount Street'.

Now, to say that Hayward dressed the great and the good would be an understatement: Sir Michael Caine; Sir Roger Moore; Sir John Gielgud; *Look Back In Anger* playwright John Osborne; Tony Bennett; Clint Eastwood; James Coburn, who once called him 'The Rodin of Tweed'; Rex Harrison; Sir Michael Parkinson; World Cup-winning skipper Bobby Moore; Tommy Steele; Peter Seller; and Terence Stamp all donned his exquisite designs.

He created suits for Mick Jagger, which resulted in him designing the wedding dress for Bianca Jagger. Steve McQueen wore Doug's suits in *The Thomas Crown Affair*, and Hayward was also the fashion designer responsible for Caine's suits in *The Italian Job*.

His female clients included Faye Dunaway, Mia Farrow, model Jean Shrimpton and actress Sharon Tate, so tragically murdered by followers of the infamous Charles Manson in August 1969. She was at the time married to *Rosemary's Baby* director Roman Polanski.

Producer of such TV hits as *Birds of a Feather* and *Lovejoy*, Tony Charles, looks back with extreme affection on those days.

'We had a special deal with the owner of Alvaro's, which was about halfway down the King's Road, 'he remembered. 'The meals cost £1 a head, and the usual number at any one time was eleven. We were all Chelsea season-ticket holders, so the idea of a slap-up lunch, followed by watching Ossie and Charlie Cooke and co seemed just great. In fact it was at one of these lunches that we hatched the idea of our movie,

Today Mexico, Tomorrow the World. That was, of course, in 1970, just before the World Cup.'

Audie Charles, for some quarter-of-a-century the welcoming and creative figure at Hayward's haven for the well-dressed at No. 95 Mount Street, reeled-off a whole list of names often to be seen imbibing and masticating at these lunchtime occasions.

'Steve McQueen used to come along,' she said, 'as did Clint Eastwood on occasion – he was living in London at the time. David Hemmings (star of cult movie *Blow Up*), Ian McShane (star of *Lovejoy*) and many others were regulars.'

My own excursions to Alvaro's were rare, as by 1970 I found myself frequenting another hangout of the luvvies, the poseurs and 'the beautiful', the Barbarella restaurant on the Fulham Road, just a short free-kick from the gates of the Bridge itself.

Lunches at Barbarellas were long, liquid affairs in the company of television scriptwriter and northern Chelsea fan Vince Powell, his long-standing girlfriend Judi, and numerous comedian friends of Vince's such as Billy Dainty and Bernie Winters.

My friendship with Vince was comparatively long, and it was close. His TV writing credentials were formidable. With Harry Driver, he was hired as *Coronation Street*'s first storyline writer, and between 1961 and 1967, the workaholic Powell penned thirty-two episodes himself, plus a further four with his partner, Driver. His *Coronation Street* immersion was confirmed in 1964 when, with one of the other regular writers John Finch, he wrote a successful stage play, *Coronation Street on the Road*.

But it was comedy shows that brought him national recognition. They ranged from the gentle fun of Harry Worth to *Bless This House*, starring Sid James, Diana Coupland and Sally Geeson (both Sally and Judy Geeson could be seen regularly at the Bridge) and the controversial *Love Thy Neighbour*, a show that to this day evokes fury amongst many people. Even back in the far less PC days of the 1970s, the show was regarded as overtly racist.

I once asked Vince about the programme, and at the time I laid my anti-racist cards on the table (I was already involved with the Anti-Apartheid Movement, as indeed was my father), and he told me that the whole philosophy of the sitcom was to expose racism, and at the same time ridicule it. Knowing him as I did, I believed him. After all, hadn't Johnny Speight done the same thing (although in a totally different way) with *Till Death Us Do Part* and Alf Garnett?

Now Vince Powell's part in the success of Peter Osgood was only small, but had a massive impact nonetheless. And like so many aspects of life – and in particular life for what John Mortimer referred to in one of his Rumpole stories as 'showfolk' – its beginnings were convoluted.

Having already explored by the back-end of '69 as many avenues as possible in which Ossie could spread his wings and not simply rely on his ability to trouble the onion bag each and every Saturday, I got wind of the fact that Vince Powell had become captivated by manager Dave Sexton's team; captivated to a such a degree that, despite his Manchester beginnings, he had adopted Chelsea as his club. So it was with some cheekiness in my heart – probably aided, I am sorry to say, by the odd pill – that I contacted a friend at London Weekend TV and obtained Powell's telephone number.

At the time, Vince and Harry Driver were receiving plaudits from the critics about their series *Never Mind The Quality, Feel The Width*, starring John Bluthal (later to garner even greater success as Frank Pickle – 'The Most Boring Man In England' – in *The Vicar of Dibley*) and Irish actor Joe Lynch, who built up a huge following in the 1970s as Elsie Tanner's boyfriend in *Coronation Street*.

The series, which ran from 1967–1971, concentrated on the activities of Manny Cohen (Bluthal) and Patrick Kelly (Lynch), two tailors in business together – one Jewish, the other an Irish Catholic.

The openings for jokes – many of which were obvious but nevertheless extremely funny – were enormous.

Anyway, I spoke to Vince, and he was very approachable. Straight away there was a simpatico between us – you get this sometimes in life with a person you've never met before. It is difficult to put into words, but I think on this occasion what it boiled down to was that, despite his comparative fame, and his age, we were one of a kind – enthusiastic and optimistic, and above all, mad about Chelsea FC.

So, after the first few sentences of, 'how are you?' etc., I asked him about the possibility of using Peter Osgood in one of the episodes, and he went for the idea, without any apparent salesmanship from me. Later he was to say to me that Ossie could in fact 'make it on TV', but life moved on and any ambitions we had of stardom away from the football pitch were never realised. Opportunity knocked, but thanks to fate, we weren't able to answer the door.

My next step was to journey down to the Thames TV studios at Teddington Lock and meet Vince, who was dying to meet Ossie; he had made his own way from the Chelsea training ground in Mitcham.

Powell and Peter were soon chatting away like old friends, and within a matter of minutes we were in the Thames TV bar downing a few drinks. Producer Ronnie Baxter then joined us, as did some of the actors. And it was Joe Lynch, buoyed by the odd glass or two, who took centre stage. Here was yet another Ossie fan, and the striker lapped it all up like the proverbial cat with the cream.

Vince told us he was going to fiddle a scene into this particular episode which would be shot on film; all Peter had to do was show off his soccer skills on a pitch adjacent to the studios. His only 'acting' was to utter just a few words, but it would, assured the scriptwriter, be an integral part of the show, and bring with it a feast of publicity for all parties.

As we were leaving, an excited Vince told Peter he'd be at the next home game, and as I made my exit, he asked me if I would like to have lunch with him at the Barbarella restaurant before the match.

All the 'Thames TV' people really enjoyed Ossie's company, and one man in particular, *Never Mind the Quality, Feel the Width* co-star Joe Lynch, became a close friend to the two of us.

Having gained a great deal of success in his native Ireland, both on stage and in TV productions, he later gained many more media accolades across the water both in the sitcom *Rule Britannia*, as well as *Coronation Street*.

By 1979 he was back in Ireland, and soon his portrayal of Dinny Byrne in the RTE soap operas *Bracken* and *Glenroe* had made him a household name. His was also the voice of Grundel the Toad in Don Bluth's hit adaptation of Hans Christian Andersen's *Thumbelina*.

Joe enjoyed a bevy or three, and after the filming of Peter's scene, we all retired to the bar where copious amounts of alcohol were consumed. Eventually, realising it was getting late, Ossie bade his farewells, and Joe kindly offered to drop me at my home in Hampstead. He lived not a million miles from me, so 'it was no trouble', as he kept saying.

Arriving in London NW11 – and by now it was very late indeed – we thought it would be a good idea if he joined me in my flat for a few more glasses. 'How about some cheese?' I asked. My speech by this time was as thick as a 1950s London pea-souper.

He voiced his appreciation and addiction to French cheeses, in particular Brie and Camembert. Once inside my front door, I dashed into the kitchen and whipped up, what seemed at the time, a tasty selection of cheese and biscuits, which we gobbled greedily while relaxing on a Victorian settee in the sitting room. We washed the food down with a variety of drinks, mainly red wine, but later we took the bull by the horns and went for something stronger, namely some ludicrously pricey cognac I had recently bought from Harrods. 'Nothing but the best' was my motto, no matter how much it dented my bank account.

As our tongues grew looser and looser, the conversation developed into inarticulate rambling bouts of fractured speech covering food and football and politics, with Joe at all times emphasising how much he admired and liked Ossie. No matter what the subject was, we always returned to the subject of Chelsea FC. Joe had been a fine footballer in his younger days, and in fact had refused professional terms in 1947 to join the Radio Eireann players as an actor. He vigorously maintained that apart from George Best, Charlie Cooke and Peter Osgood were the most exciting players in the country. I mentioned Rodney Marsh, but Joe was a bit dismissive, making the point that the QPR hero was performing his magic tricks in a lower division, so any comparisons would be invalid.

Suddenly poor old Joe's face took on a pea-green aspect, and unfortunately all the expensive Camembert, Brie, burgundy and cognac were returned to sender in most dramatic a fashion. Then, seemingly just to remain in synch with the jovial Irish actor, my insides did much the same. It was not a pretty sight! Matters did not improve when my twelve-year-old tabby cat, Pamplemousse, joined us and proceeded to investigate the 'damage' in the manner of a bloodhound on the scent for arch detective Sherlock Holmes. We felt and looked like extras in *The Night of the Living Dead*!

Somehow, Joe managed to gird his loins and spruce himself up; he even found time to thank me. As he left, I felt even more fragile. I knew I needed to go to bed, but illogically I craved another drink. Downing a quadruple brandy, I felt better, and my senses began to return to normal about the same time as my stomach felt my own again. This general feeling of mental and physical togetherness was even more enhanced after I had swallowed one of what were known in the 1960s as wake-up pills. I did not sleep, and tomorrow would never come if I didn't go to bed. Anyway, I had a very special idea to put to Peter Osgood, and his agreement to my plan would make him unique in the world of professional football. In fact, in this respect, he still is.

My manifesto was to spread my agent's wings as wide as possible, but with a marked difference to anything that had been attempted before. We already had this company, Peter Osgood Ltd, to administer all aspects of his career, but what was needed was another organisation to 'do deals', as I put it to him, for other Chelsea stars. So, Star Soccer Management was born, complete with expensive-looking blue company paper, with me in the driving seat, and Ossie the contact man. It was, on the face of it, a partnership made in heaven.

I was already doing bits and pieces for Charlie Cooke, but on our blue letterhead, we were able to add the names of Alan Birchenall, (a great singing voice, had Birch; in fact he had once formed a duo with 'With a Little Help from My Friends' star Joe Cocker in some pubs in Sheffield) Ron 'Chopper' Harris; John Hollins and the Manchester United goalkeeper Alex Stepney. Never before, and certainly not since, has a star player been part of the agency business.

However, it should be pointed out that the business of being an agent during the 1960s and 1970s was a totally different enterprise to today's wheeler-dealers. Contracts and transfers were forbidden fruit forty-odd years ago. The sole purpose of a footballer's representative then was to promote the player in terms of endorsements, newspaper columns, opening supermarkets and TV and radio. Trying to offload him to another club in order to pocket a percentage of the transfer fee was *verboten* big time.

Meanwhile, the Blues were receiving a plethora of plaudits from all and sundry. It was true that Leeds United – guided by their astute and no-holds-barred boss Don Revie – were the most effective outfit in the country, basing their whole *modus operandi* on the physical aspects of the game, whereas Chelsea could at times be unpredictable, but at the same time much more aesthetically pleasing.

Some thirteen or fourteen years before, during his time as a player with Manchester City, the grim-faced Revie had devised 'The Revie Plan', based on the system employed by Nandor Hidegkuti for the rampant Hungarians during the 1950s. Yes, he was full of new ideas, some of which were regarded as revolutionary. But to say that his players were as colourful as those of the equally intense Dave Sexton would be a gross exaggeration of gargantuan proportions.

Having despatched Birmingham out of the FA Cup on 3 January 1970, seven days later saw them host Leeds for what was already being regarded as a vital contest in terms of the league. In the encounter at Elland Road back in September, Revie's men had prevailed 2–0. The *Yorkshire Post* had given the match its very own X Certificate with phrases such as 'late and early tackles', and its correspondent had gone on to criticise both sets of players for playing 'venomously'. Some form of revenge was gained sixteen days later with a 2–0 victory in a League Cup replay, but it was the First Division fixture in the autumn that proved to be the template for all the hokum that was to follow.

So the scene was set for a right winter dust-up. Pre-match, I joined Vince and girlfriend Judi at Barbarellas for a culinary delight of a lunch. Judi was a really pleasant girl. Obviously sensitive – some would say neurotic – she made easy company and we ate and drank with relish.

It was difficult to get away from business, so during what was probably the tenth or eleventh glass of wine, he gave me the schedule for the filming and told me that he'd like me to be his guest for the broadcast of the Ossie episode. He also gave me a few pointers as far as other ITV shows were concerned, in particular the afternoon children's programme, *Magpie*, hosted by Susan Stranks. Later it was fronted by Mick Robertson – yet another follower of Chelsea – who became a great friend and a great help in my everlasting quest of attempting to get footballers on to kids' TV.

Arriving at the ground, we joined over 57,000 others to witness a debacle. Leeds bashed the Blues 5–2. Ossie notched a goal, but it was all depressing stuff.

Victories over Arsenal and Sunderland, with the Burnley FA Cup success sandwiched in between, soon revived flagging spirits, but it was the FA Cup that seemed to whet the appetite down the Fulham Road and beyond.

Struggling Crystal Palace succumbed 4–1 in round five, thanks to goals from Ossie, John Dempsey, the vastly underrated Peter Houseman and that chaser of lost causes, Ian Hutchinson. .

Chelsea *v.* Queens Park Rangers, 21 February 1970; 33,572 overtly partisan spectators were packed into that compact coliseum Loftus Road, right smack in the middle of *Steptoe and Son* territory, Shepherd's Bush. As far as Londoners were concerned, it was *the* tie in the last eight. And on a personal note, it gave me just a smallish loyalty tug.

For by this time I was also 'doing the agent bit' for a true club icon, the trendy Rodney Marsh. That Victorian teller of gothic tales and intricate mysteries, Wilkie Collins, used

Hampstead Heath in North London as the eerie setting for the opening scene of his pièce de resistance *The Woman in White*, and it was on the very same heath that I first had a conversation with the enigmatic yet extremely likeable QPR idol.

It was 1969, and The Rolling Stones were gearing up for that jam session to end all jam sessions, the free concert in a sun-drenched Hyde Park, which they dedicated to the recently deceased Brian Jones.

The plan was to meet Rodney in Hampstead, and once on the glorious swathe of Hampstead Heath, take some ultra-modish shots of the man himself, looking every inch the rock star. Our photographer, one of those precious effete guys more used to dealing with *Vogue* models than pro footballers, pouted unattractively and told me in no uncertain terms that he was not at all happy with Rodney's apparel.

It is important to remember that these posters of ours were not the common-or-garden mugshots so prevalent in the likes of *Shoot* and *Striker* and a whole host of cards pirated by suspect 'businessmen' operating out of small, smelly offices in some back alley. No, these had to be all about Carnaby Street and the King's Road and fashion and attitude.

Now, I was fortunate enough to possess a wardrobe full of flower-power shirts, marketed by that trendsetter chain of emporiums *I Was Lord Kitchener's Valet*. What type of shirt Rodney was actually sporting on that particular afternoon, I cannot for the life of me remember, but as far as the mincing snapper was concerned, it was definitely passé in the extreme.

'Look here, Greg,' snapped the guy with the camera, 'your blue flowery thing is what we're after, so could you give it to Rod to wear.'

So, a-shirt-swapping we went, and the mouthy photographer gave me his Yves St Laurent jacket to wear (a bare torso on Hampstead Heath, even in the liberal and permissive 1960s, would have been frowned upon by the more traditional populace of Hampstead).

Once it was all over, I chatted to the jovial Marsh, and dropped a few unsubtle hints about Eric Clapton and Peter Osgood. We agreed I could 'give it a go as [his] agent for a bit'.

The following day, I gave Terry O'Neill a bell, and even though he was an ardent and dedicated follower of Chelsea, like me, he was bowled over by Rod's unique brand of insolent skittishness. Rod was undoubtedly cool and he was undoubtedly photogenic with a big 'P', and after a few more telephone conversations, he was on his way to model for a series of full-colour monthlies, Yves St Laurent's brand-new collection for men, in his 'Rive Gauche' range.

The main star of the photo session – apart from Rod himself, that is – was Yves St Laurent's new very chic denim jacket, retailing at a hefty £60, (over £700 in today's values), which the QPR man showed off perfectly. As a model, he looked like he'd been traversing the catwalk since birth! I almost expected him to call me 'darling'!

Okay, so he was a guy from the East End, but he could paint and he was perfectly at home at poseur-style cocktail parties, just like the one we attended just before Christmas 1970. The room was choc-a-bloc with society wallflowers of both sexes plus the usual quota of dippy debs, but Rodney flourished in these surroundings. He was cool and he was hip, but he was also very much part of the new social strata of a country no longer completely enveloped in a straitjacket of snobbery.

Away from George Best and the Chelsea crew, Rodney was the only player of that era to truly encapsulate both the colour and the thumbing of nose to convention that was the swinging '60s.

Rodney liked freebies – I got him one of the sixty quid Yves St Laurent jackets gratis – and he also liked his money in 'readies', as he regularly put it. He owned a beautiful Lotus Europa, which I always found getting into about as hard as trying to put on your trousers with a broken arm. The motor looked lovely, but the passenger door opened up like some massive can of sardines – like it, I did not!

Not to be outdone, I scrounged a 'Rive Gauche' jacket for myself, for as Ray Davies so aptly put it: I was 'a dedicated follower of fashion'.

We would regularly pop along to the Pizza Express in Dean Street, sometimes to eat lunch and drink red wine with his old mukka Terry Venables. More than once during these drives, Rod would quip with a terrific twinkle in his eye that every time he asked QPR chairman Jim Gregory for a transfer, the well-heeled car showroom entrepreneur would make him a present of a new motor!

At that cosy but raucous enclave of Loftus Road, Rod was a big fish in a pretty small pond. He was an authentic hero – the man whose élan and improvisations had guided QPR to unlikely League Cup final glory in 1967, when the West London outfit became the first Third Division team to lift a major trophy at Wembley Stadium.

That day, 97,000-plus fans saw Albion take a 2–0 advantage before goals from Roger Morgan, Marsh and Mark Lazarus gave the underdogs victory.

Rangers were managed by the evergreen Alec Stock. Many years later, in 2000, I helped to organise a special Testimonial Dinner at Yeovil Town Football Club, where Stock's name had first reached national sporting hearts and minds in 1949, when, as player-manager, he had netted one of his side's goals in the 2–1 FA Cup fourth round ousting of the so-called 'Bank of England team', Sunderland. Marsh was Guest of Honour, and agreed, for no fee, to stay on and answer a whole series of questions from the assembled guests.

The press gave the tie the big build-up, and it all revolved around Marsh *v.* Osgood. Okay, so Rangers were Second Division, but the gulf in those days of flared trousers and flair on the football field was nothing compared to the current era of the Premier League and Middle East money and Russian oligarchs. There was also the interesting subplot of Terry Venables captaining Rangers against his former club, and another former Chelsea favourite Barry Bridges starting in QPR's line-up.

Rangers had accounted for the Brian Clough/Dave Mackay axis at Derby County at the previous hurdle, and given the fortress nature of Loftus Road, many pundits had predicted a torrid afternoon for the King's Road glamour boys. But it was not to be. Ron 'Chopper' Harris marked Marsh out of the game, and Ossie claimed a superb hat-trick in a 4–2 victory.

After the game, I wandered across the pitch – and boy was it muddy – in the company of a relaxed Charlie Cooke. I was dressed in a chocolate brown suit, recently purchased from a King's Road boutique for a pretty packet. Charlie stared at my new brown, buckled wet-look shoes, and with a twinkle in his smiling eyes, waxed lyrical about them. Talking to him, you would never have thought he had just been through a gruelling ninety minutes of blood and guts football during which he had had to deal with tackles that in this day-and-age would have a referee flourishing red cards like some manic magician on speed!

Soon after my chat with Charlie Cooke, I approached an acquaintance at London Weekend TV, and the long-and-the-short-of-it was that Ossie was required the following morning for a recorded interview in *The Big Match* studios in Dean Street, Soho.

Soho on a cold, crisp Sunday morning in late February 1970 was a somewhat eerie place. There were still some remnants of Saturday night excesses, with sartorially elegant young men and women looking bleary-eyed and zombie-like as they made their way home after a rave or whatever. In the Victorian alleyways there was more unpleasant evidence of a 'good night' going wrong in the shape of piles of multi-coloured vomit – there was even the odd discarded syringe secreted behind a sad-looking dustbin.

The bars and cafés were either open, or in the initial throes of opening their doors. The strip clubs looked bleak and unwelcoming without the neon lights highlighting the large colour photos of well-endowed young women in various states of undress.

One thing that has never changed in Soho is the morning smell, which smacks more of Paris or Brussels than it does of dear old London Town. It is doughy and at the same time sweet, the freshly-baked brioches and croissants mixing with the slightly acidic aroma of alcohol plus just a whiff of waffle. Forty-two years ago there was the added stale tobacco smell; it was everywhere, in every human pore and every nook and cranny of every building, big and small.

I met Ossie outside the small unprepossessing studios; we were both just a shade fragile after quite a celebration the night before. Upon entering the inner sanctum, we were greeted by that doyen of football commentators, Brian Moore, who for so many years graced the airwaves with his understated style. Think of that shouter-supreme Jonathan Pearce, and then imagine the opposite – that was Brian. Cool, suave, but above all very English and normal.

Moore was a true gentleman, and I remember meeting him for the first time at Chelsea's Mitcham training ground. He came up to me, smiling broadly, and without in any way sounding rude said something like: 'You are Peter Osgood's agent, aren't you?'

Peter's interview on *The Big Match* went well – he always made a perfect interviewee, and as his fame grew, not unsurprisingly he appeared more and more on the show. I remember another occasion in particular when he was the guest in tandem with one of the 'Lisbon Lions', the marauding Scotland international full-back Tommy Gemmell, who by 1971 had left his beloved Celtic to sign for Nottingham Forest.

I introduced Ossie to Gemmell, and you could see almost immediately that my man was star-struck. Later, Ossie built up this façade of being arrogant, and some would say cocky, but rest assured, much of this was an act, in my view anyway. Upon meeting Gemmell, he was as humble as any fan.

So, after a few standard 'goodbyes' and the odd 'see you later', we eventually left the studios. Ambling along Dean Street, I passed Sunset Strip, the oldest striptease joint in Soho, famed during the 1960s for a performer of Italian origin with the unsubtle stage name of 'Busty Bernicci'.

Since the beginning of the 'Me' decade, the 1980s, Soho and its immediate environs have taken on a cleaned-up air. It is now safe and sanitised and all the wonderful crazies and delightful eccentrics of past decades have all but evaporated; a bit like football itself really: now gentrified, the players all uber-fit, living Howard Hughes-like existences in a world of muesli, minders and masses of moolah.

Charlie Cooke stated recently that some of his behaviour as a player – the excessive drinking for example – was 'unprofessional'. Maybe so, but if Charlie, Ossie and Alan Hudson et al had not indulged in some serious Dolce Vita would they have been so entertaining and as exciting to watch? I don't think so. After all, the threesome didn't leave burnt-out wreckage in their wake; they just lived their own particular versions of the rock 'n' roll lifestyle.

If you were young, musical and British in the 1960s, rock 'n' roll was an irresistible career path. At the same time, if you were young, could make a football talk and were British, pro soccer also represented an enticing career road. And with George Best at the helm and several of the Stamford Bridge buccaneers plus Rodney Marsh not far behind, living out the rockstar lifestyle in the beautiful game was available as never before. For already, for just a few, the bling culture had arrived, but without the wags and all the tacky folderol of the new millennium.

As has been quoted on numerous occasions, England manager Alf Ramsey was heavily into industry and sweat – deft artistry or extravagant élan were never on his compass. So, selecting someone with Peter Osgood's supposed playboy reputation – no matter how unwarranted – was never likely to appear on his agenda.

However, I had other ideas, and in the *Daily Mail*, and more specifically the paper's sports editor Charlie Wilson, I had a leading media organisation and a respected journalist and man about Fleet Street who, like much of the football-watching population (and indeed beyond), had fallen in love with Dave Sexton's Chelsea, and in particular their charismatic centre forward Peter Osgood.

So, one day after a brief visit to the treatment room, I sat down in a typical 'greasy spoon' of the period with Ossie and told him in no uncertain terms that it was now time for an all-out newspaper assault, with 'Osgood For England' as our war cry.

Charlie Wilson, who later climbed the Fleet Street ladder to edit *The Times*, was an ebullient Scotsman, full of genuine enthusiasm. He was also extremely loyal to the people he liked and respected. He had a particularly close rapport with

Charlie Cooke. In fact so much so, that the three of us could often be seen downing cognacs in the Tudor-beamed bar of The Wig and Pen situated almost bang opposite the Royal Courts of Justice. It was evident during these afternoon sessions that the journalist Charlie and the football Charlie had more in common than just a love of the round ball.

In 1968, Wilson married fellow journalist Anne Robinson, later of course to gain national prominence as the fearsome frontwoman of the BBC's *The Weakest Link*. Early in her chequered career, she suffered the indignity of being given the heave-ho by then deputy news editor Wilson at the *Daily Mail* because of a bizarre custom that forbade married couples working in the same office!

Wilson remained by far our staunchest ally, as did the paper's sports news editor Peter Moss. During the latter part of '69 there was a cartoon on the *Mail*'s back page featuring an archetypal trainer – as the breed was called then – with the legend 'Osgood Ltd' emblazoned on the back of his tracksuit. Underneath were the words: 'It's Alf Ramsey's company you need to be in'.

Then, through a combination of subtle PR, plus the fact that all the guys at the *Mail* were anti-Ramsey – whether in Charlie Wilson's case it was that the tight-lipped manager had guided England to the World Cup, and being Scottish he found this hard to stomach I never quite fathomed – but from everything that I had garnered from the embryonic beginnings of our relationship, it seemed that whereas Chelsea FC was groovy and hip, Ramsey was definitely old news.

How it came to pass that Wilson got us on the front page of the *Daily Mail* was never fully explained. But aged just twenty-three and a few months, whatever came along I just accepted as the norm. Now having said that Ossie and Chelsea were hip, it was soon decided that to try to ape George Best was not a clever move, so the John Steed/ *Avengers* look was adopted.

Photographs of Ossie donning a bowler complete with City suit and umbrella dominated that day's front page forty-two years ago, in conjunction with a full story about him; how much he could make; quotes from me, the whole piece ending with the line that 'Pele earns £100,000 per year' – big bucks in 1970; well, it certainly put Peter's pounds' potential into context!

Mentioning the 'M' word brings me on to the saga of Ossie's *Daily Mail* column, which not only almost caused a full-scale strike at the newspaper, but later resulted in a rap on the knuckles from the Football Association and boss Sexton for some of his more controversial and forthright comments and opinions.

Having bored Charlie Wilson to death on an almost daily basis about Ossie 'writing' a regular column for the paper, it was finally agreed that we should meet the managing editor, the legendary Fleet Street figure E.V. Matthewman to discuss the idea.

Being in the presence of Matthewman in his office, all leather and telephones, power emanating from every corner, made me feel very young indeed – it was a bit like a trip to the headmaster's study for six of the best!

He looked forbidding, sitting there, master of all he surveyed. Charlie Wilson was there, but I didn't feel it was vital for Peter to make an appearance. There was talk and all kinds of questions were levelled at me about content and how it would be written. It was all very deflating.

Matthewman never smiled, and this made me even more nervous. I thought about 'The Wig and Pen' round the corner and how pleasant it would be to be sitting there now with an extra-large cognac and nothing to worry me; just thinking about how I could enjoy myself and milk my youth for all its worth.

Then – and it was just like a dream – Wilson asked me something, and I replied, and Matthewman started talking about a contract and £80 per week. This was music to my ears, and I visibly relaxed without need of a brandy.

We then shook hands, and Matthewman – or was it Wilson? – said something about contracts in the post and signatures and other such minutiae. As I left, I smiled at Matthewman, but he just stared. I was indeed out of my league.

Ossie was understandably ecstatic about the *Mail* column: apart from the tantalising prospect of a substantial

Screaming Lord Sutch and his Savages publicising the Lord's radio station.

The author drinking coffee with Press Presentations MD, Bob Baker, on the Thames quayside at the launch of Lord Sutch's radio station.

Right: Zoot Money (far right) outside The Flamingo. Also in view is Andy Summers, later of The Police.

Below: The author, far right – looking pensive – at a Flamingo reception. *Ready Steady Go!* presenter, Cathy McGowan, is on the left with producer Vicki Wickham, Dusty Springfield's manager.

The author, The Yardbirds and a train of media arriving at Lord Ted Willis' front door in 1964.

Ossie's locks being trimmed by Blues fan Vidal Sassoon.

Georgie Fame (centre) with manager Rik Gunnell (right) toasting his twenty-first birthday at a Soho party in June 1964.

Right: The author, far left, with a youthful Eric Clapton (far right) at an HMV signing session.

Opposite above: Eric Clapton (far left) playing the Blues in the Willis' garden in 1964. Ted Willis and his daughter, Sally Hook, are seated in the foreground.

Opposite below: The author's only foray into music management, The Ricochets - it wasn't a great success.

Front cover of *The Amateur Footballer* magazine in 1969, featuring George Best tackling Exeter amateur Pinkney in a Cup tie.

Vol. 3 No. 1

THE AMATEUR FOOTBALLER

1/6

The author in a King's Road suit presenting Hitchin boss, Vince Burgess, with a Manager of the Month award in 1969.

The author with Spurs and Scotland skipper, Dave Mackay. He captained Tottenham against Chelsea in the 1967 Cup Final.

Full-page ad in *The Amateur Footballer* for rock-style football posters. George Best and Willie Morgan feature.

The author, on the far left, next to Ken Adam who 'beat him' to become Alan Hudson's agent. Far right is *Shoot* editor Chris Davies.

WELL DONE SUTTON!

Says PETER OSGOOD

Chelsea star Peter Osgood writes exclusively for "The Amateur Footballer"

ALTHOUGH I don't have much time to watch Amateur Football, I have always been extremely impressed by what I have seen.

I remember very distinctly being marked by Enfield's experienced centre-half Alf D'Arcy in a friendly fixture at Stamford Bridge against the British Olympic team. He certainly gave me a rough ride that day, and I must say that I was tremendously surprised by not only his tough tackling, but also his all-round skill. I am sure he could have made the grade if he had decided to become a professional.

However, it does seem to me, as an outsider, that much could be done to improve the level of competition in the amateur game. I am sure I am not in a minority when I say that it seems incredible that there is no relegation from the

Isthmian League, which is after all supposed to be the senior amateur league in the South of England. Surely the success of any league set-up is based upon promotion and relegation to maintain interest right to the end of the season. If this vital piece of legislation was passed, I am certain Amateur Football would begin to prosper once more.

Obviously the fact that an amateur side, namely Sutton United, has managed to reach the Fourth Round of the F.A. Cup, should give the amateur game the sort of boost it so sorely needs. And what a tie for the Surrey amateurs! A home match with League champions Leeds United. I was also very pleased to see that the Sutton committee, after a great deal of deliberation, had decided to stage the tie at Sutton. They could so easily have been swayed by the financial rewards of playing at Elland Road, but I am convinced that if the Isthmian club is to win or force a draw, and at the time of writing I don't know either, then they can only achieve this on their own ground. Anyway, whatever the result I would like to send my congratulations to Sutton United on being the first amateur side to reach the Fourth Round for seventeen years.

They certainly have some fine players — Ted Powell, Micky Mellows and Larry Pritchard to name but a few. I have always thought highly of Mellows' ability as a striker. He is just the type of forward I admire — always there at the right time to snap up chances, similar in fact to our own Tommy Baldwin.

Of course, all the recent talk of "shamateurism" has done nothing to help the waning image of the amateur game. But basically whether amateurs

are "shamateurs" or "shamateurs" are amateurs, I am still convinced that Amateur Football has a future even in this day and age of high-powered commercialism.

Ossie's article on Sutton's Cup giant-killing in *The Amateur Footballer.*

ANZORA TOPS THE POPS

Anzora Hairdressings make you the master of your hair. Whatever the style you prefer, whatever the condition of your hair, Anzora keeps you perfectly groomed always.
Anzora Cream for light grooming, Viola for dry hair and Anzora Special, medicated against dandruff.
Let Anzora master your hair. 2/10 and 4/- At leading chemists

Advert for Anzora Hair Cream in a 1970 edition of *The Amateur Footballer*. The cream gave a 'greasy look', as commented upon by Ray Connolly in his interview with Ossie.

Bukta Professional Sportwear

Peter Osgood thinks it's the greatest!

Star forward for Cup-Winners Chelsea and the England World Cup Team, Peter Osgood certainly knows a thing or two about football kits! And he says 'If you're going all out to play well, you've got to have well designed kit—and for a really professional look you just can't beat Bukta Sportwear. They're winners for hard wear, too'.

Ask your **local sports outfitter** for the FREE Bukta 1970 World Cup Catalogue, packed with kits in all the top soccer and rugby club colours— over 1,000 different colour combinations of jerseys, shirts, shorts and stockings!

OR write for a copy to: Edward R. Buck & Sons Ltd., Bukta House, Brinkeway, Stockport, Cheshire.

'Bukta' advert in *The Amateur Footballer* featuring Ossie.

THE **PETER OSGOOD** COLUMN

THE use of overlapping full backs has been the secret weapon for many clubs for some eight years now, but even today many Continental teams are still baffled by this tactic. We at Chelsea have been using this ploy for some time. When we gained promotion from Division Two in 1963, both Ken Shellito and Eddie McCreadie were at times playing in the manner of an orthodox winger, and this caused a great deal of havoc among many Second Division defences.

We have continued to use this ace, and because of this we have probably scored more goals. Take Dave Webb for example. He has banged in as many goals during recent months as many so called strikers. Eddie Mac once scored the winner in a League Cup Final with one of the greatest goals ever seen at Stamford Bridge. Yes, there is no doubt at all that although teams are criticised for leaving gaps at the back, this feature of the modern game is here to stay.

The "Old Timers" say we don't attack so much nowadays. What I would like to say to these people is this: Did full backs attack in your day? Older people are perpetually telling us how good football was in the "Good Old Days". Of course, soccer was entertaining before the war, but why should top-class football lag behind other spheres of life in terms of progress? My answer to any elderly "knocker" is simple: In your day defenders were there to beat the ball away, whereas today defences are stronger and most of our successful sides bear their success on a rock-like, yet skilful rearguard.

Leeds United's English international Terry Cooper is, in my view, the most talented of the overlapping breed. His main asset I suppose is his tremendous speed and dribbling ability which obviously stems from the fact that at one time he was

A goal as a left winger has helped Leeds full back Terry Cooper develop tremendous speed and dribbling ability.

A feature of the modern game is the overlapping full back—Chelsea have a fine combination in Dave Webb (above No. 2) and Eddie McCreadie (right).

an orthodox winger. This invaluable experience of playing on the left flank also enabled him to perfect a sizzling left foot shot which he has used to great effect on numerous occasions, especially in crucial matches.

Half-backs also attack much more now than they used to. People like Billy Bremner, Alan Mullery and our own John Hollins are often up there with the marksmen, fighting it out in the penalty area. Before the 1966 World Cup a wing-half tended to be rather overrated as his play, but Dave Mackay's great influence changed all this.

The 1969-70 season will go down in the record books so probably the most hotly organised in the game's long and eventful history. Every one knew last August that this was World Cup year, yet nothing constructive was done in advance to help iron out future congestion that was almost bound to arise.

Let's look at Chelsea for instance. We drew with Leeds in the Cup Final at Wembley, and only two days later were playing at Stoke in a league fixture. This was followed by fixtures against Burnley

and Liverpool all in the same week. Hardly the sort of build-up needed for an F.A. Cup Final replay!

On top of all this, the congested fixture list meant that all the Chelsea and Leeds players involved in the Home International tournaments had to be released by Sir Alf Ramsey for club duty.

People will undoubtedly be quick to ask me what I would do if problems such as those mentioned were thrust on me to be sorted out. My solution is a simple one. In World Cup year start the season in July. If this were done we would not have the ridiculous fixture situation that we experienced in April.

Many fans are often under the impression that when a fixture becomes severe players concentrate on the field, the blokes involved bottle up their dislike after the game has finished, and only look forward to some sort of revenge. This is far from the truth.

Things that happen on the field are soon forgotten when the referee blows the final whistle. During the Cup Final, for example, Charlie Cooke and Billy Bremner were involved in a "little" incident, but there was nothing at all premeditated about it. Both simply just lost their tempers, and it was soon forgotten. This is typical, and just part and parcel of the modern game. Of course, bitterness and antagonism do

Osgood—in action against Watford in the semi-final that sank Chelsea to Wembley and eventually that fine triumph over Leeds Limited in the replay at Old Trafford.

exist, and several players that I know of really do hate one another. But basically this is rare. I only hope more fans remember this in the future.

Finally this week I would very much like to comment on the decision of Leeds' Paul Madeley, who followed in the footsteps of Evertonians Gordon West by refusing for personal reasons to go to Mexico with the England squad. Certainly one must sympathise with Madeley, who says he has had too much football, but surely as this sort of opportunity can come only once in a lifetime, to reject it is a bit of a waste to say the least. My wife Rosemary would be the first footballer's wife to admit she is lonely when I am away for long periods, but she realises that football is both my career and my life so she accepts all the invitations that go with being the wife of a football star. After all the life of a professional footballer is very short so some one like myself has, in the saying goes, got to "make hay while the sun shines". Let's face it, if I were a 9-5 man would any income be what it is today? I very much doubt it.

That's all for now.

[signature]

PROGRAMME SPOT
BOLTON WANDERERS
* * * * * * * *

Opposite top: Then Chelsea
vice-chairman Richard
(now Lord) Attenborough
with his wife. I found him
warm and friendly in 1969.

Opposite bottom:
An Ossie article in *Striker*.
The author ghosted these
for £20 a week.

Right: Ossie on the
front cover of *Striker*.
His column helped
boost circulation.

Below: Interview between
the author and Ossie
on his record-breaking
European goal-fest,
in *World Soccer* in
November 1971.

STRIKER

EVERY MONDAY   NUMBER 56   ONE SHILLING (5np)   JANUARY 30 1971

THE NATIONS CUP

PETER OSGOOD Chelsea
JOE ROYLE, JOHN HURST Everton

WORLD SOCCER, November, 1971   WORLD SOCCER, November, 1971   TWENTY-FIVE

Eight goals
equals record

I SPOKE to Peter Osgood Immediately following Chelsea's record European defeat of the Luxembourg side Jeunesse Hautcharage in the European Cup Winners Cup.

Ossie had just scored five of his team's 13 goals, and these coupled with his hat-trick in the first leg meant that he had equalled the individual European goalscoring record.

However, Osgood was not that pleased, as he had managed to score "only" five!

"You see," he told me, "I had made a bet with Peter Bonetti that I would score six, so Peter picked up an extra fiver for all the work he had to do that evening! So you can imagine I was not too overjoyed with only scoring five."

Obviously Peter Osgood is not a man to make rash predictions, and I know that from having spoken to him well before the match he was really intent on breaking the European individual goalscoring record, even though as Osgood himself put it: "This match is basically only just a canter for us, although we were all impressed in Luxembourg by the way their players stuck to their job, and accepted the 8-0 thrashing with real dignity."

Higher class

We all know that Peter Osgood has it critics, and will undoubtedly continue to do so in the future. But I think we all agree that there are not many other forwards in Europe today with so much goalscoring flair. Even though he has helped his side to smash the European record, he realises only too well that in future rounds of the Cup Winners Cup he will be up against teams of a much higher class.

"I feel that it is about time I scored goals more consistently again, just as I did in fact during the 1969-70 season. Then yes I hardly ever begin a season with a real bang, I used to build up my goal-getting output as the months go by.

"I appreciate that on paper my record so far this season looks exceptionally good. But let's be realistic about it. At the time of writing my tally for Chelsea is 12—but eight of these were scored in our matches with Jeunesse. My aim therefore is to try

and utilise my goalscoring exploits against Jeunesse as a kind of launching-pad for the rest of the season."

But can such easy opponents as the Luxembourg side really help a striker to improve his game?

"Well, frankly I think it can," Ossie replied. "My view has always been that no matter how inferior an opposition may appear, in important European Cup-tie is just what the doctor ordered as far as I am concerned. After all it does prove to you that you can score goals. And sometimes playing in the First Division regularly makes you think you'll never score many!"

I suppose all of us know by now that European competitive football is based almost entirely on a defensive concept, which obviously creates a mountain of problems for strikers such as Osgood. Yet, although aged only 24, he has had enough European experience to know that with enough

guile and skill it can always be found through even the toughest defence.

Negative

"Yes, that's perfectly true. You know I get fed up with people who are perpetually blaming negative tactics for the lack of goals. In my opinion if a forward has enough of a soccer brain to match his ability with the ball near the box, then there should always be goals—even in a really tight European Cup away leg.

"After all, guys like George Best and our own Charlie Cooke, with their own unique brand of trickery, are players who can always break down even the most uncompromising of defences."

Peter Osgood in action against
Coventry City.

Are you saying in fact that the only way to counter packed defences is by placing a great deal more emphasis on the old-fashioned skills of the game such as dribbling and being able to body-swerve?

"Yes, you've hit the nail right on the head! I have always believed football to be a game of skill. In other words being able to do something with the ball as opposed to simply hoofing the ball for safety, something we see too much of today.

Runners

"Of course you have got to have your runners. But that does not mean football SHOULD be for the runners only. Real Madrid and the Brazilian national team have proved that vision is what makes soccer tick, and I agree with this."

Many of you are probably thinking that some of Peter Osgood's ideas about football are old-fashioned. Maybe they are, but after all his attacking flair prevented Brazil from dominating world football!

Peter Osgood shoots towards the Derby goal during a First Division match at
Stamford Bridge which ended 1-1.

Left: Blues fan Michael Crawford with his ex-wife Gabrielle. She moved on to striker Tommy Baldwin.

Below: The author and The Yardbirds' lead singer, Keith Relf, at a signing session in HMV Oxford Street, 1964.

PENALTY

April, 1965   Vol. I   No. I   Price 1/6

See inside:
**FULL PAGE PHOTOGRAPH
OF CHELSEA F.C.**

Front cover of the
one-off magazine,
Penalty. It was 1965
and Chelsea were
riding high under
Tommy Doc.

VOGUE

**50 PAGES OF
BRITISH FASHION**
THE BEST CLOTHES THE BEST PRICES
AND ALL READY TO WEAR NOW
SUPER PROTEIN DIET · ONE-DAY TOTAL BEAUTY PLAN
CLOTHES FOR CHILDREN · 10 BEST BREAD RECIPES
THE NEW BATH ROOMS · EXTRA MEN IN VOGUE SPRING EDITION

Front cover of *Vogue* in
1971. The piece by the
author and Charlie Cooke
was a first for football!

Right: What a line up! Best, Osgood, and Hudson in Chelsea shirts before Ossie's testimonial in 1975.

Below: Julie Driscoll (with Brian Anger). The author worked with Julie in Soho. She was The Yardbirds' fan club secretary – greatly loved by all!

Right: Ossie and a 'Dolly Bird' model in Piccadilly, publicising his poster.

Above: T. Bone vocalist Gary Farr at The Marquee in 1975. The author and Gary's dad, former boxing champion Tommy, had a run-in on one occasion.

Terry O'Neill
and his All-Star
team. Terry
(front row, second
from the right)
is beside *Porridge*
star Richard
Beckinsale. Also
featured is *Lovejoy*
star, Ian McShane.

David Hemmings
with his wife,
Gayle Hunnicutt.
The *Blow Up*
star was an
Alvaro's regular.

(in those days) improvement in his income, he fully realised that it would help to spread the Peter Osgood Ltd gospel of 'Osgood for England'.

Several days went by, and still no definite confirmation of a start time for his first piece. By this time I was becoming edgy. 'Why the delay?' I asked Charlie Wilson. Eventually, I got to the bottom of the problem, and boy what a bombshell that was!

Believe it not, the prospect of a regular Peter Osgood column in the Conservative-supporting, right-leaning *Daily Mail* had caused the National Union of Journalists to, shall we say, adopt an intransigent stance.

'Peter Osgood is not a journalist,' was the kernel of their argument. 'If he writes for the newspaper, we'll call our members out on strike!'

This was serious stuff. Even though I had always been a firm believer in the general ethos of Trade Unionism, I thought the attitude of this group of newspaper scribblers was just a tad over-the-top and definitely picky in the extreme.

Another conflab was arranged at Matthewman's inner sanctum in order to try to untangle this web of what, in my opinion, was a bitter stance adopted by people still trying to live a pre-war life.

The *Mail*'s managing editor sat behind his desk looking unusually benign. The desk seemed even more grandiose than since my last visit, and his bank of telephones had surely grown, hadn't it?

In essence, the conference was all about diplomacy and meeting our 'adversary' halfway. The experienced combo of Matthewman and Wilson assured me they had the answer, and once explained, it was simplicity itself.

'We'll get Brian James to interview Peter Osgood each time,' I was told. 'And Brian's byline will appear at the bottom of each column. This should solve the problem.'

James was the paper's chief football writer, and one of the most respected journalists of his generation. I found him reserved and unapproachable, but having said that, when it came to reliability and quality he was definitely your man.

The plan was put to the NUJ Chapter, and rather reluctantly, it was accepted. As far as Ossie's column was concerned, we were back in business, but this was not the end of controversy.

Peter Osgood was a true child of the post-war era. The 1950s had witnessed Jimmy Porter in John Osborne's *Look Back in Anger* on a personal rant against British society and in particular that bugbear of Charles Dickens, hypocrisy. But essentially, the 1950s were all about the status quo. Certainly, as far as sport was concerned, life had not altered since the 1930s. In fact, the only professional footballer to coherently articulate dissatisfactions with aspects of his profession during the '50s was, the elegant Northern Irish Spurs skipper Danny Blanchflower. But he was very much a lone voice.

Sportsmen and women had to do what they were told, but late on in the 1960s, this altered as freedoms of all kinds were embraced. Footballers became more and more frank in print, and Ossie was at the forefront of this sea change. So, when he made a few disparaging remarks about Derby County boss, the equally controversial and vocal Brian Clough, the stuff really hit the fan.

Both Chelsea manager Dave Sexton and the Football Association gave him a rap on the knuckles, but in my book, it was more grist to our publicity mill. He was fast developing into an archetypal 1960s anti-hero, and the media salivated en masse in the manner of a first-timer at Paul Raymond's Revuebar.

Having conquered the threat of a strike in Fleet Street, and having assured those in the corridors of power within the game that Ossie would be good boy from now on, it was now time to develop not only his potential as a footballer selling traditional products such as boots and the like, but also to nurture the whole fashionable side of the football club. But, first things first: now was the time to get Peter Osgood's face and name on products, and my first stop was that prestigious British sporting goods manufacturer, Bukta.

TEN

ENDORSEMENTS AND THAT CUP FINAL

It was a clammy day in Chelsea. A fidgety wind kept rustling the skeletal trees, so that in spite of the thin sun and the mild air London was filled with a sort of unease and the threat of a storm.

At Stamford Bridge, the pitch was caked in pudding-like mud. Ossie was in his Chelsea colours, kicking a ball left and right as a fawning photographer snapped incessantly. 'I'd like Peter to head a few balls into the net,' said the man with the camera in a reedy voice.

'Okay,' I said. 'What would you like Peter to do?'

'Well, if he could stand near the penalty spot, could you send in a few crosses from the corner flag?'

I swallowed, and the butterflies in my stomach took on a life of their own and went on a rampaging dance.

'Well, I'm not really dressed for kicking a football,' I moaned. 'Surely you can do without me.'

'Oh, don't worry,' said the reedy voice. 'Just do your best.'

Now, I was almost neurotically fastidious in those days about my sartorial appearance. And the thought of giving a football a host of heavy whacks from the corner flag quadrant filled me with horror. You see I was dressed in yet another King's Road suit, complete with the same wet-look buckled shoes that Charlie Cooke had commented on after the QPR Cup-tie.

'Can't somebody in the club office fix you up with some gear?' enquired the reedy voice.

'No, don't worry,' I replied. 'I'll have a go.'

By this time I was more than just a shade embarrassed by my obsession with my clothes, and God knows what Ossie thought of me. This was hardly the stuff of a macho man, but he took it all in good spirit. After all, the payback was several hundreds of pounds in endorsement lolly from the Bukta people, plus the promise of more work in the future.

I felt a lonely figure as Ossie handed me the ball, and I placed it by the corner flag at the end opposite The Shed. My first effort was far too low for the Chelsea striker, but once I forgot about my trendy suit and my ultra-expensive footwear, the corners just flowed, and there was Peter heading in left and right as the man with the camera became more and more animated.

At the end of the session, Ossie was effusive in praise of my corner kicks. 'How nice he is,' I thought. 'Always so generous in his praise of people.'

After a few inane pleasantries, the Bukta photographer left, no doubt to constantly regale his friends and family of his Stamford Bridge exploits.

As for Peter, he changed back into his civvies, I attempted to wipe mud off my shoes, and we went off for a cuppa at a local café.

The irony of the whole Bukta photo session was that, despite taking seemingly endless snaps of Ossie heading home my corners, the majority of images used in the company's major advertising campaign revolved around the Chelsea star looking supremely elegant just kicking a ball! But at least I could include in my CV that I had crossed a ball to the great Peter Osgood and he had deftly headed it home!

A period of run-of-the-mill engagements followed for Peter, mainly opening sports' shops and supermarkets and shaking hands in the manner of a prime minister or president seeking re-election – all that was missing was kissing a few squealing babies!

But our prime concern – forcing him into the England team – hadn't been forgotten, and when the team to face Belgium in Brussels on 25 February 1970 was revealed, Osgood's name was there.

His selection had the press boys buzzing round us like bees round a honey pot. Some of the more enthusiastic of their number were becoming a nuisance to Ossie's long-suffering wife, Rosemary. So much so, that in the early hours following the team selection, she phoned me.

'I don't know what to do,' she said – her voice all of a quiver. 'BBC Radio 4 want to interview me on the *Today* programme.'

I told her not to worry, and a little later I received a call from the *Today* presenter John Timpson, outlining to me the sort of questions that would be thrown Rose's way.

It was all fairly straightforward; and when I got back to her I explained what was going to happen, and essentially just told her to be herself.

The upshot was that the interview proceeded better than expected, with Rosemary's modest character shining through. In 1970s terms, she came across as just a typical British housewife. 'How refreshing,' I said to myself. 'She is the total antithesis of the whole playboy Chelsea image and reputation.'

The match itself, played at the Parc Astrid in Brussels, was a successful one for Ramsey's side. England, with two goals from Alan Ball and one from Geoff Hurst, came through with an impressive 3–1 in front of over 20,000 fans. Ossie didn't manage to find the net, but he played well and from the off built up a positive understanding with the industrious Hurst. 'This was just the beginning of a long England career,' I shouted out loud to all and sundry in a Fleet Street hostelry on the day after the game. That was what I thought, anyway.

So, thanks to the efforts of the *Daily Mail* and Charlie Wilson in particular, my persistence, Ossie's form on the park, and Chelsea's all-round image as *the* swinging soccer club, he had made it into Ramsey's eleven. With the Mexico World Cup just round the corner, the chances of him developing into an authentic world star had increased dramatically.

It was about this time that my association with photographer Terry O'Neill eventually blossomed into something more than just a conventional business relationship.

Throughout 1968 and 1969, I had had numerous meetings with him, mainly in connection with photos of stars such as Tom Jones and Elvis Presley and Robert Redford, likely to be used as full-colour images by our family business, Star Posters. But, early on I discovered that Terry was a committed Chelsea supporter, and an admirer of the likes of Osgood and Cooke and Hudson. He was forever coming up with ideas for photos and publicity stunts, many of which bore positive fruit. There were so many, but probably my favourite – and I know that Ossie had a particular fondness for this photo shoot – were the *Borsalino* pictures.

Borsalino was a cult movie, released in 1970, starring those icons of the French cinema, Jean-Paul Belmondo and Alain Delon. It was a French-Italian production, and well received by the critics on both sides of the Channel.

Set in that hotbed of dealers and drifters and grafters and gangsters, Marseilles, during the Great Depression years of the 1930s, it cleverly mixed comedy, drama and violence, without at any stage making the audience feel awkward. Down on the King's Road they loved it – in fact anything with subtitles was regarded as elitist, which was of course just what the doctor ordered as far as the Chelsea cognoscenti were concerned.

The word 'Borsalino' essentially translates as fedora. It is the name of the hat company established in Italy in 1857 by Guiseppe Borsalino, which popularised the style of titfer so closely associated with gangsters (and controversial football coach Malcolm Allison during the 1970s).

Terry had once compared Ossie's looks to one of his most famous 'subjects', Steve McQueen, and he felt that wearing one of the Borsalino suits would only enhance the striker's reputation as an authentic model. It would also fit in perfectly with the whole King's Road mystique, which had been created and nurtured by so many of the upmarket glossies.

Unsurprisingly, the PR gurus for the movie gave the seal of approval to the idea, combining as it did all that was chic in France with the unique style of this new breed of English footballer, still regarded as eccentric elsewhere in the world, but fast developing into the norm in what were now, sadly, the dying embers of Swinging London.

We managed to acquire a Borsalino suit in pure silk from Simpsons in Piccadilly, plus a beautiful fedora hat, purple silk shirt and matching purple silk tie, topped off with gleaming white loafers. The suit was a double-breasted job with vibrant blue vertical stripes and turn-ups. When I say I acquired one suit, I should in fact say two, as I was mad keen on getting such an ensemble myself. You see, I wanted the two of us to be seen out-and-about dressed liked Belmondo and Delon, for we were ever the exhibitionists!

Terry O'Neill's photos were sensational, and the *Sun* newspaper turned them into a major feature. Terry had this way about him of making his subject so relaxed that once the lights were turned on and the shooting started, any signs of tautness and tension in the muscles evaporated away. What you got were, despite all the trappings, some very natural photographs; striking images that raised the character of the face to new heights.

As for me, I once wore the Borsalino outfit to a meeting I had with a small-time crook at a drinking den in Soho. This guy, Ron, was a rather dubious contact man I had 'befriended' because despite his unsavoury image, he was a dab hand at outlandish ideas. I once played pool against him, dressed in the suit, with several West End Central detectives looking on! I think they thought I was more disreputable than my crook friend. However, once I told them about Chelsea and Ossie, they succumbed to my charm (or to put it more accurately, they were just mad about Chelsea).

Ron was youngish – it was difficult to put an age to him – and he had black curly hair, which was naturally oily. He looked somewhat like a malnourished Sylvester Stallone. He owned a large Alsatian dog, of which he was overtly fond. He had a brother, who was not blessed with good looks, and despite being on the whole as friendly as a cocker spaniel, was not someone whose nose you would want to put out of joint.

Someone who was also mad about Chelsea was actor Michael Crawford. He was also mad about Alexander's restaurant in Chelsea, frequented by several of the Blues top stars as well as a whole galaxy of showbiz and society icons.

As Terry O'Neill once said: 'The girls loved the footballers. They loved a bit of rough, I suppose, or whatever. So, it was a whole mix – lords, ladies and the working-class heroes who took it over. That's the sort of crowds you got down regularly at Stamford Bridge.'

Certainly Ossie enjoyed the ambience of 'Alexander's' enormously.

Owned by the late husband of fashion innovator supreme Mary Quant, Alexander Plunket-Greene, it opened its doors in the 1950s. In fact, Quant's first shop, Bazaar, which first saw the light of day in 1955, was above the restaurant. However, it was during the '60s that Alexander's, in Quant's own words, 'had become the most fashionable in Chelsea, with a chic clientele'. Quant said that she remembered Grace Kelly and Prince Rainier being there with two friends. 'Once, I was invited to join Brigitte Bardot and her second husband, the French actor Jacques Charrier. Bardot was preening herself deliciously as the entire staff fell into disarray with excitement. Playing up to all this, she had no idea they were actually fans of Charrier!'

The reason they were fans of his, as opposed to sex kitten BB, was simply because, in Ossie's words, 'the waiters were all gay, but we really liked them. Everyone used to go to the place – Michael Crawford, actress Jane Seymour – everyone.'

Unlike the culture of the twenty-first century, which would without question frown sanctimoniously on any behaviour that reeked of late nights, over indulgence and hedonistic pleasures, the fact that Chelsea's star names adopted the personas of Hollywood celebrities and rock idols rather than sportsmen only increased the ongoing infatuation of the general public with these eccentric young footballers. What helped, of course, was also the pervading attitude of the media. Nowadays, it is enough for a photo to appear of a Premier League footballer taking a drag on a cigarette to cause all kinds of pompous preaching and condemnatory ructions.

Also, these guys had opinions, which they aired. They were not yet slaves to the robotic post-match '1984'-style 'newspeak' favoured by the majority of the leading managers and players of today – talk about boring!

The likes of Cooke, Hudson and Osgood, and indeed Best and Marsh, possessed such innate talents with a football that any rumours of carousing were never on the public agenda because they continued to enthral supporters up and down the country with their sublime artistry and improvised brilliance.

Having despatched QPR so thrillingly in their quarter-final, the Blues were given another favourable pairing in the semi-final at White Hart Lane on 14 March 1970, in the shape of Second Division Watford.

This Cup-tie was the cheese and tomato between the two slices of bread of two vital league games – vital, if Sexton's men were ever to have more than just a smell of title glory. The first was 'a-bit-of-a-let-down' 1–1 home draw with Nottingham Forest, watched by over 55,000 vociferous fans. The second, three days after the semi, saw Charlie Cooke fire in the only goal against Stoke City. Just four shy of 29,000 saw this game – another example of the erratic nature of Stamford Bridge attendances in those days. Probably the reason was that there were more genuine lovers of the game during that era, and they, as neutrals, would decide to turn up for a game often as a last-minute thing on the day itself.

The 14 March 1970 was cold. In fact it was bitter. Earlier in the month, a band of heavy snow had hit Southern England, and combined with strengthening north-to-north-west winds, it felt more like New Year's Day than the cusp of spring. By the 14th, despite it remaining raw, the snow had turned to rain, and the White Hart Lane pitch resembled a beach that had had clay poured over it.

Watford were the underdogs, and once the pugnacious Dave Webb had put Chelsea ahead, they eventually sauntered their way into the final with a 5–1 success,

Peter Houseman helping himself to two goals, with one from Ian Hutchinson plus the obligatory Osgood net-finder.

However, during the first period, Watford gave the favourites the odd shock or two, and soon after Webb's opener, the Hornets conjured an equaliser through Terry Garbett, whose spinning effort completely deceived Peter Bonetti. But despite looking a shade jaded, the favourites upped the ante and in the end it was all a bit of a formality.

The other semi-final, involving Leeds United and Manchester United was one of those long drawn-out affairs so prevalent in the days before TV schedules determined kick-off times, and the police were content for Cup replays to take place just a matter of days after the first contest. Eventually Revie's Leeds prevailed: 1–0 in the second replay at Bolton's old ground of Burnden Park.

So, the two old enemies; the two football teams that summed up in so many ways the North-South divide, were to meet in the FA Cup final at Wembley Stadium on Saturday 11 April. It is fair to say, without displaying a semblance of bias, that much of the nation was sitting with baited-breath waiting for this final of all finals.

The perceived animosity between South-West London's club of cavaliers and Yorkshire's grittier roundheads had its roots in the mid-1960s after successive promotions by the two clubs from the old Second Division.

The whole saga, which was to come to a dramatic head in 1970, all started back in 1966 when a Bobby Tambling goal saw Docherty's Diamonds squeak through 1–0 in an FA Cup fourth round clash at Stamford Bridge. Leeds laid siege to the home goal for much of the game, but a combination of extreme obduracy from the home defence and more than a slice of Lady Luck saw Chelsea prevail.

Then, of course, there was the semi-final twelve months later: once more, luck played its hand in Chelsea's favour when Peter Lorimer's 'goal' via a dynamic free-kick was controversially ruled out.

The two league meetings during the season of 1969–1970 went the way of Leeds, and in both encounters there was this continuing undercurrent of repressed violence – it was all edgy and flaky and almost neurotic – it was Alfred Hitchcock without the love interest.

Recently, Norman 'Bite-yer-Legs' Hunter, that cornerstone of Leeds' line-up, stated that there was no real dislike of the Chelsea players. However, Norman's rose-tinted summation of those epic contests of forty-odd years ago is not borne out by some of the comments made by the likes of Ian Hutchinson and company, most notably in the definitive history of football shown on BBC TV in 1995, *Kicking and Screaming*.

This series, which debuted in October, received praise aplenty from the critics, and personally I felt extremely flattered when the programme makers asked me to be part of the whole project, in particular one episode dedicated to the whole Chelsea/Leeds relationship and its cultural and social significance during a period of seismic change in Britain.

I developed a really good rapport with Hutchinson. I was never actually his agent, but did manage to arrange a few mini-deals for him. And, in fact, much, much later in the 1990s I was more than pleased to be in a position to make him a few bob with several television appearances as a pundit during Chelsea's European Cup Winners' Cup run of 1994–95.

Hutch was always candid, and certainly didn't suffer fools, but I always found him friendly and generous to people he respected. During several interviews for this episode of the documentary, he summed up his attitude to Revie's Leeds with these no-punches-pulled words: 'They hated us and we hated them.' Later he said: 'There was no love whatsoever. The only person I really got on with was Norman Hunter.'

As for Alan Hudson, he once said to several of the Yorkshire club's number during a particularly boisterous battle: 'You're just robots.'

Football writer John King summed up the whole Chelsea *v.* Leeds soap opera with these words: 'Leeds were portrayed as dour Yorkshiremen with a reputation for playing dirty. Chelsea, on the other hand, were the wide boys of London, dedicated followers of fashion. While Leeds were drinking tea and playing cards, Chelsea were out boozing and chasing girls, but when it came to games between the two, however, war was declared.'

Then, of course, there was the famous – or infamous – Jack Charlton 'little black book'. In it were supposedly two names; two players that Charlton would punish for on-field misdemeanours, or as he so succinctly expressed it: 'If I get the chance to do them, I will. I will make them suffer before I pack this game in.'

Charlton came out with these quotes during a Tyne Tees TV interview with broadcaster Fred Dinenage on 3 October 1970. Dinenage asked him the following question: 'You have had your fair share of cuts and bruises. What is the worst thing that has happened to you?'

Big Jack replied: 'I cannot remember names, but I have a little book with two names in it, and if I get the chance to do them I will. I do not do what I consider to be the bad fouls in the game, such as going over the top. That is about the worst foul in the game, but I will tackle as hard as I can to win the ball, but I will not do the dirty things, the really nasty things. When people do it to me, I do it back to them. Because I am not noted for doing so, people don't do it to me, but there are two or three people who have done it to me, and I will make them suffer before I give this game up.'

He refused to divulge who these players were, but stated in no uncertain terms that 'they know who they are'.

This frank and hard-hitting interview was given a nation-wide airing seven days later, and soon the flak started to fly. Those dark-suited grey gentlemen of the Football Association must have choked over their port or mild and bitter or Newcastle Brown or whatever it was, as Charlton's words became – in their eyes – more and more inflamma-tory. On top of all this, some of our national newspaper sports' columnists climbed on their high horses of morality and spouted words of righteous indignation.

The *Daily Mirror*'s Peter Wilson, for example – never a man to turn down the odd snifter – wrote: 'Have these petulant, primp-ing, overpaid, under-principled gladiators no responsibility?'

Wilson, an authentic eccentric, resembled that arche-typal breed of upper-middle-class Englishman that in many ways almost became parodies of their real selves during the immediate post-war years.

Red-faced with luxuriant moustaches, they could undoubt-edly hold their liquor. In fact talking about that word of Wilson's, 'responsibility', I remember sitting near the great scribe at the Lord's Tavern. It was during a Test match, and he was consuming his lunch, which comprised one rather sad-looking cheese sandwich on white bread with a bottle of something much more expensive and very red on the high-class claret list.

Wilson was there in his role as correspondent for the *Mirror*. I liked his style – vintage wine with a sandwich – but as his eyes became more and more glassy, I could have posed the same sort of question as he had done in print: 'As a highly-paid professional, was he behaving responsibly drinking so much booze whilst on duty?' But I didn't. I have never been sanctimonious.

FA secretary Denis Follows and his colleagues felt Charlton's words were likely to bring the game into disre-pute, and that 'the committee has further decided that until the matter has been resolved, the England team manager should be informed that Charlton won't be eligible for any FA representative teams'.

Later, Charlton consumed a portion of humble pie, saying: 'Looking back, I realise I was wrong to say the things I said, the way I said them. It's not because of the fact that Jack Charlton was hurt. That's nothing. But it gave people the opportunity to hurt through me the game I love. I regret that very much.' And later, he said: 'The truth is there was never any little black book. It was just my way of saying there are a couple of players who have had an unfair go at me at one time or another.'

At about the time that Charlton was letting the old moggy out of the carrier, Ossie was being interviewed on a daily – sometimes it seemed like hourly – basis. However, one newspaper interview stood head and shoulders above the rest. The journalist was Ray Connolly, the venue was Peter's house in Windsor and the result was a candid conversation with Connolly that gained Ossie both new fans and new friends in the media.

His 'Connolly On Saturday' column in the *London Evening Standard* was one of the standout showbiz features of the time. Ray had replaced the snooty Maureen Cleave, and despite a truly bad stammer, his career was very much on the up and up.

During his time at the *Standard*, Ray interviewed many of the most famous people on the planet, ranging from Elvis Presley, The Beatles, Mick Jagger and Keith Richards to David Bowie, Jimi Hendrix and Dusty Springfield. Only three sportsmen were included in his impressive list of subjects: Joe Frazier, Muhammad Ali and Peter Osgood.

Later in the 1970s Connolly would receive worldwide recognition for his screenplays of critically acclaimed movies *That'll Be the Day* and *Stardust* in which he worked with David Puttnam, the producer of Oscar-winning *Chariots of Fire* in 1981. He also wrote and directed the definitive documentary about the '50s screen idol James Dean entitled, *James Dean: The First American Teenager*.

I spoke to Ray on the phone, and we arranged for the interview to take place at Ossie's house in Windsor. The Chelsea star had been interviewed many times before, but he fully realised that this one was special. You see, a chat with Ray Connolly in 1970 meant that as a performer you were very much in the big league. This was not lost on Ossie and he performed superbly, as indeed did his wife Rosemary.

Connolly described Ossie thus: 'At 23, he is possibly the most exciting footballer in the country. So far this season he ties as leading goal scorer in the Football League with 28 goals. With fan mail running up to 200 letters a week he can truly be described as the Golden Boy of Stamford Bridge.'

He was also quick to pick up on Os' informality: 'Peter Osgood is sitting in his socks at his Windsor home. Rosemary, his wife, in fluffy new blue carpet slippers, is knitting and listening, and occasionally correcting (almost pedantically), while Gregory Tesser, his agent, supervises from beneath his hair cream.'

Ray never asked me about my hair cream, but if he had done, I would have told him exactly what I thought of this product. It was called Anzora, it had been on the market since before the First World War, and despite its claims, I found it to be bloody awful! It made my hair feel like it weighed a ton, and even though the company was a regular advertiser in *The Amateur Footballer* magazine, there was no doubt that in the load-of-rubbish-stakes it was number one!

Ossie tells Ray that life has never been so positive: 'I have an agent to earn me money and to get me known as a name. I'm doing posters. I'm tied up with a sportswear firm, and I hope to sign a contract with a very large advertising agency. And then I have a deal with Ford from which I get a basic salary as an area sales manager – I don't work, no, they just use my name in advertisements in the local papers, and people who want to buy cars, ring up – and then there's a column in a national paper. One day I'd like to own a nice boutique, with trendy gear like they have in Cecil Gee.

'Really, George Best has had it too good up to now. There's been nobody to challenge him. I will – although I've got a different image from him.'

Ray then outlines the persona that Osgood is trying to project: 'His image is, in fact, almost the complete opposite to Best. There's no narcissism about Osgood. He is a handsome, regular, old-fashioned-looking sportsman, and his hair is short, and neatly cut away from his ears. He doesn't like these long-haired types, he says. He's open and garrulous and honest, to the point of naiveté.'

As his agent, I made sure that Ossie kept to this clean-cut, yet at the same time very modern image. However, as the King's Road was catapulted into world consciousness as the 'hippest place on earth', and sideburns in London became bushier and bushier and longer and longer, so Ossie adapted accordingly, and effortlessly altered his style, without ever attempting to ape Best.

I have already made mention of Rosemary Osgood's 'ordinariness', which is not a criticism; she was literally a breath of fresh air.

As Ossie himself said: 'No, Rosemary doesn't like to go out much, she'd rather sit in. She's a quiet type, you know, she likes to do the gardening.'

You could see from the outset that Ray had real simpatico with Rosemary. 'Rosemary Osgood,' he wrote, 'is the same age as her husband. She's terribly house-proud, something that Peter is proud to mention about her. He likes to get home to a spick and span house at night. She hardly ever goes to football, because she can't get baby-sitters, since all their relatives and friends go to the matches. She won't be at Wembley today (for the Cup Final) for that reason. She admits, however, that she isn't really that interested in football, and often wishes that Peter had an ordinary nine to five job.

'She isn't looking forward to the World Cup, particularly because she gets lonely sitting in by herself: and she doesn't like it when Peter goes out at night. He likes to go out to clubs for dinner and a cabaret.'

Some of what she then admitted to Connolly sounds somewhat sad: 'Course I'm used to it by now. I know he don't [*sic*] talk to me when he's in – just sits there watching television all night, but it is nice to have someone else in the house.'

Peter married Rosemary when both were aged seventeen. Later, two children were born, Anthony and Mark, and as Rosemary once admitted to me: 'Do you know, by the time Peter's thirty-five years old, he could be a grandfather?'

As the conversation continued, Os' frankness about his ambitions and his life in general increased sentence-by-sentence. He told Ray that his number one ambition 'is to be a rich man'. Connolly, a man so adept (like that great TV inquisitor of the past, John Freeman) at getting behind the façade of the particular celebrity he was interviewing wrote: 'He wants to make enough money and to collect enough business interests around him during the next six years or so to make sure that he never has to work at a full-time job again as long as he lives after getting out of football.

'He wants, he says, to be able to sit back and enjoy himself. To be a playboy ('Well, a married playboy'), to be able to buy racehorses, to be able to go anywhere to play golf, or just to go off to the Continent for a couple of weeks should he feel like it. He never wants to have to worry about money again.'

As for his 'playboy image', Rosemary made the point that 'when he started going out with me, his parents were very surprised because he'd never bothered with girls before'.

Ossie wasn't slow to highlight past misdemeanours and in an extremely frank admission of his shortcomings when making the breakthrough into the Chelsea first team, he said: 'It happened so fast then that I didn't know how to handle it. I had a bad image then, but really I was just growing up and I thought I could get away with pranks and being silly, but I just couldn't. Docherty fined me about £500 in six months. I was getting fined just about every week.

'The only thing I'm really ashamed about was when I hung a contraceptive on someone's back on an aeroplane. I was just a country bumpkin, but I got fined about £80. Docherty went mad. But it really was funny at the time. It was tremendous. It just hung there getting longer and longer.'

Peter Osgood loved being interviewed. He was always articulate, and on this occasion, he was refreshingly honest, as well being naturally amusing. As I glanced at my watch, Ray Connolly rose from his chair. It was nigh-on ten o'clock and Rosemary was in the process of preparing her husband's Ovaltine. It was almost time for bed. We bade our farewells, and Ray offered to give me a lift. I told him I lived in Hampstead, north-west London, and I think he was residing somewhere near Twickenham, so it was decided he would transport me to a convenient station.

During the comparatively short journey, we spoke, or most probably I did. However, he was extremely complimentary about Ossie, and when I left his car and gave him a wave and a smile, I felt contented. An interview with Ray Connolly was another feather in our collective cap, as it would, in my view, enhance the Chelsea striker's reputation enormously. It would also show to the public that unlike so many sportsmen of his vintage, Peter was a real character: a rebel, but unlike James Dean, a rebel with a positive cause.

By this stage my phone – one of those dinky Trim Phone jobs, so popular in the late 1960s and early '70s that chirped like a demented garden bird – was chirping almost every second with desperate scribes demanding to get a few quotes on the 'Little Black Book Affair'. Anyway I asked Ossie more than once about this storm in a teacup. As far as he was concerned, Charlton did have a little black book, and Ian Hutchinson later had his own take on the whole affair with a story of how Ossie pricked more than one nerve of big Jack's after a benefit match. Thinking that he, Ossie, was in it, he asked Jack about it.Charlton responded by saying: 'It's not for you, it's for that big twat next to you.' As Hutchinson so succinctly put it: 'I was that twat!'

During the filming of *Kicking and Screaming*, Hutch was very candid about Leeds. 'They'd stand on your foot,' he stated. 'They'd say "you're only a youngster, come over here and I'll break your leg". And, "You go past me again and you won't do it again". But it's not like one or two of them, there's like eight or nine of 'em all doing the same thing. As soon as you started giving it back to them, then they started what we called "crying". They used to shout, "Referee, referee". They were terrible.'

Ossie was often dismissive of the Leeds' football philosophy, telling me that 'they were a machine, and when it came to a one-off cup-tie we were so much better than Leeds because we were capable of enjoying ourselves, whereas they always stuck to the same plan. They were rigid.'

It had a build up like no other, this FA Cup final, which without knowing it, displayed in a sporting context the new landscape of this 'sceptred isle'.

On 11 April 1970, the ill-fated Apollo 13, commanded by Captain James Lovell Jr, was launched from the Kennedy Space Center, Florida. The Beatles' 'Let It Be' – their swansong, so to speak – was number one in America. The weather was murky with strong northerly winds and smacked more of John Keats (his 'face hath felt the winter's wind') than of spring and gambolling lambs.

Just prior to the big day, I had spent a relaxing afternoon in the company of Peter Osgood strolling along the King's Road.

Our main port-of-call had been that temple of the trend-setters, I Was Lord Kitchener's Valet. Ossie, who often complained that the shirts he bought were always 'far too short for my very long arms', really liked this emporium, this epitome of 1960s' style, and because of my association with the company – our family business supplied them with a seemingly endless supply of 'personality posters' – I was able to obtain a selection of sleek shirts for him, gratis of course.

The whole chic King's Road sartorial scene never really came naturally to Ossie. Alan Hudson was a natural cool dude, whose every garment displayed impeccable taste, whereas Os was not a King's Road natural in the fashion stakes.

Now, discretion is something you learn very early on in the PR business, so when Ossie asked me to 'sort out a few shirts' for a guy called Stan Flashman, I didn't ask any questions as to why. The only problem about this was that Flashman had, in Ossie's words 'a massive neck', so my task was far from easy. Twenty-odd inch collars back in 1970 were rare, to say the least.

Some people would maintain that Flashman was, in every respect, larger than life. Others would be just a shade more jaundiced in their opinion of the man. He was, to all intents and purposes, a 'successful businessman'. As he himself said: 'I call myself a ticket broker. Some people call me a ticket tout, and some people call me a spiv. They can call me what they like if the colour of their money is right.'

'Fat Stan', as he was known, claimed he could provide a ticket for any event, from the men's singles final at Wimbledon to a Buckingham Palace garden party. It was even said – probably by the man himself – that he had sold an invitation to Princess Anne's wedding!

He operated out of a seedy office in King's Cross, and there was no doubt that football was his bread-and-butter, major Wembley finals and the like in particular. He relied heavily on players 'supplying' him with these tickets, and to be fair in an era when professionals were paid just a mere drop in the ocean compared to today's £100,000 a-week-plus stars, surely no blame should be attached to these players for attempting to garner just a few extra quid.

He was always a shadowy figure, and later he gained a fame of sorts as chairman of Barnet Football Club, this fame later turning sour as his whole dodgy business operation placed this once-famous amateur football club in the mire. By the early 1990s, his 'empire' had crashed and he was a broken man.

The son of an East End tailor, his first attempts at making money involved selling pots and pans and sheets and ties in Houndsditch. It was during the early 1960s that he had his 'eureka moment'.

'I was a Spurs fan and saw a bloke selling tickets outside White Hart Lane,' he later recalled. 'So, I bought a couple and then sold them on to a punter and made a quick tenner. I soon realised that if you go up to someone offering to sell something, there are only two things he can say – yes or no. So I hung around buying and selling for a couple of hours and made £40. That was more than a whole week's wages for me in those days.'

He soon adopted the archetypal gangster persona, prowling the mean streets of the capital in dark glasses, dealing solely in cash. There were rivals out there, and these hard-nosed individuals soon became so worried about this new kid on the block that they became determined to thwart him before he was able to rule any kind of roost. Once they even resorted to handcuffing and gagging him, as they rifled his pockets and took wads of FA Cup final tickets plus £1,000.

But he had staying power – that there was no doubt. He was an extremely volatile character, and I suppose the only similarity with the other famous Flashman, the character created by Thomas Hughes in his classic novel *Tom Brown's Schooldays*, was the fact that both were infamous bullies.

One such example of Flashman's 'erratic behaviour' was when he screamed at a female fan: 'Do you want me to permanently mark your face?'

One-time Barnet boss Barry Fry, who had an ongoing love-hate relationship with 'Fat Stan' summed it all up like this:

'If you didn't know Stanley you would think he was an ignorant pig. He's certainly a Jekyll and Hyde character.'

Judging from the brief conversations I had with the
man, I would say there was definitely more of the latter
than the former!

The first time I was introduced to him, I must admit I felt
more than just a tad nervous. He was an intimidating individual;
a great hulk of a man, coarse in his habits and lacking all those
natural social graces we take for granted. His massive neck
– bulbous gargantuan mounds of greasy looking flesh – wob-
bled every time he uttered a few words. I immediately likened
him to the actor Sydney Greenstreet in *The Maltese Falcon*,
for despite his bulk and lack of class, he seemed to move like
some grotesque ballet dancer.

He didn't actually ever directly thank me for obtaining
those elegant shirts from I Was Lord Kitchener's Valet;
he just grunted his version of thanks. A bit like Rik Gunnell
back in '64, he gave me the willies. I always made sure that
on the rare occasions I met him, I was the typical fawning
sycophant! What a coward!

Much, much later when all kinds of cats exited a variety of
different bags, and the game was up for Flashman, he was
declared bankrupt, undoubtedly avoided being a guest of Her
Majesty because of ill health, and disappeared to suburban
normalcy in Ilford. The million dollar question was: 'Where
had all the money gone?'

He died, aged just fifty-nine in 1999, following a lengthy
battle with Alzheimer's disease.

I must say you soon find out that all the many acquaint-
ances you have made all want to be 'matey peeps' when
it comes to tickets for a big occasion. Taxi drivers and taxi
controllers and trades people of all shapes and sizes bom-
barded me with incessant phone calls, and it was always
the same patter: 'Hello Greg, how are you? Hope you're
well? How's Ossie – looking forward to the final, I guess.
I forgot to mention, by the way, I have this case of wine or
this suit or this bundle of LPs or don't worry about that trip
to Slough or Windsor or wherever, I'll put it on the office

account.' Then came the punch line: 'You couldn't do me a favour, could you? I'd be so grateful: any chance of a ticket for the final? I'll pay you, of course, and I don't mind paying well over the odds.'

Time and again, I had to bite my tongue, pretend to be 'ever so sorry', and somehow say no. Even a mere twenty-four hours before the final, I was taking such calls. By this time I was thoroughly cheesed-off with the whole thing.

Unlike so many of the surfaces that the professional player of the late 1960s had to contend with, Wembley Stadium was known throughout the world for its playing area. There was always a beautifully manicured bowling green; a green swathe so perfectly produced that even the most mediocre journeyman of a footballer would surely be capable of at least trapping the ball in one movement. Yet, this was not the case on 11 April 1970, and it was all down to some deranged individual's madcap idea and a load of horses.

Having collected my ticket – left for me by Ossie – I took my seat and gazed in bewilderment at the sight before me. Gone was the elegant green pitch with its broad brushstrokes of uniformed patterns, and in its stead was something that resembled Brighton beach following a particularly nasty Mods and Rockers rumble!

To understand life in 1970, it first has to be understood that the 1960s ethos of expression and fairness and services before profit was still dominating the British landscape. The current obsession with screwing as much money out of people as pos-sible without necessarily providing a top-class service had yet to permeate the thought processes of either business or sport. But the seeds were there, and the decision to hold the Horse of The Year Show so close to the showpiece of the English game at the home of English football was an example of this folly.

The amateurs of Enfield and Dagenham had experienced these nightmare conditions a mere seven days before in the FA Amateur Cup final, and club secretary C.S. Taverner had been scathing in his post-match comments.

'We'd sooner have played on our own pitch,' he moaned. 'It was pretty grim; in fact I have never seen it look so bad.'

Leeds boss Don Revie used even more vociferous language: 'If they are putting 100 tons of sand on Wembley then it is goodbye to good football. A hundred tons will deaden the pace on the ball. It will be like playing on a beach.'

Skipper Billy Bremner echoed his manager's verdict with these words: 'The pitch was in a terrible state. There was not a sign of the normally immaculate turf, which everyone associates with Wembley. The pitch had been sanded, but you found yourself almost ankle deep in mud and sand, at times, and if Wembley's once lush turf was stamina-sapping, I can tell you that pitch on which we played destroyed the energy of the players, as the game wore on. The pitch didn't run true – the ball came at you from awkward angles, bounced and bobbed about, as you tried to ply passes with precision.'

BBC Television commentator Kenneth Wolstenholme made these comments at the kick-off: 'The pitch is rather like Goodwin Sands. Quick turns might be very dangerous manoeuvres this afternoon.' And later, 'the players are already sinking into this soft, sanded surface.'

Peter Osgood later told me that the 'pitch was just like some kind of pudding, but you just got on with it. It was certainly tiring though'.

However, despite the pitch and the plethora of pre-match protests, the contest itself proved to have as many surprises and twists as an Agatha Christie whodunit.

Sitting in my vantage point at the old Wembley, I was soon struck by how well Leeds were coping with the conditions compared to their opponents, whose more cavalier and some would say more arty approach to the game, floundered in the sinking sands of the famous old stadium.

Poor old Dave Webb was being given the run-around by Leeds' young silky-skilled winger Eddie Gray, so it came as no surprise when Revie's men took a twentieth minute lead through Jack 'Black Book' Charlton. It was a mess of a goal, and probably in many ways best summed up the infamous track; a downward header that you would expect a schoolboy to clear, but it died a quick death on the surface and as Eddie

McCreadie attempted to clear, he understandably completely mistimed his kick, and the ball almost apologetically found the net. Chelsea appealed to referee Eric Jennings that Peter Bonetti had been impeded, but all to no avail. The Leeds lads were one up, but the goal was all about the pitch.

Four minutes before the break, one of Chelsea's so often unheralded heroes, Peter Houseman, levelled matters with a low shot that Leeds keeper Gary Sprake somehow managed to fumble.

A few words on Peter Houseman, so sadly killed in a car crash with his wife and two friends, in 1977, aged just thirty-two.

During my time as agent, when I seemed to live and breathe and eat and sleep Chelsea, what always struck me was how different Houseman was to so many of the others. When photographer Terry O'Neill likened the Chelsea team to the cast of the film *The Dirty Dozen*, Ossie became Clint Eastwood, 'Chopper' Harris was Lee Marvin, Hudson a young Robert Mitchum and so on and so on. But Houseman was not part of this fit.

He was like a throwback – and I mean this as a compliment. He was modest almost to a fault, very polite, quiet and in all respects the complete antithesis of the King's Road hellraisers so beloved by the red tops. He was definitely a professional footballer more in keeping with the deferential years of the 1950s. It was in a way to his credit that the Swinging '60s seemed to have passed him by.

As a player, he was a tireless worker and a clever winger; there were not many more proficient crossers of a ball in the game at that time. He was not a robust performer, and it was not unusual for some of the crueller members of the Stamford Bridge faithful to refer to him as 'Mary' when he seemed to be backing out of a tackle.

But Chelsea and manager Sexton relied on him just as much as the side's flashier players, and sometimes even more. As for me, I never even thought of adding his name to my list of clients, which in a way was to my everlasting shame. I, like so many, got caught up in this new world when football and the '60s counterculture climbed into bed together for an affair; not long-lasting, but long enough to consummate a marriage without the vows.

Half-time and the Blues were lucky to be level. The second period followed much the same pattern as the first, and with six minutes left on the clock, Leeds' Mick Jones was the first to react when Allan Clarke's header had hit the post, and put away what was surely the winner. But these Blues never knew the meaning of defeat, and two minutes from time the always-brave Ian Hutchinson headed in the equaliser.

Extra-time couldn't separate the two teams, so it ended two-apiece – the first-ever Wembley Cup final draw. At the end of this pulsating encounter, the two squads jogged round the pitch in a joint lap of honour. As agent and fan, I knew my team had been let off the hook. As a romantic, I thought, maybe destiny beckoned.

Unlike so many Wembley occasions, before and since, this tussle was terrific – a real nail-biter that had the supporters of both sides roaring their heads off for the entire 120 minutes.

Don Revie had a dour, almost forbidding image – well, he seemed dull to us soft Southerners anyway – but he came out with an unusually succinct quote, laced with irony, in the dressing room at the end: 'Just think what sort of game it would have been on a pitch!'

Views on Revie, both as a man and a manager, veer from the complimentary from fans in his old stamping ground of Elland Road to the outright insulting, from lovers of the game in other parts of this green and pleasant land.

Respected journalist Michael Henderson summed it up best in his volume *50 People Who Fouled Up Football*: 'Don Revie should be regarded as one of the towering fig-ures of the English game. Instead, beyond a few parishes in Yorkshire, where keepers of the flame maintain a lonely vigil to defend a reputation that curdled long ago, elsewhere he is considered a deeply flawed man who made his club's name mud and betrayed his country.

'Neutrals took against Leeds for perfectly sound reasons. They kicked like mules, and cheated like Sicilian bandits.'

Harsh stuff, but thousands of fans in the early 1970s would have shouted 'Hear! Hear!' if such language had been used over forty years ago: as it was, many of Leeds' 'robust tactics' were dismissed as just part of the game. After all, 'it was a man's game, wasn't it?'

After the dust had settled and the moans about the pitch had continued apace, the Football Association decided that the Wembley playing area was in such a deplorable state that Old Trafford would be used for the replay in eighteen days' time.

Talk about fixture congestion! The FA had decreed that the season should reach its climax in April. There was sensible reasoning behind this decision; the idea being that as World Champions, England, should be in a position to properly pre-pare for the World Cup by having an early acquaintance with the vagaries of a Mexican summer.

The upshot of all this was that Chelsea's programme resem-bled some kind of endurance test. On Saturday 4 April, 45,000 fans at the Bridge saw them beat Spurs 1–0, thanks to a Tommy Baldwin strike. Seven days later they were, of course, embroiled in the Leeds marathon. Two days after that there was a trip to Stoke and another victory, Ian Hutchinson netting one of the goals in a 2–1 score line. Only another forty-eight hours elapsed before the King's Road boys were on the road again, this time to Turf Moor where they found Burnley in unforgiving mood in a 3–1 defeat. Their league campaign ended on 18 April with a 2–1 home win over Liverpool, Osgood scoring both goals.

Such an-end-of-season treadmill prior to an FA Cup final replay would have the likes of Arsenal manager Arsene Wenger spitting blood in this day and age, but footballers back then were made of sterner stuff, and to be fair the pressure that managers had to endure was nowhere near the often ludicrous and over-the-top matter-of-life-and-death attitude which currently exists, and will continue to exist until the media reassesses the values of the game and some semblance of perspective returns.

However, on the upside, there was now an eighteen-day gap before hostilities were to be resumed – enough time for aching limbs and knocks and springtime tiredness to be manipulated and massaged and generally treated. As Charlie Cooke pointed out: 'There was a lot of time to work up to it and think about it, so it was unusual in that sense.'

Thankfully, the fact that the rematch was at Man United's ground, which had a capacity of just over 62,000, as well as being scheduled for a Wednesday evening, put paid to most of my litany of 'ticket scroungers'.

My own travel plans for the match were, to put it mildly, chaotic (as indeed was so much of my life during those heady days), but I was eventually given a lift by *Striker* editor Tony Power. The journey itself was a talking-shop as we were both high on FA Cup final fever. Well, actually I was high on more than that, having downed the odd Mandy or two in the morning. I am not sure about Tony, but he did enjoy the odd snort of Colombian marching powder.

Ensconced in my hotel – I cannot for the life of me remember exactly which one, as I ended up eating breakfast at some ungodly hour the following morning with the Chelsea players and a few of the more celebrated scribes in the Piccadilly Hotel – I got ready for the game.

Now we come to the replay itself: described by a host of hacks as 'epic' and even 'iconic', it was indeed a blood-and-guts extravaganza with lashings of skill and tackles that had people throughout the UK wincing in front of their TV sets.

Noted former referee David Elleray, who refereed Chelsea's 4–0 1994 FA Cup final defeat to Manchester United, stated categorically that if this game had been played today, six red cards would have been issued plus a massive twenty yellow cards. As it was, referee Eric Jennings booked just one player, Chelsea's Ian Hutchinson.

After a few minutes the heat was turned up to Gas Mark 5 when Ron Harris kicked the back of Eddie Gray's knee, thus halving the Scottish international's potency on the wing. Hunter and Hutchinson then indulged in some fisticuffs. Charlton kneed and headbutted Ossie, and so on and so on. Some of it was X-rated stuff, but what drama; what a spectacle; what a denouement.

Over 28 million watched this football match, the second largest for a sporting event, only bettered by the 32 million-plus TV audience for the 1966 World Cup final. In fact, incredible as it may seem, the Chelsea *v.* Leeds replay is number six in the all-time list, a mere 1 million shy of the Apollo 13 splashdown, and just under 1 million more than tuned in to watch the wedding of Prince Charles and Lady Diana Spencer in 1981.

Chelsea's man between the sticks Peter 'The Cat' Bonetti was injured when he was bundled unceremoniously into the net by the bustling Leeds striker Mick Jones, and it was the same player who gave Revie's charges a deserved advantage ten minutes before the break.

But despite this setback, the men from south-west London soon discovered renewed energy levels, and with the charismatic Cooke beginning to weave his magic and link-up more effectively with Ossie, an equaliser looked very much on the cards. But the Chelsea fans, whose support was absolutely out of this world, had to wait until twelve minutes from the end of the match to find parity, and what a goal it was!

It was a flowing move, encompassing as it did all the innate élan, improvisations and talents of this group of players. There he was, the supreme ball artist Cooke on the right; he looks up, and with the blink of an eye, he despatches what is a perfect cross; meanwhile Ossie, all elegance and predatory instinct, anticipates the Cooke cross to find the net with a thrilling diving header.

The Blue section of the ground erupts as Ossie, displaying his full repertoire of matinee idol mannerisms, clutches his clenched fists to his face almost like a child crying to attract its mother. He knows, and we of a Blue bent know: the force is now with Chelsea.

Extra time, and we're all exhausted, players and supporters alike. It has become a slog, with the tackles still raising a few eyebrows. Then, with a mere sixty seconds remaining, Chelsea had one final chance via a throw-in from surely the longest thrower of a football in the game's history, Ian Hutchinson.

Hutch possessed a throw that would make the efforts of Stoke City's rocket-launcher of touchline torpedoes, Rory Delap, look insipid. The movement of his arms, when projecting the ball, resembled a windmill on speed – it was indeed unique.

He held the ball in the manner of some Victorian anarchist cradling a bomb before launching his missile into a packed penalty area. The ball adopted a life of its own as it soared over every single head, eventually finding the head of Charlton, only to fall to the never-say-die Webb, who bundled home the winner.

Talking of Webb, some thirty years later we worked together during his short tenure as manager of Yeovil Town. Club chairman John Fry had given me a part-time consultancy role as PR man and press officer and general media factotum, and I worked hand-in-hand with the former Chelsea stalwart on such aspects of the club as the phone line and match programme. On meeting the colourful East Ender again after so many years, my first words were: 'You're my hero! Remember Dave, you are the man who won the Cup for Chelsea for the first time.'

He smiled – he has always possessed a most infectious grin – and said: 'Gawd bless yer!'

Chelsea had won the FA Cup for the first time in the club's history, and soon the atmosphere in Manchester was to ape that of a Hogmanay rave in Edinburgh or Glasgow. It was going to be a long, long night, resulting in fat heads and memories that would be impaired forever.

There was one Chelsea player, a King's Road dandy if ever there was one, who sadly missed out on this momentous moment, and his name is Alan Anthony Hudson. Alan was the one player I craved to sign; the missing link, you could say, in my list of supreme entertainers. But Alan's career at that stage was very much in the hands of his father Bill, and eventually it was decided that the up-and-coming agent Ken Adam should handle his affairs.

He and Ossie were close; in fact Huddy owned a black poodle called 'Ossie'. Cooke and Hudson and Osgood – the names just roll off the tongue like a glass of Chateau Lafite. In my opinion, if life had been kinder to the rebel that was Huddy, then he could, and in fact should, have blossomed into one of Europe's premier players. But don't take my word for it. Others – legends of the game – lavished more and more plaudits on the young Hudson as his embryonic skills developed and his performances for Dave Sexton went from being seven or eight out of ten to the maximum week-in-and-week-out.

For example, after Hudson had given the fans a masterclass at the Loftus Road FA Cup quarter-final, England manager Alf Ramsey said: 'There is no limit to what he can achieve.'

The legendary German midfield maestro Gunther Netzer, he of the wild heavy-metal-rock hair, said of Hudson, who made his international debut in England's 2–0 victory over the World Champions in 1975: 'where have England been keeping this player? He is world class.'

Equally enthralled by the natural control and elegance of the midfielder was West German boss Helmut Schoen, who made a comparison between Huddy and a national football treasure when he stated that: 'At last, England have found a replacement for Bobby Charlton.'

Bobby Moore was equally lavish in his praise: 'Alan Hudson looked like conquering the world, and perhaps for a short while he did.'

The staggering indictment of English football during the 1970s was that neither Ramsey nor Revie, who replaced Sir Alf in 1974 as England boss, did mavericks. Marsh, Hudson and Osgood: three of the most talented performers of that era – and indeed any era – mustered a measly 15 caps between them. The ethos of these two coaches epitomised the schizophrenic nature of English football at the time: Ramsey's intransigence and Revie's obsession with slide-rule planning.

Hudson ran the show that March evening at Wembley Stadium, and at the still tender age of twenty-three, the world, in the words of *Minder*'s Arthur Daley 'was his lobster'. George Cole starred as Arthur in the TV series, alongside Chelsea nut and great mate of Hudson's, Dennis Waterman. But, as I have already indicated, football was obsessed with this world of robotic runners – no place here for the artists, the poets of the game. In international terms, English football's slogan should have read: 'Up the workers!'

By the time of his England bow, Huddy was a Stoke player, having left Stamford Bridge in 1974 for £240,000. Later he signed for Arsenal for £200,000 before moving to America. He returned to both Chelsea and Stoke in the early 1980s, but his career on the biggest stages by this time was over.

Never blessed with the luck we all deserve in life, there is no doubt in my mind that if he played on the Premier League stage today, he would be a shoe-in in the England set up. One journo colleague of mine said of his England debut: 'He passed the ball better than anyone.' Oh, that that was the case in 2013!

Some twenty-one years after his stellar display against West Germany, I was sitting with him in Terry Neill's Sports Bar in Holborn, discussing some publicity angles for his auto-biography *The Working Man's Ballet*, and he outlined how his life changed on Easter Monday 1970.

'We were away at West Brom,' he told me. 'And having gone for a ball – there was nobody near me at the time – I landed badly, severely tearing my ankle ligaments – the pain was terrible.'

Despite all kinds of treatment, including an Irish faith-healer massaging his ankle – he watched the Wembley confrontation from the touchline. The portents for the replay were a little more positive, and he returned to hospital for seven days of intensive treatment, and even paid to see a distinguished Harley Street practitioner, which irritated the powers-at-be at the club, but it was all in vain.

So, once more Huddy was to be a spectator. As he himself said, 'When I woke up on the morning of 29 April 1970, I felt like a failed suicide.' Whether his subtle skills would have influenced the outcome of the first encounter is open to debate. Des Lynham once said of him that 'he was a superb tactician', and my opinion is that with Hudson in the team, Chelsea could have prevailed in game one.

Returning to my hotel, I was already drunk, but as yet not a trace of alcohol had even kissed my lips. Mind you, I was hoarse, what with shouting and having puffed and dragged upon a shop-load of fags, but the world had suddenly changed its hue; it was now a universe of pure happiness and joy. All I needed was a quick wash, and then join up with a few of the guys to paint the town red – or should I say blue.

I met up with Ossie and Eddie McCreadie, and after a few drinks we set off for one of Manchester's premier night clubs. It was a smoky place, and as you can imagine, our small party was on this cloud of euphoria – in fact we were like bipolar people on a massive high. What the club looked like was secondary to us, as we just inhaled the whole experience like some huge drag on some super-duper joint.

Memory banks play tricks. I am sure the club in question was part owned by George Best; he was certainly in attendance. Later, I was to ghost a few Peter Osgood articles for the great man's yearbook.

By this time, we had downed a few more glasses, and I found myself in deep conversation with McCreadie, another real cool dude who smoked Rothmans cigarettes with the refinement of Noel Coward. He wore chic Buddy Holly-style spectacles, and later sported a pencil-thin Viva Zapata moustache – as I say, he was the King of Cool.

He was also an extremely thoughtful guy, and how he put up with my know-it-all views on such things as player bonuses for winning the FA Cup and other such financial aspects of a player's wage structure, I'll never know.

What I was saying to him smacked of the kind of greed so rampant in the modern game. He disagreed with me (quite rightly, looking back) when I blurted out that 'the money you get is not enough'. Looking at the money-side of football circa 1970, it has to be remembered that for the first time in this country, the elite players – the crème de la crème – were being paid, by the standards of the day, top dollar. And to someone like Eddie, who had joined the club in 1962 for a paltry transfer fee of £5,000 from East Stirlingshire, some trendy-looking London smart-arse telling him he wasn't being paid enough must have rankled with him. However, to his credit he remained silent and diplomatically changed the subject.

Scotsman McCreadie gained 23 caps for his native Scotland, and was an innovative full-back, blessed with express pace and tackles that would have modern coaches and managers jumping around in their dugouts in extreme agitation. His wild back-flick of a kick on the head of fellow Scotsman Billy Bremner in the final was more *West Side Story*, all George Chakiris or Russ Tamblyn, in its execution – you could almost say Kung Fu – than standard FA coaching book. Looking at it now it undoubtedly highlighted McCreadie's undoubted commitment to the cause, but it also illustrated how times have changed. In 2013 it would have resulted in a spot-kick, possibly even a red card, but forty-three years ago referee Jennings just waved play on!

Ossie was always extremely effusive when talking to me about the Scotsman with the craggy good looks. Later he was to say to me that in his opinion it was Eddie Mac, during the days of Tommy 'Doc', who had developed into the first authentic overlapping full-back in England.

After over 400 appearances, he retired in 1973, and joined the Stamford Bridge coaching staff. Two years later, in April 1975, he was appointed manager, just at the time when the club's fortunes were at rock bottom. Relegation to Division Two was an absolute certainty, and the club was riddled with debt. Eddie, always a firm believer in youth, rebuilt the side and made some brave decisions along the way, the most controversial being taking the captaincy away from his old Cup final-winning skipper 'Chopper' Harris, then aged thirty-one, and handing it to a precocious teenager, eighteen-year-old Ray Wilkins.

This McCreadie-created outfit, brimful of young talent complemented by some veterans of the club's halcyon years, reclaimed their top-flight status in 1977. Then came one of those bizarre incidents bordering on the surreal that have dominated so much of the club's history since its inception in 1905.

Boss McCreadie requested a company car, which was fair enough, you would think, considering what he had achieved in so short a time. The way it all panned out was convoluted in the extreme, but the bare bones are these: Eddie's request for a car was initially turned down by chairman Brian Mears, but later Mears backed down and offered the manager a brand-new Rover. It is said that Eddie craved a Merc, but the club turned this down flat.

Now it all depends on whom you believe in this whole sorry saga, but a friend of the flying Scotsman – with friends like these who needs enemies – has gone on record as saying: 'It was Eddie's fault, really. They offered him the new Rover, which was the car of the year, but he was holding out for a Mercedes.' Talk about trivial. Anyway, Eddie had obviously had enough and decamped to the USA to sign for the Memphis Rogues.

Just a little aside here linking Joe Meek, The Tornados and Eddie McCreadie: in 1963, Heinz Burt – who died of a stroke aged just fifty-seven in 2000 – an integral member of The Tornados, who had a stormy and some say sexually-charged relationship with enigmatic Meek, released a single, 'Just like Eddie'. It was a tribute to the late rocker Eddie Cochran, and with McCreadie's overlapping charges now seducing Blues fans en masse, a chorus or two of this ditty could be heard emanating from the terraces whenever Eddie was on fire.

More and more drinks were downed, and we somehow found our way back to the hotel where all kinds of eccentric happenings were going on, most notably *Till Death Us Do Part* scriptwriter Johnny Speight somehow ending up in a bath clutching a bottle of whisky. How he ever got there I never did manage to find out! It is said that Johnny, who died in 1998, was a follower of Fulham, but on this famous night there was just one club for him: it was based at Stamford Bridge, not Craven Cottage.

By this time I was so intoxicated that I felt like I was part of the audience at a theatre; all these events were taking place, but I was looking on from the outside. 1 a.m. clicked over to 2 a.m. and I found myself chatting and drinking with a guy called David Morgan, one of the senior directors of I Was Lord Kitchener's Valet; the wafts from my breath must have been like a gale of brandy fumes.

Ossie had gone off somehow – later he told me he had met up with some woman; a blonde. 'She was a nice girl,' he told me – but I was more than content to just gas away with Morgan, who, like everyone at Lord Kitchener, was an ardent Chelsea fan.

Morgan looked arty; in fact if I had been asked to describe him in some witness-type statement for the police, I would have said, 'He looks like a well-nourished version of Vincent Van Gogh'.

Who will ever know exactly when I and the others at last slid between the sheets to try to get at least the odd hour or two of sleep. By this time it was all so mad that thanks to Ossie, I was given a room at the Piccadilly (I'd sort out my bag at the other hotel later). None of this mattered one jot.

There is one thing about being young and a pill-popper, and that is you have no fear. Hitting the mattress, I was soon in touch with the god of dreams, Morpheus. I slept for maybe two hours at most. I awoke, my tongue feeling like a plumber's handkerchief, took a couple of pills, gulped some water and dressed. No shaving, no teeth cleaning – yuck! Then down to breakfast for a big, greasy fry-up paid for by Chelsea FC.

Sauntering into the dining room I was met with a few half-hearted hellos and smiles by several of the players. I joined Marvin Hinton and Ron Harris at their table, and having placed my order – for by now the pills had kicked in and I was as ravenous as a kid at Christmas – I poured some coffee and proceeded to chat to my fellow eaters ten-to-the-dozen.

Seated opposite us was *Daily Mail* football journo Jeff Powell. I was and never have been a lover of the *Mail* – in my circle these days it has been given the appropriate nickname of 'the Hate Mail'. But during those 'Make Love not War' years, the paper had some of the foremost sports writers in the business. Apart from Powell, there was Ian Wooldridge and Brian James, and I will forever be thankful for the support the paper gave me in our campaign to persuade Ramsey to select Ossie.

Time was precious that April morning as the plan was that we were to catch an early train back to Euston, but that didn't prevent me from going through the whole gamut of the hotel's breakfast menu at breakneck speed.

Mention the name of Marvin Hinton to any supporter of a certain age, and he or she will tell you that 'Lou', as he was called, was surely the best central defender never to be capped by England. Signed by Tommy Docherty in 1963 from Charlton Athletic for £30,000, he always looked in control on the park, and in many ways he was the perfect foil to some of the 1970 team's 'wild men'.

'Lou' Hinton was a quiet man – the sort of guy you'd want in a crisis; the sort of guy able to keep his cool at all times. A soft word here and there would be enough to quell any potentially damaging situations.

On a personal note, I was once 'protected' by him at a nightclub, following a lavish dinner at the Meridiana' Restaurant on the Fulham Road, to celebrate Chelsea's FA Cup success.

The dinner had been organised by one of the Lord Kitchener directors, and it proved to be a riotous occasion. There was a colossal cake, shaped like Stamford Bridge Stadium, complete with goalposts and club colours – it was absolutely immense.

The champagne flowed like water and even though all manner of luxurious goodies were available, our Lord Kitchener high-flyer, who had arrived in a brand-new Bentley, ordered eggs, bacon and chips!

Unfortunately, owing to his England commitments – he was in Ramsey's World Cup 22 – Ossie was not there. But there was a good sprinkling of first-team squad stars including Alan Birchenall and the urbane Hinton.

After we had gorged on the fodder and drunk enough bubbly to sink a few ships, we staggered to some nightclub in Chelsea where I continued my liquid intake by ordering champagne cocktail after champagne cocktail. By this time I was beginning to behave like a bit of an idiot, and when I started to demand that the DJ play some tracks from the *Sergeant Pepper* album and in particular 'A Day In The Life', that great homage to counter-culture, I was being boorish in the extreme.

This boorishness reached its peak when I began mourning the passing of the 1960s and announced to the assembled throng that things 'would deteriorate from now on. All your dreams, all your ideals have now gone!'

By this time, 'Lou', realising I was tanked-up to the gills, told me in that soft voice of his just to calm down. It was amazing how the tone of his voice did the trick. In a matter of moments, I was 'normal' once more, and having apologised profusely – Hinton merely said 'don't worry' in that soft voice – it was all over.

Well, this is how he was on the pitch, and even though his involvement in the replay was of the cameo variety – just eight minutes before the end of extra time when he replaced Ossie – his performances were always efficient. And on more than one occasion his stability, and in those days when a centre-half was more often than not a big lump, his technical ability with the ball and the quality of his passing were almost continental in ethos. The old adage of 'if in doubt, kick it out' was never on the Marvin Hinton agenda.

Having demolished this gargantuan breakfast, it was now time to make our way to the station. I say 'our' way because I was to join the whole Chelsea party in the train back to the Smoke.

I managed somehow to collect my bag from the other hotel, and there we were on the platform, hunched and hungover and definitely a bit puffy round the eyes – like some mass group of serial partygoers. Personally, I was feeling just like Dorian Gray on a bad day. Thank goodness I didn't look at myself in a mirror!

Once aboard – and here I was ensconced with all the players – manager Dave Sexton attempted to adopt a more human face. In fact he even smiled at me. It was of the patronising variety, and I almost read into it that he forgave me for not shaving; and that he forgave me for the length of my hair; and that he forgave me for my Viva Zapata moustache; and that he wouldn't normally forgive me for this lack of discipline, but that today was a special day, and because of it, 'anything goes'.

Sexton was a religious man. A devout Roman Catholic and devotee of the Jesuit philosopher Teilhard de Chardin, he had been educated at St Ignatius College, a Jesuit Comprehensive School for boys in Stamford Hill North London; ironically an area of the capital more associated with Judaism than Roman Catholicism, which, in my opinion explained much of his over-all persona: severe and unforgiving.

The college has produced a list of famous alumni, most notably former Archbishop of Westminster Cardinal Heenan, film director Alfred 'Psycho' Hitchcock, former BBC News Diplomatic Editor Brian Hanrahan (his famous words whilst standing on the deck of HMS Hermes during the Falklands War – 'I am not allowed to say how many planes joined the raid, but I counted them all out and I counted them all back' – has gone down in journalistic folklore), and legendary record producer Sir George Martin, whose list of credits reads like a pop music Hall of Fame. His recordings of the music of The Beatles resulted him being widely known as the fifth Beatle.

So Dave Sexton, professional footballer and coach extraordinaire, who died last November, aged eighty-two, could quite rightly be added to this distinguished company. The son of former professional boxer Archie Sexton, he was a cerebral man, who was never, in my opinion, able or indeed capable of either relating to or understanding this new breed of pro that he had in his ranks.

Another aspect of life he abhorred was publicity. Think of Jose Mourinho, then imagine the complete opposite to the suave Portguese, and you have in your mind's eye Dave Sexton.

Sexton believed in discipline and established values. He was modest almost to a fault, but there was one thing he lacked – humanity. Professional footballers are people, often very young people. Even as long ago as the late 1960s and early '70s, players were beginning to make big money. As never before, they were beginning to mix with an eclectic range of humanity: people from screen, stage and the world of rock music; even the aristocracy. Unfortunately, Dave could not or would not buy into this – a great shame, for I feel that had he made even a small effort to understand the character of the likes of Cooke and Hudson and Osgood, that magnificent Chelsea side could and indeed would have gone on to even greater things.

As Alan Hudson later told me: 'Dave just did not understand Os even though he 'understood' his talent. I could have sat down with Dave and given him the low-down on his main man – that is, if he bought me lunch and allowed me a glass of wine or two. I jest. After all, it is a little like Fletch in *Porridge*: he would tell you more about his cellmate Godber than anyone else in the entire world – he knew his every move. Well, although I did not know every move that Osgood made, because we weren't under HMP rules, I knew a darn sight more than the man who should have.'

Later Sexton was to remark, following a complete breakdown in his relationship with what he regarded as a recalcitrant Osgood, which eventually resulted in his transfer to Southampton for £275,000 that 'maybe it would have been best if Ossie and I had sorted it quickly between four walls of a locked room. But it wouldn't possibly have remained private with Ossie. He doesn't know when to be a good lad or Jack the lad.'

As a coach, Dave was one of the most sophisticated of his generation. As a player, he is best described as a journeyman professional, his career taking in a variety of clubs from West Ham in the early 1950s to Crystal Palace in 1959.

His first managerial appointment was at Leyton Orient in 1965, and after having coached at Stamford Bridge, he replaced the sometimes combustible, but always flamboyant Docherty two years later, remaining boss until 1974.

QPR was his next port of call where, having signed a couple of Chelsea old boys, Hollins and Webb, he took the Loftus Road club to within a point of the First Division crown in 1976.

Next stop was Old Trafford. Once more he stepped into Docherty's shoes, following the sacking of the colourful Scot for his an affair with the wife of club physiotherapist, Laurie Brown.

Losing one FA Cup final to Arsenal and finishing second in the top flight was a poor return for a club of United's aspirations and pedigree, so in 1981 he was on the move again – to Coventry City, a position he retained for two years. This was his final club appointment. However, from 1977–90 he coached the England U-21 side, taking on the role full-time from 1994–96.

Whenever I encountered him, I felt a bit like a schoolboy in the presence of a headmaster with a particularly fearsome reputation. I never relaxed in his company, and even though on more than one occasion he was pleasant and even smiled, something that he obviously didn't find easy, I always got the impression that in his eyes I was someone who was too interested in having a good time to be of real benefit to any of his players.

My rock PR background gave me this awareness of the value of publicity. But with Sexton, all publicity angles were bad angles. How he would cope with the modern obsession with the media, and the acres of managerial pronouncements that we read in our papers at the breakfast table and online, would make an interesting debate. In my humble opinion, he would be out of his depth. But having made all these points, he was as relaxed as I had ever seen him as we sped through the countryside on this excellent state-owned British Railways train to Euston Station and the waiting hordes of ecstatic fans.

ELEVEN

EUSTON STATION AND BEYOND

Arriving at Euston, we were greeted by what seemed like hundreds of cheering people of all ages. By now, the alcohol intake amongst several of the playing squad and the press corps was back to immediate post-Cup final replay levels.

As we climbed, or should I say staggered, on to the waiting bus to escort us back to the Fulham Road and its environs with the Cup, I was joined in my section of the vehicle by both Charlie Cooke and an extremely lubricated Hugh McIlvanney, now rightly regarded as one of the leading sports columnists in the United Kingdom.

Charlie Cooke was one player who was regularly singing Hugh's praises to me, and there is no doubt that there have been few more articulate purveyors of sports writing than the articulate Scotsman, then aged thirty-six.

Now I have never been that broad or that big in stature, whereas even forty-three years ago, Hugh was not exactly a lightweight. So, when he came soaring towards me, obviously having consumed more than just a wee dram, I had to be on my toes to avoid his well-proportioned frame. All I ever remember of that 'meeting' with him was the smile – no, it was more of a broad, almost cartoon-like grin – on his face that captured the whole mood of the occasion perfectly.

Driving through the London traffic, we were cheered incessantly by Londoners – were they all Chelsea supporters? And after what seemed like an eternity we reached our destination, Fulham Road, where mayhem ensued. This was joyous mayhem, however, with the crowds lining the pavements on either side cheering with such undiluted joy that I must say that the odd tear ran down my cheek. No doubt the emotion I displayed was increased in intensity by the amount of booze I had consumed in only a matter of hours.

I remember Ossie telling me later that 'after an evening out, I'd get myself a glass of port, turn on the video, and watch the replay again'. Like me in 1970, I am sure he shed the occasional tear or two. After all, why not? These were emotional guys – the class of 1970.

This Cup Final had captured the imagination of the country as never before. No longer could football at club level in television terms be regarded as esoteric, and all of us with blue blood in our veins just hoped and prayed that this first-ever FA Cup triumph would at long last remove that music hall tag from the name of Chelsea FC.

The Cup euphoria continued for days and days, but for Ossie and Chelsea keeper Peter Bonetti, the pressure was only just beginning, as they prepared to embark for Mexico and the 1970 FIFA World Cup Finals. Alan Hudson would also have been included, I am absolutely convinced of that, but his ongoing ankle problem was probably the deciding factor for Ramsey.

While Osgood was away in Mexico, the cash kept coming in from the Ford deal – more and more each month. Just prior to his departure, I had said to him, 'Ossie, there's no need to worry, I'll give your wife Rose a ring when the money comes in and drive to Windsor and hand over the notes over a nice cup of tea. How does that sound?' His head nodded in contented agreement, and over the coming weeks I enjoyed several pots of Typhoo or whatever it was and some biscuits and some cakes in the Osgood garden with his charming spouse. These were tranquil afternoons for us both, and maybe it's simply another case of rose-tinted glasses, but the sun always seemed to shine, never too hot, but just right; balmy days indeed.

Away from all this rapture, my life had taken a different course. So much of it was all about putting on an act, pretending to be arrogant and devious à la Andrew Loog Oldham, trying with all my might to 'do deals'. However, when it came to Charlie Cooke, I was able to revert to my real self.

As I have already made clear, Charlie was in so many ways not the ideal footballer to try to promote. He didn't enjoy the publicity razzmatazz at all, and even when I managed to arrange a first-person column in the likes of *Inside Football* for example, he insisted on being the writer in charge.

He was also not a great one for actually talking about the game. My everlasting image of the young Cooke will always be of an intellectual – yes, intellectual – seated in his small Mini, eating shellfish. We often did this together. It was all pretty messy really: two guys sitting in his car, having gulped down loads of chardonnay, attempting in a ham-fisted way to extract some crab or lobster or giant prawn meat.

One such occasion sticks in my mind. I was lunching with Cooke and an old friend of his, Alan Sharp. Like Charlie, Alan was Scottish; also like Charlie he was a writer. But whereas Cooke's twinkling feet earned him his bread and cheese, Sharp was already making a big name for himself in Hollywood. In fact, the first time I met him, he had just completed the film script of *The Hired Hand* for Peter Fonda.

Later, Alan would achieve some limited critical success with his play, 'The Long Distance Piano Player', which hit our TV screens in the BBC series *Play For Today* in October 1970, starring The Kinks' Ray Davies.

Over a lunch of pizza and lashings of wine in one of those chic King's Road eateries that sprung up in the 1960s – well actually we were sitting outside, for it was a warm sunny day – I asked him about the play, and he openly admitted that his work was based on Horace McCoy's cult novel set in Depression-era USA, *They Shoot Horses, Don't They?*, an extremely frank observation I thought.

The film of *They Shoot Horses* was released in 1969, but it is only fair to point out that Sharp's play made its debut on the radio well before the film was available at the cinema.

In Sharp's drama, Davies plays Pete, who in a run-down Northern town, embarks on an attempt to break the record for non-stop piano playing. During the course of the play, Davies' playing becomes more and more eccentric and off-key, which led *The Spectator* critic Patrick Skene Catling to comment 'that he was beginning to sound like Thelonious Monk!'

Lunches with Charlie were always fun and extremely liquid. He had a wide knowledge of modern literature, the books of Ernest Hemingway being his passion. I remember *Daily Mirror* football writer Nigel Clarke having a conversation with me in a taxi, comparing Cooke to that 1920s American genius F. Scott Fitzgerald, and he wasn't referring to Fitzgerald's prowess with a soccer ball.

No, what Clarke had in mind was that, like that doomed idol of the Jazz Age and writer of that great American novel *The Great Gatsby*, Cooke was on a downward spiral, fuelled by booze.

Whether he was or not, and many people have told me since that when 'in his cups' he would more often than not morph into an aggressive and obnoxious man, I always found him charming, albeit a trifle introverted; except, that is, when the conversation veered away from the round ball game to the world of arts and literature.

I personally have always admired the quality of Hemingway's writing, but I must say that I never found his 'man's man' kind of machismo at all attractive. I admired his bravery and principled liberalism in fighting Spanish Fascist dictator General Franco in the Spanish Civil War with that group of intellectuals and communists, the International Brigade. I used to say to Charlie that I found Fitzgerald's more poetic prose more appealing to me, as I did his obvious sensitivity and vulnerability plus his beautiful satire in such works as *The Diamond as Big as the Ritz* and *Gretchen's Forty Winks*.

His admiration for 'Papa Hemingway' was in my eyes surprising in a man I always thought to be both sensitive and susceptible to the vagaries of life as a professional footballer.

Our other meeting place was the world-famous pub in Hampstead, the Bull and Bush. We would meet outside, sometimes on a Saturday evening, just to shoot the breeze.

Charlie would always down just a couple of pints and then say to me that he had to go.

'Where are you going – anywhere nice?' I asked.

'Oh, just a bit of business,' he would answer, *sotto voce*.

Like Ossie, Charlie had an absolutely charming wife. Edith had a sort of Moira Anderson-type beauty about her, and her Scottish accent was soft and velvety and smacked of compassion and friendliness.

She would telephone me sometimes, and it was always the same question on her lips: 'Have you seen Charlie recently?'

My answer was always the same: 'Sorry, Edith, not since Saturday when we had a couple of drinks in Hampstead at the Bull and Bush. Has he not phoned you at all?'

And her reply was always the same: 'No, I've not heard or seen him for a few days.'

She was always so polite; so softly spoken. Our conversations always ended like this: 'Well, not to worry,' I would say sympathetically, 'I'll definitely let you know if I hear from him.'

Some ten months later, Charlie would break into an environment never before traversed by a professional footballer – and in fact football has not broken into this rarefied world since. It was a one-off, and in many ways something that even in today's 'classless' society would not be possible. It was the world of high fashion: a world of class, elegance and glamour, but more of this anon.

The summer of 1970 was dominated by two major events. One was the General Election, in which Tory leader Edward Heath was attempting to defy the pollsters and oust incumbent Harold Wilson. And the other was the World Cup in Mexico.

England were World Champions, but by no stretch of the imagination were Bobby Moore and company regarded as favourites. In Mexico's Latin American culture in which refereeing decisions in those days in particular tended to favour the likes of the hosts and the Brazilians, plus the problems of altitude and extreme heat, the holders' chances were rated as comparatively slim.

Their quest was hardly helped by the Bobby Moore/ Bogota incident in which the England skipper was accused of stealing a valuable bracelet after Ramsey's troops had taken on Colombia in a warm-up contest.

The whole sorry saga has been well-documented, with the full facts actually not being placed in the public domain until 2003 under the thirty-year rule.

The date was 18 May 1970: the venue, the Tequendama Hotel in Bogota. The England team were in the country, preparing to face Colombia later the same day. Moore and Bobby Charlton were looking intently at the wares in the Green Fire jewellery shop, situated in the lobby of the hotel only a few yards away. Within a few minutes one of the shop's assistant, Clara Padilla, began throwing accusations at Moore that he had stolen an emerald and diamond bracelet, valued at £6,000. The police were summoned, and statements were taken. Both Moore and Charlton agreed to be searched, but their offer was refused.

England strolled to a 4–0 victory, and they later flew off to Quito to take on Ecuador, in order to gain more experience of performing at altitude. Initially, it all had the makings of a big storm in very small cup of Darjeeling.

After a 2–0 win over Ecuador, the plan was to make their way to Mexico via Bogota, as there was no scheduled direct flight. Upon arrival at Bogota airport, the England party was met by what seemed like a battalion of armed police, who were there to arrest the England skipper.

It was only the intervention of British charges d'affaires Keith Morris, who arranged for Moore to voluntarily attend a police station that prevented the affair from becoming one of international embarrassment.

The 'police station' turned out to be a courthouse where Moore, after hours of the third-degree, was arrested. He was about to be marched off to prison when the home government butted in. Following this intervention, Bobby was placed under house arrest in the home of Colombian Director of Football Alfonso Senior, with two armed guards for company.

The England players had flown off to Mexico, and the bewildered Moore, in a bid to keep fit, decided to go for a walk the following morning, accompanied by the guards. That same night these guards, obviously feeling bored with life, embarked on a serious drinking session, which left them the worse for wear the following morning. In fact they were feeling so ill that they agreed that Bobby could go for his walk unaccompanied, on the understanding that he would return, which, of course, he did.

At 10 a.m. on the morning of 27 May, it was decided in the manner of a South American Hercule Poirot, to hold a reconstruction. The small jewellery emporium was packed with a senior judge, police, witnesses and a huge press presence.

During this farce of a reconstruction, Moore was able to cross-examine Padilla, and it soon became clear that the whole charge was an absurdity. Bobby was dressed in an England tracksuit, and Padilla, having been asked if he was dressed in the same attire when he allegedly stole the bracelet, answered: 'Yes'. She was then asked to repeat this, and the ever-alert England captain, quick as a flash, showed the judge that his outfit had no pockets!

Eventually, after further posturing by the Colombian authorities, the Colombian people themselves took a hand by venting their displeasure at the way Moore had been treated, and that it was a 'national disgrace'. So, on 28 May the judge signed the release papers, and twenty-four hours later he was on a plane bound for Mexico.

There was a serendipitous moment on the plane when Bobby found himself in conversation with Argentine international Omar Sivori, who told him that these 'frame-ups' were common in Colombia. Later, the manager of World Cup favourites Brazil, Joao Saldanha, told Moore that he had experienced exactly the same thing.

It was only in 2003 that it was revealed that the Colombian police knew that Moore was innocent and that his release was down to the intervention of Prime Minister Harold Wilson.

This was hardly the ideal preparation for an England team attempting to retain the Jules Rimet trophy, and Ossie later told me that even though the whole sorry episode was something they could have done without, it did in fact 'pull us together even more'.

In Chelsea terms, Mexico '70 was not a good World Cup. Goalkeeper Bonetti was made the scapegoat for the quarter-final defeat by West Germany. And as for Osgood, his input was minimal – scandalously so. Ramsey and Osgood: it was never going to be a marriage made in heaven. In fact I remain utterly convinced to this day that but for the clamour from the press to get Ossie international recognition, which even the tight-lipped England boss could not ignore, the King of Stamford Bridge would have remained an international outcast.

Having replaced Franny Lee midway through the second period in England's far-from-convincing opening 1–0 victory over Romania, the betting was that Ossie would be on the team-sheet for the pivotal meeting with those kings of flair from Brazil.

However, it was not to be. Os told me all about it over lunch later that summer. 'I'd been working really hard in train-ing – doing all the right things – in fact I hadn't had a drink for a few weeks! I was doing everything I was told. In one of our practice games, I put two goals past Gordon Banks – I was really flying: on top form. Afterwards Mooro (Bobby Moore) said to me that he was certain I'd be in the team for the Brazil match. Then when Alf Ramsey read out the team he said: "The side that finished the game with Romania will play against Brazil".'

Ossie's euphoria was soon dispelled when Ramsey cor-rected himself: 'I am sorry, I meant to say the team that started the Romania match will play the Brazilians.'

Alan Hudson's take on the whole 'Chelsea/Mexico experi-ence' certainly makes interesting reading.

'If Os was very disappointed with the outcome, then Bonetti was, I can only think, inconsolable, as his worst nightmares came true against the West Germans,' he related to me. 'Osgood was by far a stronger character and although Mexico hit him hard – or the lack of Mexico – the other Peter (Bonetti) was, although a very confident character and per-former, not made of the stuff that Osgood was. Os would shrug and say, 'Well, if last season did not show you, then watch this season'. And that is exactly what he did, he was that special under pressure.'

Bonetti, a last-minute call-up for the West Germany quarter-final, following Banks' illness, was crucified by many for his supposed poor goalkeeping, which allowed the Germans to net two goals when they were so patently second best. However, in my view – and that of Hudson – it was Ramsey who was at fault.

'Oh, how I felt for him – the other Peter, that is. To this day, I can still make a case for him. I know that the Franz Beckenbauer goal looked like a soft one, but I think it looked far worse than it was, and given what was to follow, it kind of escalated and highlighted it out of proportion.

'What Alf Ramsey did with his substitution was far more damaging, and after all we were still a goal to the good. Then the wheels fell off, and all through bad substitutions.'

The bare bones of the game are that England took a 2–0 advantage through Alan Mullery and Martin Peters, and were still 2–0 ahead with just over 22 minutes remaining. It was at this crucial stage that the ultra-cautious Ramsey substituted both Bobby Charlton and Peters (no doubt in attempt to keep them fresh for the semi with Italy on 17 June), and it was then that the Bonetti 'blunders' changed the whole course of the tie.

Beckenbauer pulled a goal back, and the Germans obtained parity with a goal from their diminutive striker Uwe Seeler. In extra time Gerd Muller plundered the winner, and poor old Bonetti's life was turned upside-down as he became the national focus of blame.

Four days after this soul-destroying reversal of fortunes for the national team, the voters dumped Labour's pragmatic Prime Minister Harold Wilson out of office, and the far less charismatic Edward Heath took charge.

To this day, many leading figures in the Labour Party remain convinced that Bonetti's 'blunders' or Ramsey's poor use of substitutions – you pays your money and takes your choice – which led to England's demise were the prime reasons for Labour's own shock defeat.

When the wily Wilson called the election, Labour was some seven points-plus ahead in the opinion polls, but as it turned out the favourites lost – the Tories gaining an overall majority of 31 seats.

Wilson himself dismissed the World Cup debacle, as a reason for his own defeat, stating – 'governance of a country has nothing to do with a study of its football fixtures'.

Yet Wilson was a football fan, supporting as he did his local club Huddersfield Town, and many years later Denis Healey, Defence Minister at the time, told another story about a strategy meeting at Chequers in April 1970 in which 'Harold asked us to consider whether the government would suffer if the England footballers were defeated on the eve of polling day?'

Local Government Minister at that time was the suave and urbane Tony Crosland, and he was even more worried about the election being held during the World Cup. He blamed the defeat on 'a mix of party complacency and the disgruntled *Match of The Day* millions'.

One government minister with an authentic football background was Denis Howell. A former Football League referee, the then Minister of Sport had no doubt why the election had gone wrong.

'The moment goalkeeper Bonetti made his third and final hash of it on the Sunday, everything simultaneously began to go wrong for Labour the following Thursday.'

The portents were surely there on the Monday morning after the German disappointment when Home Secretary Roy Jenkins held a meeting in Birmingham. Howell said: 'Roy was totally bemused that no question concerned either the trade figures or immigration, but solely the football and whether Ramsey or Bonetti was the major culprit.'

Howell has since become an almost mythical figure of history. A plain-looking man with a soft Brummie accent, he was appointed Minister for the Drought during that long hot summer of 1976, and whether he was in touch with the gods or not, his presence influenced the sky to form clouds and eventually, loads of the wet stuff followed.

This England performance, which has gone down in international sporting folklore as one of those rare occasions when a side seemingly in charge of its own destiny managed to 'snatch defeat from the jaws of victory', divides opinion. Some blame Bonetti, but like Alan Hudson, I am on the side of the other camp, questioning the decisions of manager Ramsey.

As Huddy made clear to me many years later: 'What Alf Ramsey did with his substitution was far more damaging (than Bonetti's performance in goal). And after all, Ramsey – since 1966 – had made quite a few ricks.'

TWELVE

COMMUNISTS AND FASCISTS AND FASHION

The new campaign for Chelsea was full of much promise. The only problem was how both Bonetti and Osgood would react to the massive let-down of Mexico. Would this lead to a cloud of depression, or would the two Peters pick themselves up, dust themselves down and get on with the business of 'trophy collecting'? Only time would tell, of course.

The Charity Shield match-up with League Champions Everton was very much one of those 'after the Lord Mayor show' occasions. Much joyous singing as the team paraded the FA Cup, but as I have already outlined, not a Stamford Bridge afternoon to live in the memory.

The highlight for me was meeting DJ Ed 'Stewpot' Stewart, who, prior to presenting Ossie with his *Striker* award, paid him huge compliments: one in particular I shall always remember was, 'maybe if he had played in the Brazil game, things could have been different'.

This Brazil theme continued later that month when I met Peter Pullen for the first time. Peter wrote for *World Soccer* magazine, but away from his writings on the game, he was also at the time the Brazil Sports attaché in London. Later he was part of the Brazil Football Federation's failed bid for the 1994 World Cup, and later still a FIFA delegate.

To cut a long story short, he contacted me purely for a chat about Peter Osgood. I think I had written something for a magazine along the lines that Ossie played football in the manner of a boy brought up on the Copacabana beaches, not in the Royal town of Windsor. These words obviously fascinated Pullen, in essence because at the time in England shouts of 'Get Stuck In!' were common at most grounds. For many fans, sweat still counted more than improvisation, languid skill and technical ability.

Upon entering his office, I was struck by both his elegance and obvious sophistication. The dour, monochrome worlds of Ramsey and Revie were as far away from Pullen as Mars.

Reclining in his chair, he listened intently to what I had to impart. 'It's a shame,' I said, 'that Peter Osgood couldn't play for a club in Brazil – I am sure he would be idolised out there. What do you think?'

Now, I wasn't attempting to try to arrange a transfer to Corinthians or Santos. Life then was just not like that. The world was a much bigger place, and anyway, even though I was his agent, I was not allowed to involve myself in any contract or transfer dealings. No, I was just making a point, and I simply wanted Pullen's immediate reaction.

His answer to my rat-a-tat-tat of a question was frank and unsolicited. 'Peter Osgood would grace any Brazilian team,' he replied, his voice both soft and soothing. 'The problem we have in Brazil is all about money, so competing with what he earns in England would be difficult. What is most unusual is his style – the power that he possesses, which is typically English, but mixed in with this is finesse and subtlety, which you associate more with players from the Latin countries.'

Before I left, and as we shook hands, he reiterated his comment that if Osgood had been born in Rio, he would have made the Brazil national team. 'Take that, Mr Ramsey!' I said to myself as I climbed into a black cab.

The next time I shared a glass with Peter, I related to him what Pullen had said about his ability, and his eyes lit up like small beacons. He was flattered – there was no doubt about it. Like any artist, Ossie needed his ego massaged from time to time. In an environment in which you are only as good as your last game, and the chant of 'Osgood Is Good' was often corrupted by opposition supporters to 'Osgood Was Good', Peter needed his fair share of flattery.

Having lifted the FA Cup for the first time, the Chelsea players were straining at the leash to get their teeth into Europe and the European Cup Winners' Cup.

The first round saw them drawn against the unheralded Greek outfit Aris Salonika. No problem here, we thought. But what we hadn't taken into account was the powder keg political situation in that country at the time.

On 21 April 1967, there was a coup d'état in the country, led by an influential and ruthless group of colonels. Their military rule lasted for some seven years, during which Western-style democracy and basic freedoms were denied to the population as a whole. Essentially it was pure Fascism. Some politicians, in both Britain and America went even further, labelling it as 'unadulterated Nazism'. The American ambassador in Athens, William Phillips Talbot, complained that the colonels' rule 'represented a rape of democracy'.

By 1970, this odious regime was probably at its most potent. Political parties had been dissolved, and torture of political opponents was widespread, with Amnesty International representative James Becket declaring in 1969 that 'a conservative estimate would place at not less than two thousand the number of people tortured'.

The Greek citizens' right of assembly had been overturned and political demonstrations were declared *verboten*. Widespread surveillance was commonplace, which understandably resulted in people looking nervous and tense in bars and cafés, as any political discussion or even minor criticism of the government was outlawed.

The men at the helm of the junta were by no means purely and simply mindless thugs. They were subtle, and realising that such entertainments as the odd rock concert and the showing of an occasional liberal film would garner the regime some semblance of credibility, they set about what they regarded as a PR campaign. But it was all a vast sham.

Initially the monarchy was retained, and in December 1967, King Constantine II launched an unsuccessful counter-coup. Eventually after hiding out in various villages, he and his family decamped to Rome, eventually ending up in London where they lived in comparative anonymity in Linnell Close, Hampstead Garden Suburb. I lived opposite the ex-King for some twenty-four years, and I was struck almost immediately by the personae of the Special Branch men that kept guard outside his front door. They were so archetypal it wasn't true – dark suits, dark glasses – the whole Hollywood Secret Service baggage – the lot.

So, arriving at some ungodly hour at Luton Airport on 15 September 1970, this was the land that I was to encounter in a matter of hours. I was with a small group of 'Chelsea People' plus a few journalists, most notably former captain of Spurs and Northern Ireland Danny Blanchflower, then putting pen to paper for the *Sunday Express*.

I was dressed in a light blue King's Road three-piece suit – flared trousers of course – and shod with yet another pair of wet-look loafers complete with obligatory buckle. My hair was long and I sported an impressive – well I thought so anyway – drooping but well-nourished Viva Zapata moustache.

The journey on the plane was, to put it mildly, eventful. There was just the one female attached to our group, a perky Lulu-lookalike who walked in the manner of a fashion model, often wiggling her neat bottom à la Marilyn Monroe. She was a kind of courier, and she wore a perpetual smile. Needless to say, the men became her number one fans.

Also on board for some unfathomable reason was a paltry party of Coventry City people on their way to Bulgaria for a European Fairs' Cup-tie against Trakia Plovdiv (they won 4–1), so we were obliged to stop off in Sofia for a few hours.

By today's high-tech standards, the plane was rickety and looked past its best-before date. Therefore, like the tie itself, our journey was a two-legged affair. Sofia, the capital of the then hardcore Communist country Bulgaria, was those days locked in a Stalinist shroud of repression, and the airport itself was rudimentary with a capital R.

It was just like walking on to the set of some Cold War spy movie shoot. You half-expected a well-preserved Californian film-maker, all trendy shades and perma-tan, to come out of the shadow of an antiquated plane and bellow: 'Action!'

But this was no film-set; this was colourless Communism down to the seedy bar, with a smell of what I hoped was just cabbage, where we had to twiddle our thumbs drinking, or trying to drink, weak-as-water Bulgarian beer – 'gnat's pee', as someone wryly observed.

The surly, sour-faced woman behind the bar became quite animated when she thought we might be in possession of the odd Deutsch mark or US dollar, but when she discovered that all we had (apart from Greek drachmas, of course) was good old British sterling, her cracked-face smile reverted back to a half-hearted snarl.

Eventually she softened a shade and agreed to hand over the beer, giving us worthless Bulgarian currency in our change. It was during this what seemed interminable wait that I got into conversation with the articulate and erudite Blanchflower.

Chatting with the Northern Irishman over this dubious Bulgarian brew, we soon got round to chatting about Chelsea and Peter Osgood in particular.

'So, you are his agent then,' he said.

'Yes, I'm doing my best to promote him,' I responded nervously, for the pills I had swallowed to counteract my fear of flying were, in conjunction with the alcohol, making me extremely dopey. 'Sometimes it's not that easy because being in my early twenties, so many of the people I have to deal with are very sceptical about my qualifications.'

How different it was in 1970 to today's society in which everything we listen to, read or watch is geared totally towards the 'yoof' market.

I then did my best to get away from all things Stamford Bridge, and asked him about his own career – he was extremely unassuming about it – and he told me of his early days as a player with Barnsley in the 1950s and how he had upset the Oakwell hierarchy with his forthright opinions.

It seems incredible to relate, but in those less-enlightened times, players were never given the ball in training. They were told in no uncertain terms that being deprived of this so-important sphere would make them hungrier for it on a Saturday afternoon! Danny expressed his dismay at such archaic training methods and opined his concerns to the coaching team. These concerns were met with cries of 'we know best'.

When Danny went on to inform the manager that ball retention and technique were how it was done abroad, again his viewpoint was pooh-poohed.

He was man born before his time, that there is no doubt. A professional who displayed intellectual leanings and articulate thought in an era when these working-class heroes were essentially slaves to their clubs, earning a pittance even though week-in-and-week-out they would attract crowds in excess of 50,000.

All-told Danny won 56 caps for Northern Ireland, and he also managed the national side for three years between 1976 and '79. His crowning moment came at Wembley in 1961 when he captained Spurs to a 2–0 victory over Leicester City, thereby becoming the first twentieth century club to complete the League/Cup Double.

In 1978, he had a short and unsuccessful go at managing Chelsea, but it was as the fulcrum of that great Tottenham team that will forever remain in the memory.

Clambering aboard plane number two at Sofia Airport, I was by this time out on my feet. 'Are we ever going to get to Greece?' was the question that kept running through my brain, which by this time had more than a touch of the scrambled egg about it. What I needed was a pick-me-up, and fast!

Arriving at Salonika Airport, two things struck me: firstly, the heat. Boy, was it intense! There I was dressed up to the nines in my new suit, complete with waistcoat, walking, or should I say staggering, like some out-of-condition zombie into this oven. Later, a local told me that even by Greek standards, the temperature levels were exceptional for the time of year.

The second thing that caused some alarm bells to ring was this posse of machine-gun-wielding soldiers of the junta, looking mean and obviously itching to shoot someone. It was with trembling hands that I approached the passport area. I'm no coward, but these gun-toting guys with their dead eyes gave me the creeps.

Arriving at the desk, I was confronted by this smiling official: well I say smiling, it was more of a leer. He looked at my unkempt hair and moustache and was about to demand from me, in his quirky version of the English language, the full SP about my political affiliations. Thankfully, before I could point out that I was here with Chelsea, someone in authority spoke to him *sotto voce* in Greek to tell him of my Chelsea affiliation, and with a friendly wave and a Cheshire cat-style grin he waved me through. However, before he did so he did tell me that I would have to hand over my passport at the hotel, and it would be returned to me upon departure.

Once I was ensconced in the coach to ferry me to the team hotel, I was informed by the driver – who spoke extremely good English – that essentially long hair and what were termed 'Revolution Moustaches' were a big no-no as far as the junta was concerned. I thanked him and made some quip on the lines of: 'Well, more than half the Chelsea team resemble Che Guevara!'

Arriving at our hotel, I was impressed by its luxury. The bar in particular was outstanding, and needless to say, having handed over my passport at the desk as requested, found my room and unpacked at 100mph, I was soon sitting with a few of the players, imbibing tall glasses of gins and tonic.

To the sound of clinking glasses, I began chatting to Ossie. He smiled affectionately at me, as he did every time I had a glass in my hand. In a matter of minutes, a thirty-something English couple, obviously intent on talking to us about Chelsea's chances in the game, sat down and joined us.

Soon it was bonhomie all round. The guy – he was one of those typical golf club blokes of old – and Ossie soon built up a real rapport; he was good like that with fans, he always made them feel special, a rare talent. After a while, the stranger and his wife disappeared and we were left to our own devices. Despite all its drawbacks and inconveniences, this was undoubtedly my favourite football excursion. I had more adventures in Salonika than were good for me – but what fun. Or as Joe Gargery put it so succinctly in *Great Expectations* – what larks!

Later I was to say to Alan Hudson, 'How the hell did we fit all that 'stuff' into one night?'

He just chuckled and said quietly: 'Well, we just did.'

Before talking about the game, let us look at the environs of the Harilaou Stadium. Walking jauntily to the entrance, I was struck first of all by the amount of police and soldiers on duty. These were grim-faced guys with the expressionless eyes of psychopaths. Each one had some kind of automatic weapon over his shoulder. Some even clutched machine guns. The stadium itself had the look of Stalag Luft 111 in the classic British war movie *The Wooden Horse*: all Everest-high barbed wire and soldiers, and there was a moat as well – it was the eeriest football ground I had ever visited.

As for the game itself, it was a particularly poisonous encounter, which included some of the worst on-the-pitch behaviour I had ever witnessed. Without sounding too biased, I am, of course, referring to the 'tactics' employed by the Salonika players.

I'll let Alan Hudson describe some of the Salonika 'tactics': 'The Greeks weren't smart at all. There was all this spitting, and the worst thing was when they lifted you up if you'd fallen down in a tackle and then they would pull the hair under your armpits.'

After the game, Ossie also condemned the Salonika players' behaviour to me, as indeed did Ian Hutchinson, who as usual had been as brave as the proverbial lion.

The match was not one to savour in any aesthetic sense, but there was much admiration for the Chelsea players from the media, taking into account all the provocation they had to endure from first whistle to last.

Around 50,000 screaming Greeks (with the odd Chelsea fan) were packed into this fortress of a ground, and the noise was deafening when Alecos Alexadis put Aris ahead. Late on, Hutchinson deservedly levelled, and the verdict was that it had been a 'thoroughly professional job' in which Sexton's men had displayed both patience and restraint, words that certainly could not be used about the hours that followed on this hot and sultry night in Thessaloniki.

Once the dust had settled and the Chelsea party was back at its hotel, it became like a scene from the Keystone Cops as player after player spruced himself up. Suitably suited and booted, they were ready to face their hosts at a banquet laid on by representatives of the Greek FA and Aris Salonika officials.

It was a lavish affair, and much wine was quaffed. Sexton, displaying surprising friendliness and warmth told me I could sit down with the Chelsea squad at the Downton Abbey-type dining table, laden with all kinds of sumptuous goodies, in one of the hotel's largest private rooms.

Considering all the nastiness that had gone before, the dinner was all sweetness and light. Each Chelsea player was given a couple of gifts each. Whether the Greek football powerbrokers knew who I was, I wasn't sure, but my place setting was empty – no gift. However, Ian Hutchinson put that right.

Hutch was a hard man on the field of battle. He never shirked a challenge, and after retirement his body was testament to all the bashings and beatings it had taken. However, off-stage, so to speak, he was a softly spoken 'nice guy'. He always struck me as someone whose sensitivity could be taken advantage of by some sweet-talking, smooth operator. Anyway, seeing that I had been left out of the gift stakes, he smiled at me and, handing me a bottle-shaped wrapped parcel, said: 'Here, Greg, you take one of mine.'

We all unwrapped our parcels like some mass Christmas Day Morning present-fest for children, and inside 'mine' was a bottle of Metaxa Greek brandy, which proved a good friend to me for the remainder of this strangely surreal trip.

How much food we ate, and how long this dinner lasted; all these facts are now buried in the mists of time. But, having put on a good show of British diplomacy and phlegm, we slowly but surely left the room for more hedonistic pleasures,

I teamed up with Ossie and full-back Paddy Mulligan. I didn't really know Paddy at all, but he was good fun and an extremely matey guy. What we were going to do, I hadn't a clue, but somehow Osgood had been given some info about a nightclub in downtown Salonika.

A bit about Paddy first: born in Dublin, he was signed by Sexton for £17,500 from Shamrock Rovers in 1969. He made 58 appearances for the Blues before moving on to Crystal Palace in 1972. He was a regular in the Ireland national team, winning 50 caps; in his day he was a buccaneering type of right back, but he could also be inconsistent. He was comparatively short, with long, luxuriant dark wavy hair that had the look of a perm about it.

After hanging up his boots, he was on the short-list for the Ireland manager's job in 1980. The list was eventually whittled down to two candidates: Limerick City boss, Eoin Hand, and Mulligan. Hand won by a solitary vote, and later one Irish FA committee member explained why he had voted against Paddy. It seems this official thought he was the player who once tossed a bun at him on an away trip!

So off we went, this trio of disparate human beings in a taxi, to this nightspot. I must admit I was very sceptical about the whole thing. In a country in which long hair and moustaches and Dylan were banned, I didn't honestly think that the nightlife would be anything to write home about. How Ossie knew exactly where to go remained an unfathomable mystery to me; maybe he just asked the driver or someone in the hotel for a nearby bar with bit of oomph – who knows!

Arriving at this neon-lit, seedy establishment, I was struck by how empty the streets were. No one was abroad it seemed. Mind you, the junta's ban on late night assemblies by the populace undoubtedly had more than a tad to do with it.

The bar itself was virtually customer-less – I later described it as 'gruesome'. There was a shabby counter with a small, dark woman, looking unerringly like the Italian actress Anna Magnani, obviously in charge. She greeted us with a smile that would have gone down well with the director of the latest Hammer production. Opposite the counter, which was in desperate need of some good spit and polish, was a small, poorly-lit stage, on which pranced a squat young woman, fondling her ample though pendulous breasts. Her movements were gauche: the same ridiculously simple steps over and over again. In the far corner there was a little fat man, lit up by too much ouzo, showing his appreciation by making lascivious noises. I must admit it was about as erotic as painting a wall with white emulsion.

I ordered a brandy – Metaxa – and Ossie stuck to lager. As for Paddy, he tried to order a particular beer – I think it was Guinness – and in attempting to describe his poison to the Anna Magnani clone, he managed to utterly confuse her. We three thought this was the funniest thing ever, but we were by this time in that limbo world between being tipsy and just plain drunk.

Ossie was always good company, whatever it was; wherever it was; and even if it was all just bloody awful, he somehow managed to see the positive side and enjoy himself.

By the time we had advanced to our third libation, another lady was on stage. She was slightly better than the previous one, but thinking about my meeting with the King of Soho, Paul Raymond, I don't think he would have gone on his hands and knees to put her under contract.

Despite the time – it was now well past one in the morning – we were still game for more, so having hailed a taxi, which was some kind of miracle in itself, we arrived back at the hotel, with one aim in mind – the next drink.

Once in the hotel I dashed to my room and threw some cold water over my face. Relaxing once more in the hotel bar, attempting unsuccessfully to look languid, I encountered Charlie Cooke, who had obviously 'had a few'. Ossie had gone off somewhere, so I sat down with Charlie, and we both ordered our favourite tipple – large brandies. At about 3.30 a.m., I started to feel ravenously hungry, as did Cooke, so we managed to find a waiter, and gave him our order: eggs and bacon!

How he managed to understand our English, uttered as it was with the thickness of Devonshire clotted cream, but he did, and within what seemed only a matter of a few minutes, our early bird breakfast arrived. I tell you what, it tasted absolutely superb – you couldn't have found better at The Ritz!

And so to bed, and not to 'perchance to dream', well not for long anyway, because the following day we had to catch the plane back to Blighty, but not before a couple more chance encounters with some of the locals.

Little shuteye, tongue like sandpaper; but who cared, we were young and invincible – in fact we were immortal. Plenty of coffee, a pill or two to get the body and brain at full throttle again, then off into town with Ossie. We found a café, and with the sun still beating down relentlessly, we ordered a couple of refreshers. The café itself was pleasant, but there was one major drawback: it was literally opposite a sort of open-air butcher's shop, which had a whole collection of un-plucked chickens hanging from hooks in long lines and completely open to the elements.

The proprietor, a tall, wide-hipped middle-aged man, wearing spectacles, came over to us and within a few minutes started chatting in competent, though somewhat eccentric English. He immediately made it clear he was a football man, and he recognised Osgood straightaway – his mugshots were all over the sports pages of the Greek dailies. He then went on to say that the people of Greece were extremely fond of the British. His compliments were mainly in reference to the Second World War, but believe it or not he managed to bring Lord Byron – who many Greeks regard as the saviour of their country – into the conversation. I didn't have the heart to mention Byron's liberal credentials.

I think he was trying as hard as he knew to convince us that everything in Greece was hunky-dory, and that the Government was doing its best for the people. The fact that I obviously didn't believe him, and that all right-minded people would never believe him, and that apart from about fifty Fascist politicians in Italy, nobody in the West would ever accept what he was imparting to us as gospel, made me smile, and I tried to change the subject.

As a boiling hot wind began to swirl and the humidity increased to around 100 per cent, so did the smell of the dead birds. The aroma was positively pungent and, as my stomach was still on the fragile side, I glanced at my watch and said to Ossie that it was about time we got back to the hotel. He laughed, and at the same time he rose, and we left. So my date with Fascism was all but at an end.

The flight back was a real anticlimax, for by this time all I wanted to do was to go to bed. My conversation had dwindled to the odd pleasantry and my smile could only be described as an apology. I also knew that Basil Jawett, accountant for Peter Osgood Limited, had a major project he wished to discuss with us at his office in Fleet Street, and that it all revolved around fish. However, a combination of Hammersmith Council and the Arab-Israeli Conflict combined to scupper our plans.

A few days after our Greek odyssey, I was wandering down Fleet Street in the company of Peter Osgood. We had just enjoyed a good lunch, steaks as usual, salad and chips. As we entered No. 54 Fleet Street, Peter asked me about his taxes. 'Don't worry,' I said. 'Basil Jawett will sort it all out: he's a dab hand at these sort of things.'

Fleet Street forty-three years ago was a wondrous place. The newspaper offices of the *Daily Telegraph*, the *Daily Express* and the other nationals dominated a street that in so many ways was like a tatty Toff – elegant, yet at the same time needing a clean and a press and a spruce-up. El Vino's, that bastion of pre-war sexism, where even during the early 1970s a lady could not order a drink at the bar, was always, even by noon, packed with a mixture of journalists, barristers and solicitors, imbibing glasses of vintage reds and whites. The Wig and Pen was another watering-hole for journalists and lawyers – its beamed façade conjuring up images of Charles Dickens, sitting with glass in hand, holding court as he regales his companions with outlines of new stories. Opposite were the Royal Courts of Justice, built in 1882; then, further down, going towards Ludgate Circus, a small alleyway called Gough Square and the famous 'Cheshire Cheese' eating house, once the home of Doctor Johnson, who used to feed his cat Hodge oysters. Indeed a romantic place.

Behind No. 54 Fleet Street, it is but a short walk to the Inns of Court, unchanged since Georgian times. It was a London that had somehow miraculously survived the Blitz, not quite intact, but it still retained every aspect of the old London that, thanks or should I say no thanks to the madcap architects of recent years, is slowly disappearing.

We walked up the stairs into the offices of Berman, Abrahams and Jawett, Chartered Accountants. We went into the reception area, and there were Basil's trio of typists banging away on their keys. 'We're here to see Mr Jawett,' I informed one of the secretaries. 'If you'll wait here, I'll tell him,' she said, smiling insincerely.

After a matter of seconds, Basil called us in. He smiled in his standard ingratiating way, for he loved meeting Ossie; it was all about reflected glory, I guess. I think he was a Spurs supporter, and he loved his golf, going off each and every spring to Augusta, Georgia for the Masters. But Peter Osgood was the 'in thing' at the time, and Jawett was the sort of person that thrived on name-dropping – it made a good topic at the Golf Club and all those Rotary Dinners that such a man would be obliged to attend.

Jawett was always dressed in the manner of the typical City gent. He had style, and the cut of his cloth reeked of quality, but he was never flashy. He wore stylish glasses, which gave him the look of an American corporation vice president. His facial expression was always on the grim side, and my mother, who never liked him, once told me that he had the 'look of a shark about him'.

Without further ado, Basil came to the point – an unusual occurrence for accountants and solicitors. 'How do you both feel about a fish and chip restaurant not far from Stamford Bridge utilising Peter's name?' he announced.

'Sounds great,' was my very obvious response. And even Ossie, who I don't think ever quite trusted the accountant completely, also displayed in obvious terms his unbridled enthusiasm for the idea.

'Yes,' continued Jawett, 'we could give it a name like "Ossie's Plaice". I think I have just the man to back the idea, so the next thing is for me to arrange a meeting.'

He then went on to explain in more detail his overall business plan, and after a few more questions to Ossie about football matters, we rose and left, but not before Ossie had signed a few autographs for some of Basil's female employees.

The idea was a sound one, and after what seemed like interminable meeting after interminable meeting, a property in the Hammersmith area was found. The backer, an Arab, was a pleasant individual, but unfortunately his relationship with Jawett was an edgy one. This was all down to the various conflicts and wars that had taken place, were taking place and were going to take place between Arabs and Israelis. You see, Basil was a Jew first, and an Englishman second. If he felt Israel was under threat, his patriotism would always be geared to that country, and not the country of his birth.

It has to be remembered that the famous – or should I say infamous – Six-Day War was still fresh in the memory. The war, which involved Israel and much of the Arab World, but primarily Egypt (known at the time as the United Arab Republic), Jordan and Syria, proved to be a military success for Israel. As a result, they captured the Gaza Strip and the West Bank (including East Jerusalem) from Jordan and the Golan Heights from Syria.

Despite being so short in duration, it was extremely bloody, and for the Arab countries as a whole it proved a disaster. The war made a star of Israel General Moshe Dayan, he of the black eyepatch, but it was, in essence, a human tragedy. As such, relations between Jews and Arabs were at an all-time low.

Basil Jawett was forever telling us that this 'Jew/Arab situation didn't matter', but it obviously did; why did he keep telling us day-after-day?

There were more meetings with the council, who out of the blue decided that our fish and chip emporium would be 'too noisy' for the particular part of Hammersmith we had selected. No one, neither Basil nor the backer, fought our corner with any conviction, so the whole deal was given the big heave-ho. What a waste of time!

Chelsea's league form during the early months of the 1970–'71 season was patchy to say the least. They remained unbeaten for six games, but this included three draws, and it was their old adversaries, Leeds United, who ended this far from convincing run on 6 September with a 1–0 victory at Elland Road, witnessed by over 47,000 fans.

From a personal point of view, it was Ossie's goal tally – or more accurately the lack of it – that was causing me concern. Thankfully, on 26 September, his drought was ended with a goal in the 2–1 home success over Ipswich Town.

The second leg with Aris Salonika came four days after the Ipswich win, and Chelsea made light of the opposition on this occasion, John Hollins and Ian Hutchinson netting a couple each in a 5–1 score line as the Greeks completely caved in. As Hudson quipped to me many years later: 'Aris were like Greek yoghurt – runny everywhere!'

Next up was a trip behind the Iron Curtain, and CSKA Sofia on 21 October. A 2–1 win at Derby County on the Saturday before the Bulgaria trip was just the confidence booster that Sexton's men needed.

Tommy Baldwin put away the only goal of the game in Bulgaria, 2 minutes before the break, so the second leg looked a formality.

It was then that, during a conversation with Terry O'Neill, the idea of a footballer actually being featured in an upmarket magazine came to me. At the time to most people, such a thought would have made them laugh hysterically; 'football was not classy enough', they would say. But I knew they were wrong, as indeed did Terry, who, like me, fully realised that football, George Best-style anyway, was throwing off its 1950s dress and shackles and replacing it with a swanky new suit from a top-of-the-range tailor. And whereas at Manchester United it was all about Best, at Chelsea it was about the team as a whole. 'It's just like another branch of the rock business,' I said to Terry, and, believe it or not, he didn't laugh – not a titter.

The plan revolved around Charlie Cooke, and to get him to pen a feature on what it was like in the Stamford Bridge dressing room before a big match: what was required were real insights, and not just 'the usual ghosted rubbish', as Cooke so aptly described most of the footballers' literary output in those days.

It was Terry who suggested *Vogue* as the outlet for Cooke's undoubted writing talents. My brief was to help him write the thing, but before any thoughts of pen being put to paper, I had to make contact, via Terry, with a senior member of the *Vogue* magazine editorial team.

Terry's prowess, plus his international reputation as one of the leading photographers on the planet, was going to be used as an extra carrot to entice the people at the magazine into agreeing to this idea.

Terry's enthusiasm knew no bounds, and he offered to take some shots of Charlie in action, so I arranged for a photographers' pass for him for the European Cup Winners' Cup second round second leg tie at Stamford Bridge on 4 November. This would, I thought, be the clincher.

Another added bonus for us was that *Vogue* had begun a 'Men In Vogue' section, and Charlie's efforts would, therefore, be a perfect fit. The next edition of this supplement for men was due out during the middle of March, and following a few subsequent meetings at the Conde Nast headquarters in Hanover Square, this off-the-wall idea was finally given the green light. Charlie Cooke, Chelsea FC professional footballer in *Vogue*; 'had the world gone stark staring mad?' would surely be a question emanating from the mouths of many.

When I lived in Maida Vale, DJ Alan 'Fluff' Freeman lived in the penthouse flat above me, and I remember telling him about the *Vogue* article (we were in a taxi at the time). He actually said to me that I had broken new ground – 'football will never be looked at in the same way again', he said. Needless to say I was flattered.

Terry O'Neill's Charlie Cooke pictures were just extraordinary. They not only captured the grace and movement of this special player, but somehow he had managed to bring into focus Charlie's facial expressions when on the ball – the contractions, the grimaces: the lot.

The match itself was a cagey affair, with Chelsea doing just enough – Dave Webb scoring the only goal five minutes before half-time.

Having broken the ice with the *Vogue* ensemble, and armed with Terry O'Neill's pictorial treasures, now was the time for me to sit down in the secretary's office at Stamford Bridge with Charlie and attempt to write something that was not just the standard football stuff, so enjoyed by the readers of *Shoot* and *Striker* and the other soccer comics of the day, but a new take on a footballer's pre-match mental state and all the rituals that he goes through prior to any big contest.

There we were sitting cosily in this shabby office, throwing ideas at one another in the manner of Hollywood scriptwriters. Looking round at the décor of this Stamford Bridge inner sanctum, I thought what a contrast it made to the plush, sleek home of *Vogue*, and its perfectly-dressed, well-bred upper echelon ladies of high fashion.

I don't know why, but I always felt somewhat intimidated by Charlie's undoubted intellect; it was said that he had the IQ of a genius – good enough for MENSA and all that. How true this was I never did find out, but what was true was that he had a way with words, albeit often very American in construction and usage. For example, he often came out with that de rigueur 'yoof' word of 2013, 'awesome'. No one else I knew then – apart from some American cousins – used this American/English word with such impunity as Charlie. As I have already stated, he was Hemingway-obsessed in those days, but having said that, his turn of phrase was better than any football journalist of the period – at times his phrases were possessed of an almost poetic quality.

Well, we differed a bit about how the article was to be formulated. I wanted something relatively simple, but Charlie thought we should go out of the norm somewhat and try to add drama to each and every line.

A few coffees were downed, and we got to work – it was a very basic pen and ink job. Once we had decided upon the direction we were going to take, the first paragraph just happened, and Cooke's pen wrote these words: 'It's different below in the dressing room before a match. There's no cool beer or King's Road dollies, none of the euphoria of up-top.'

It all flowed after that; some words here from Charlie, then more words from me. 'How are we going to end it?' I thought. 'What's going to be the denouement?'

I said to Charlie that we should utilise the first few lines, and after a few false dawns with lines that frankly were pretentious to the point of being stuff ready-made for *Private Eye*'s 'Pseuds Corner', we eventually decided upon: 'And you? Right now you wouldn't mind being up there, with the cool beer and the King's Road dollies, immersed in the collective euphoria. Yet you know that when the concrete yields to turf, when your studs cease their chatter, and you start to swing the ball about in those long looping practice passes, it will start to be all right again and the game will take over.'

It all sounds simple when told in retrospect, but the amount of crossings-out on our sheets of paper, as we attempted to get Charlie's ideas across to a readership totally unused to the doings of a footballer as he prepares for a game, were testament to how difficult the task was. 'We're writing for *Vogue*, for God's sake,' I said, half under my breath. 'This puts the whole bloody thing on another level. Some of their readers won't know a cross from a corner-kick!'

Mission accomplished, all I had to do was to type the thing out on my new Olivetti, show it to Terry O'Neill, and hope for the best. I thought it was good, and thankfully so did the ladies with the cut-glass accents at *Vogue*.

The Blues' league form continued to be no more than satisfactory, and at no stage did they display the kind of devil-may-care football that had marked their FA Cup-winning campaign. Following the European tie in Bulgaria, there was a 4–3 success by the seaside at Blackpool; a 2–2 home draw with Southampton, and 1–0 victory at Huddersfield Town three days after the CSKA second leg. A 1–0 reverse, in front of over 61,000 at Spurs seven days later was a setback, but faith was restored on the 21 November with a 2–1 victory against Stoke, Ossie at last finding the net again. And so it went on: more victories than defeats, but the successes more often than not by the odd goal.

In the domestic cup competitions, Manchester United put paid to their hopes at the end of October in the fourth round of the League Cup, and they also exited the FA Cup in round four, the other half of Manchester banging in three goals without reply. So, it was Europe or bust for the Blues.

As for Os, it was proving to be a season that never really saw him replicate the deeds of twelve months before. Apart from a dearth of goals, his cause wasn't helped by a draconian ban he received of eight weeks, plus a fine of £160, on 20 January 1971. He had been booked six times in a year, and had already been handed a suspended sentence, so when he had his name taken at Goodison Park against Everton on 16 January in a 3–0 defeat, he knew that he was for the high jump (his misery was further compounded by a penalty miss).

At the time the Football Association, ruled by 'a generation of ghosts', and apparently dismayed by the dramatic increase in bad behaviour on the pitch, set about waving the big stick. In their minds there were several players – shall we call them the characters and entertainers – who never seemed to toe the line, and as far as officialdom was concerned were just a big pain in the fundament, to quote Horace Rumpole.

George Best was certainly one, and Os was another 'naughty boy'. Apart from his ban – which, by the way, was given top-three billing during that evening's BBC TV News – their dossier on Osgood was forwarded to the England Selection Committee for them to study. This undoubtedly seemed to put the kibosh on his chances of winning more England caps.

As you can imagine, my Trim phone chirped incessantly, following Peter's ban: 'What is he going to do during his lay-off? How will he keep fit?' Never-ending questions, which frankly I found difficult on occasions to give the right – or should I say – diplomatic answer. It was definitely a touch of 'them and us' in those final years of Swinging London. The Bests, The Marshes, The Osgoods – these were young men at odds with the shiny blazer brigade at FA headquarters. They were part of a new breed, and the FA establishment just didn't get it; a bit like Dave Sexton, really.

So what I said to these newspaper guys was often con-troversial. I knew Os wouldn't mind a jot because it was all part of our plan. After all, if he hadn't ruffled a few feathers, would Ray Connolly have been interested? Os was no Bowie or Hendrix or Jagger, but to Connolly he was as much a part of the whole scene as any rebellious rocker.

But Ossie was always the supreme sporting actor and entertainer. When I say actor, I don't mean that he ever indulged in what is referred to these days incongruously as 'simulation', I mean that he knew how and when to take centre stage. And what better stage than the quarter-finals of the European Cup Winners' Cup.

Chelsea had been drawn to face the obdurate Belgians of Bruges, with the first leg to take place on 10 March 1971 away in that delightful city – 'the Venice of the North'.

The Bruges players were no mugs and proved it, prevailing 2–0, thanks to goals from Raoul Lambert and Gilbert Marmenaut. It didn't look good for the Boys in Blue for the second leg in a fortnight, but cometh the hour cometh the man, and in this case it was the irrepressible Osgood.

Stamford Bridge, Wednesday 24 March, and Os was back in town, with 45,558 spectators cheering the Chelsea players on to the pitch. This was going to be a tall order, and the team's talisman, Peter Osgood, was not match fit. It represented Sexton's last grab at a trophy, so was it going to be one of those special nights?

From the off, Chelsea attacked. The fans were raucous; it was a frenzied atmosphere cracking like thunder with emotion: tempers became frayed as the Bruges back line adopted both fair and foul methods to thwart the Blue hordes.

Then, there he is, the understated and underrated 'Nobby' Houseman advancing on goal – it's a goal! – 1–2. The curtain rises and on to the stage comes the star of the show to grab all the headlines – Peter Osgood – it's in the net! – 2–2. Extra-time, and there he is again, Osgood, making it 3–2 to the Londoners. Baldwin added number four, as the Belgian bubble burst, and the Bridge erupted as referee Kostovski from Yugoslavia blew the final whistle – Chelsea had made it through to the semi-finals on a night to remember.

Alan Hudson has fond memories of this titanic tussle: 'Osgood was eight weeks short of his best because of long-term injury, and I was still looking for my best form. We took an early lead, and they (Bruges) seemed to become more leg weary. Cooke was showing his intricate skills, and with Os struggling with his fitness and me with my ankle, we needed to dig deeper than ever before.

'In extra-time Cooke was magnificent, and Sponge (Tommy Baldwin) was living up to his nickname as he soaked up so much work, and thoroughly deserved his goal. Overall, it was quite a performance, although a lot of people tend to forget the one man who kept our faint hopes alive, John Phillips (again deputising in goal for Bonetti). He had been in such incredible form in the first leg in Belgium, and but for him the second game would have proved to be the kind of mountain that had never been found, let alone climbed!'

Believe it or not after such drama and nail-biting tension – and having grabbed a quick drink with Ossie and co. – I left the ground and made for the Paris Pullman cinema in Chelsea to see one of the most acclaimed post-war French films, *Le Grande Meaulnes*, based on the cult novel of the same name, written by Alain-Fournier in 1913. Talk about from the sublime to the ridiculous!

Away from Ossie's European exploits, I found myself busy with another player, one of a totally different hue to the King of Stamford Bridge; midfield dynamo John Hollins, whose contribution to the success of that team was in many respects as telling as the more gung-ho guys. Clean-cut, articulate and polite, here was a King's Road hero without flower power, but possessed of a football brain and work ethic that were second-to-none.

Hollins signed for Chelsea as a teenager and made his first-team debut in September 1963 in a League Cup-tie at Swindon. I actually witnessed his debut, but it was an evening to forget in Wiltshire for any Chelsea fan, as Docherty's youngsters went down 3–0.

He left Stamford Bridge in 1975 for QPR, signed by previous boss Sexton for £80,000. Four successful years at Loftus Road, and he was on his way, this time to Arsenal, where he remained for four years.

He returned to Chelsea in 1983 for a twelve-month period, but by then he was thirty-seven-years-old, and despite his most potent days being behind him, he still proved invaluable to the team cause as the club gained promotion back to the top flight. He was immediately appointed team coach, and following John Neal's departure, he became manager, but in 1988, following a series of poor performances, he was sacked.

He won just the solitary England cap against Spain in May 1967, and there is no doubt that in another era, he would have donned the England shirt on many more occasions.

I enjoyed the task of pushing the name of John Hollins. I was by this time writing regular interviews and such-like for several football magazines, and interviews and first-person features for John were starting to appear on a fairly regular basis. But I wasn't satisfied – I wanted something different.

Cooke's *Vogue* opus was above-and-beyond, but there was still the matter of cracking the chat-show radio circuit.

Probably the most popular show on radio in the early 1970s was *Open House*, presented by Pete Murray. At its height it attracted over 5.5 million listeners on BBC Radio 2. It was a two-hour magazine-style show broadcast five days a week, and it ran for some ten years. During this period, Murray was voted Radio Personality of the Year on two occasions.

Now, Murray was an authentic celebrity; he was also a football fan – an ardent follower of Arsenal. When I use the word celebrity, I mean it in its truest sense. An actor by profession – he studied at RADA – he joined Radio Luxembourg in 1950 as one of its resident presenters. It was television in the shape of *Six-Five-Special* that elevated him to the national consciousness.

To people of a certain age, the *Six-Five-Special*, which went out live at five past six on Saturday evening, was their first introduction to rock 'n' roll on TV. Jack Good, later to go on to greater things with ITV's weekly rock show, *Oh Boy!*, and even having hit records of his own with Lord Rockingham's XI and their novelty rock number, 'Hoots Mon', was the producer. Josephine Douglas and Murray co-hosted the show, with Murray's catchphrase 'Time to Jive on the Old Six Five', soon becoming one of the 'in-phrases' of the 1950s.

After *Six-Five*, Murray's career blossomed. He was one of the regular panellists on the hit TV show *Juke Box Jury*, and when *Top of The Pops* was launched on New Year's Day 1964, Murray was selected as one of regular frontmen. Three years later he was one of the original DJs on BBC radio's new youth-orientated station, Radio 1. He moved to Radio 2 in 1969, and by 1970 his stock was sky-high.

In many ways life as a PR person back then was a doddle. Okay, so there were limited outlets for publicity and promotion, certainly in respect of footballers, but making that initial contact was so much simpler. For one thing, people were far less suspicious. So, speaking on the blower to Murray was no problem, and suggesting that a Chelsea player be a guest was met with a warm affirmative.

Broadcasting House, Langham Place: so much history, so much that was part of the fabric of British culture. Arriving there with John and his attractive, bubbly wife Linda, I was immediately impressed by Murray's easy-going manner, and the almost boyish pleasure that he was obviously getting from meeting and chatting to a top footballer, even one from such bitter rivals of Arsenal as Chelsea.

John had sideburns to die for, but unlike several of his colleagues, he was never remotely associated with a rock 'n' roll lifestyle. But as a radio guest, he made the ideal interviewee, and this one show with Pete Murray did so much to dispel the standard image of professional players – inarticulate and thick.

I'll always remember many years later, listening to a Somerset County Cricket Club committee lady, who mocked footballers with these words: 'Thick as two short planks compared to cricketers.' Blanchflower, Cooke, Pat Nevin, to name but three – more cranium activity there, I would have thought, than the likes of the celebrity cricketers of today. This lady was living in the past – in the era of Mike Brearley and David Gower, when cricketers could converse on TV with the late John Arlott on subjects ranging from Apartheid to the latest wine vintage. Those days are long gone – gone forever.

As we bade Pete Murray adieu, he smiled broadly and said something like: 'We must do this again sometime.' Well, we didn't, but we should have.

Thirteen

FILM STARS –
FLIM-FLAM AND ROCK 'N' ROLL

The second clash with Bruges was seminal. A season that seemed at one stage to be run-of-the-mill suddenly took on a totally different complexion. A first European trophy for Chelsea was now fast emerging as more than just a pipedream. Holders of the Cup Winners' Cup, Manchester City, who earlier in the campaign had dumped the Blues out of the Cup, made it a home-grown semi-final – revenge, as they say, is best served cold!

Raquel Welch was sexy, and she liked Peter Osgood. Fact. Terry O'Neill knew Raquel well – he took photograph after photograph of her; often scantily clad, but always tasteful; never tacky. Our family business, Star Posters, had bought one such photo from Terry, and it was turned into a best-sell-ing colour poster. It was a striking embodiment of feminine beauty with her hair, all luxuriant curls, discreetly covering her ample breasts. I showed the poster to Ossie and he liked it. Well, why wouldn't he?

Next stop, the office of Terry O'Neill's agent, Rex Features in New Fetter Lane, off Fleet Street. How the conversation devel-oped I cannot actually remember, but what I do remember is that Terry told me that Raquel was giving a major interview to a guy from *The Times*, and that, thanks to his 'prodding', she was going to say a few very complimentary things about Os. Wow! This was better than I expected – sensational stuff.

Raquel Welch's interview in *The Times* raised more than a few eyebrows, not because she said anything particularly outlandish or profound or even dramatically revealing, but her comments, and in particular her compliments about Peter Osgood, were unique in the sense that never before had such an international movie star – and an American one at that – raved about an English football (or should I say soccer?) star; for me it was the proverbial manna from heaven.

Once more my phone was overdosing on a handful of black bombers. 'Did Peter Osgood know Raquel Welch?' or 'Do you think they'll see each other at a game at Stamford Bridge?' and so on and so on and so forth – the journalists' questions were often banal and inane, but it was up to me to make the most of the situation. After all, hadn't I said to Terry O'Neill that publicising life at Chelsea was much like the rock business? Or was it Hollywood in London SW6?

The phone trills again – this time it's Terry at the end of the wire, 'Hi, Greg,' he says, 'just an idea, but why don't you phone Dave Sexton and ask him to give his permission for Raquel to come to the ground to see a match: or maybe even training.'

I thought it was a great idea, but Terry didn't know what sort of man Sexton was, but I did. So, it was with a negative feeling that I phoned the Chelsea manager. The conversation was short, not so sweet and went something like this: 'Good afternoon, Mr Sexton [I always addressed him as Mr]. This is Peter Osgood's agent here, Gregory Tesser [the full version of my name was often used then]. You probably saw the interview that film star Raquel Welch gave to *The Times*, and the complimentary things she said about Ossie.'

Initially, utter silence reigned at the other end of the line, and I held my breath.

'I think so,' was the reply, cold as ice.

'Well, I was just wondering: would it be all right if Raquel Welch came to the ground, or even saw Ossie in training?'

Dave Sexton's manner evolved from being cold to being positively Antarctic, and his answer was both brusque and terse. He knew how young I was, and that I would never argue with him or try to influence him in an aggressive manner. As I have stated, Dave didn't dig baby boomers, and he certainly struck me as being strait-laced.

'No, I can't allow that – goodbye.'

That was that. Looking back, I probably should have pressed it a bit, but Sexton intimidated me, and I always felt – rightly or wrongly – that he 'blamed' me for some of what he termed as excesses by Os and Cooke and co.

However, on the positive side, despite Dave Sexton's rejection of utilising Raquel Welch's publicity value for the club, the story just ran and ran.

The fact is that without Terry O'Neill's 'in' with Welch and her immediate entourage, none of this Raquel/Peter Osgood 'love affair' would have taken off as it did. First and foremost Terry was a Blues fan, and he and I got on very well, so it came natural to him to try to raise the international profile of not only Os, but also the club as a whole. There is a touch of irony in all this, in the sense that since Roman Abramovich bought Chelsea Football Club, the big noises at the Bridge have had an ongoing love affair with America. Such a link today between a star player, in particular an indigenous one, with a US screen icon would have the Chelsea publicity people with their tongues out, salivating.

I never quite understood Dave Sexton's problem with the show business side of Stamford Bridge. At most home games, the main stand was packed to the gills with glitterati. One such doting fan was hairdresser extraordinaire Vidal Sassoon. I met Vidal on several occasions in the bar at the Bridge, and found him charming. He went on to cut Ossie's hair a few times, and even attempted to make sense of my unruly locks. I always remember him telling me how marvellous the whole King's Road scene was and that 'at Stamford Bridge, you had Peter Osgood – now there's a man with style'.

Of course, what I should have done was to have just gone ahead and done it, without the manager's rubber stamp. Of course as it turned out, that professor of self-publicity, Jimmy Hill, garnered all the column inches by accompanying Raquel to the Chelsea *v.* Leicester City encounter in February 1972 – the early groundwork laid down by Terry O'Neill and myself having been conveniently forgotten.

But even though Hill hit on the Raquel Welch stunt for his own reflected glory, the photographs taken of the lady herself, looking radiant in full Chelsea regalia – Os' No. 9 shirt, the lot – were all the work of Terry O'Neill. And soon these photos were wending their way around the globe.

Cup Winners' Cup semi-final day first leg: 14 April. Stamford Bridge was electric once more. Just 48 hours before, the Blues had sneaked a 1–0 home win over Liverpool, grateful for an own goal from full-back Alec Lindsay, he of the receding blond hair and Pickwickian mutton-chop sideburns. However, any thoughts of a tilt at the title had long gone; both Arsenal and Leeds were dogging each other's footsteps at the summit, but Chelsea had shown what might have been with a scintillating 3–1 home win over Leeds on 27 March. Over 58,000 packed into the Bridge saw Houseman grab two and Osgood the other as the old foes from Yorkshire were summarily dismissed.

But on the whole this was not the free-flowing Chelsea of the previous campaign. The old problem of superb one week and poor the next was very much the order of the day, yet when it came to a fixture that really mattered or a one-off contest, Os and his pals were capable of testing the best there was.

The first game with Manchester City was no classic, and Chelsea's ranks were depleted by the loss of both Bonetti and Osgood through injury, but Derek Smethurst's strike one minute after the break was enough to give them the slenderest of advantages to take to Maine Road a fortnight later.

Derek Smethurst: It is not a name that trips off the tongue when the conversation comes round to extolling the virtues of the King's Road kings. Yet, his short and undistinguished career at the Bridge did have this one magic moment. A South African – he was born in Durban in 1947 – he signed for Chelsea in 1968 from Durban City, and made eighteen appearances for the club before being transferred, at his own request, to Millwall for £35,000 later that year. His contribution to Chelsea's European glory gave him the unique distinction of being the first overseas-born player to win a European winner's medal in England, as well being the first player from abroad to score for the club in Europe.

Yet despite his limitations, he proved an acceptable substitute for Osgood, and he was called upon for more action in the second game. Once more it was cagey and edgy and nervy, with City keeper Ron Healey, a stand-in for the regular custodian Joe Corrigan, handing the Blues a 1–0 victory with an own goal. The Cup-holders were out, and it was to be another final for the Stamford Bridge faithful to enjoy. On this occasion it was to be opposition just a shade more glamorous than the lads from Leeds; it was to be Real Madrid, a name synonymous with all that was enticing and extravagant about European football; premier purveyors of the beautiful game.

Alexanders; Alvaro's; Barbarella; Meridiana; Mirabelle; Quaglino's: I could go on. These are just a few names of eating houses frequented by the great and the good, and indeed Chelsea footballers, during that unique era of change. On a personal level, I must have spent literally hour upon hour at these places day-in-and-day-out. How I ever got any work done remains one of those unsolved mysteries, but somehow I did. And I know for a fact that Os enjoyed one particular lunch at the world-famous Mirabelle in Mayfair.

Roy Stewardson was the chairman of Cheshunt Football Club. A large man – he was built a bit like Stan Flashman – he was, according to sources, a multi-millionaire. He possessed an impressive mop of black hair that would shine when the sun was out, nourished no doubt by dollops of Brilliantine. He had an expansive smile, and like most people, the thought of meeting a footballer of such national celebrity as Peter Osgood thrilled him in the manner of a kid getting his first autograph.

His aim was to make something of his club, an amateur outfit playing in those days in the Athenian League. Roy had big plans for the club, and he wanted Ossie involved in some way to try to further his grandiose ideas. At the time Cheshunt sold literally hundreds of copies of *The Amateur Footballer*; he even booked a series of adverts in the mag for some of Cheshunt's off-field enterprises – its restaurant and conference facilities etc. I used to visit the club on numerous occasions, and often Os would accompany me to games. Roy seemed to like me, and he loved the company of Ossie. After one such evening game, Roy's manner became even more over-the-top in its conviviality as he pitched a few ideas at us.

'I'd very much like Peter to be involved with some of our plans,' he announced; his voice booming like some massive drum. 'Why don't we all three meet up for lunch somewhere very soon.'

'Fine by me,' I said. 'Maybe in the West End somewhere?'

'Oh, I thought I'd take you both to lunch at the Mirabelle in Curzon Street,' he responded with a grin. 'The best in the world, they say.'

He was not wrong. Opened in 1936, by the 1950s and '60s it had become probably the most fashionable eating-house in Mayfair. Sir Winston Churchill was a regular. Royalty loved it too, with Princess Margaret being an oft-seen diner. Now, the restaurant would have the pleasure of greeting the King of Stamford Bridge in tandem with his long-haired, moustachioed agent!

In 1998, Marco Pierre White bought the restaurant, but sold it nine years later. It was closed in 2008 for refurbishment, and has remained closed ever since.

It was a sumptuous meal, beginning with shrimps on solid silver hooks attached to a burnished silver Georgian display that was shaped like a miniature Marble Arch. The sauce, served in miniature Regency-style tureens was both delicate and fragrant. We had vintage wines, some as old as 1945 – a famous year. During the meal, the ebullient Stewardson kept saying how much he would like Osgood to be part of his business operations. It all looked as rosy as the elegant flowers on our table; the money would be sloshing all over the place, or so we both thought.

The place was by no means packed, and we were waited on in the manner of *Upstairs Downstairs*. Orson Welles was holding court a few tables from us, his immense frame seeming to mask the whole table.

Richard Burton was there as well. He looked morose, but only for an instant. His large round face, cratered like the moon, then broke into a broad smile, which must have been difficult as he had a cigarette glued to his top lip. I said to Os and Roy that he was 'probably staying at his regular place, The Dorchester, just round the corner'. This small slice of showbiz knowledge seemed to impress them, which was nice. I tried not to stare; after all, staring is rude, I was told as a kid, but in a place like the Mirabelle in the 1970s, staring was almost unavoidable.

Having lunched well, and with the mellowness and 'Goodwill to all men' feeling growing by the minute in our alcohol-addled brains, Stewardson shook hands and said, 'don't worry, I'll be in touch'.

He kept to his word, and thanks to his initial enthusiasm, we were able to take advantage of his wealth – how rich he actually was I never discerned – but like so many aspects of life, the whole thing fizzled to nothing.

After the Stewardson nosh-up, the Mirabelle became a favourite haunt of mine. I escorted all manner of people through its elegant portals, only putting a stop to it when the dollars ran short. But looking back, this very first meal there in Osgood's company was certainly the most memorable.

Another lunch of note with Ossie was in the company of Terry O'Neill and Adam Faith. Terry was really pally with Faith; in fact they had known each other for years. The first time I was meant to meet the 'What Do You Want' star (the disc topped the charts in 1959), it was with Rodney Marsh, but he failed to appear. On this occasion, however, he was on time, and the lunch was yet another liquid affair, with everyone round the table heaping praise on Osgood's exploits on the pitch.

It is a funny thing, how life can go round and round in seemingly never-ending circles. Take Adam Faith. Here I was drinking Chablis or whatever at a five-star watering hole; having as a thirteen-year-old watched him on TV in the pop show *Drumbeat*, having even bought a record or two of his. He didn't know me, and I didn't know him. But later in the 1970s he was to be one of the stars in the hit movie *Stardust*, written by Ray Connolly, the same Ray Connolly who had interviewed Os for the *Evening Standard* on the eve of the 1970 Cup Final. I will always remember Os glancing up at him, and Faith smiling and saying that 'you really bring entertainment to the football pitch'.

Later, in 1987, Faith was part of a consortium, led by Terry Venables that failed in a bid to buy Queen's Park Rangers from owner Jim Gregory.

Adam Faith: lovely name, and in many respects, rock music's very first thinker. I remember seeing him on TV in the very early 1960s discussing sex before marriage with the Archbishop of Canterbury. At one stage his was the voice of disaffected youth. Yet having achieved fame and fortune, he somehow managed to lose it all, and he was declared bankrupt. He died in 2003, aged just sixty-two.

It has been said that Chelsea's three supreme entertainers, Cooke, Hudson and Osgood, courted publicity everywhere they went. And whilst it is certainly true to say that in those times they were undoubtedly flattered by all the attention and praise heaped on them by – for all intents and purposes – bigger celebrities than they were ever likely to be, it is also (from my experience anyway) true to say that the actors and singers and models just loved being in their company. One such star was actress Jane Seymour, and Hudson remembers their meetings at the Red Lion pub on the Fulham Road well.

'It would always be about 5.15 in the afternoon, after a home game, of course,' he outlined to me recently. 'A load of us players were there, and there was one particular day – she had just been chosen to star in a James Bond film, *Live and Let Die*, I think – and the atmosphere was really good. I used to see a lot of her at the Red Lion.'

The part Alan was talking about was that of 'Solitaire', and she co-starred with Roger Moore. The theme song was a massive hit for Paul McCartney and Wings.

The connection between beautiful Jane, Alan and his mates was obvious. In 1971, she married theatre director Michael Attenborough, son of Richard, who was of course Chelsea vice-chairman. Unfortunately, their marriage was a short-lived affair, as two years later they divorced.

Another Chelsea fan was Michael Crawford; probably bluer than most. He was a regular presence in the stands at Stamford Bridge. His rise to the top was very much part of '60s culture, and during the 1970s his name and that of his wife Gabrielle became linked with the club as their marriage fell apart.

Crawford had married Gabrielle in 1965. At the time she was working at the Pickwick Club, the same club where, in 1964, I had dined in the company of photographer Jeremy Fletcher after organising a publicity shoot for Larry Page's band The Pickwicks with Harry Secombe. As I have already written more than once: in this sort of environment it just goes round and round, like some Kafka-esque never-ending circle.

They divorced in 1975, Michael later citing the following reasons: 'I acquired a business manager who lost all my money through bad investments.' In 1971 he got a plum part in *No Sex Please, We're British*. 'I went into the theatre at 12.30 in the afternoon. I needed the feeling of being there, but Gabrielle wanted me home.'

Gabrielle was having an affair with Blues striker Tommy Baldwin – known as Sponge. They were undoubtedly what is termed today 'an item'. Alan Hudson referred to Sponge when reminiscing about Chelsea's epic battle with Bruges, stating his nickname derived from the way he 'soaked up as much work as he'd ever done', other Chelsea players of that era maintained at the time that this moniker was all about his ability to absorb alcohol! He even used to arm-wrestle hellraiser and Hollywood superstar Richard Harris in nightclubs: no mean test of endurance, considering the Irish actor's ability as a rugby player – he represented Munster at both junior and senior level.

Tommy once summed up his whole Chelsea experience like this: 'It was a good time at Chelsea and we had a good time too. We were down the King's Road every night with all the actors and actresses. We had a real showbiz team: we had Ossie and Charlie Cooke and Alan Hudson. Boy, we used to entertain. The players don't seem to be having the same sort of fun now. We used to go to the local boozer after games and see the supporters. They would tell you if you'd had a good game or not. Nowadays, they go their own way after matches. There's not the same camaraderie.'

Tommy was a terrific player, and in my view never quite received the accolades and plaudits he deserved. Signed in 1966 from Arsenal by Docherty in part-exchange with George Graham, he remained at Stamford Bridge until 1974. By then the wheels had come off down the Fulham Road, but for any Blues fan of baby boomer age, those cavaliers of the King's Road would have been far less potent without the donkey work and vital goals of Sponge. Charlie Cooke said Baldwin was 'the perfect foil for Ossie'. And Os himself once told me that he and Tommy 'worked really well together'. Nice understatement, there, Os: in my book you were like caviar and champagne!

The tabloids made hay while the sun shone over Baldwin's relationship with Gabrielle, but frankly by the standards of today's red tops – phone hacking and all that – it was comparatively small beer, despite being emotionally disturbing for all the 'actors' concerned in the drama.

As I say, Crawford was Chelsea through and through, and even shared a flat in Kensington with FA Cup hero Dave Webb at one point.

Moving away from Stamford Bridge for a minute, it should not be forgotten that I was also knocking my pipe out plugging Rodney Marsh. Marsh was big, but unlike Ossie he was a gargantuan fish in the small pond that was QPR and Loftus Road. His skipper at the club was the shrewd midfielder with a cheeky chappie, almost Max Miller persona, Terry Venables.

Terry had made his name at Chelsea, and critics have maintained that he never quite fulfilled his true potential. As a precocious teenager he was compared by some pundits to the late and truly great Duncan Edwards, who so sadly died in the Manchester United Munich air disaster of February 1958. He was a character, and he also possessed a razor-sharp brain.

I used to regularly hang out with Venables (and Rod Marsh) at the Pizza Express in Dean Street, Soho. I did a few interviews with him for various football magazines, and the odd ghosted piece as well. At the time he was developing into quite the author. Writing in collaboration with Gordon Williams, he penned a whole procession of *Hazell* books in the 1970s, these volumes later spawning a hit TV series.

Now aged seventy-nine, Williams' writing career has been quirkily varied. Like that other creator of unique detective fiction, Belgian-born man of Paris, Georges Simenon, he began his working life as a journalist, in his case on the *Johnstone Advertiser*. After National Service, he returned to the *Advertiser* before moving to south-west England and the *Poole and Dorset Herald*.

It was during the 1960s that his career path took a turn into the world of football, a game that had always been one of his prime passions. Having ghosted a series of autobiographies for some of the sport's heavyweights, most notably Tommy Docherty – whose story he once described as 'a stream of consciousness on a par with *Ulysses*' – and Bobby Moore, he went on to become Chelsea's commercial manager.

I first met him in 1971, soon after the publication of *They Used to Play on Grass*, a futuristic football novel written in conjunction with his old mucker, Terry Venables. Williams' most famous – some would say infamous – book, *The Siege of Trencher's Farm*, had been published two years before. The film version, *Straw Dogs*, starring Dustin Hoffman and Susan George, was about to hit the screens, and to put it mildly, create quite a stir.

Williams himself described Sam Peckinpah's film as 'utter crap', and to this day remains utterly embarrassed that, despite refusing to write the script, his name is associated with the cinematic end-product. Initially, Roman Polanski was to direct the movie, but in the end the gig was given to Peckinpah, a man Williams obviously overtly loathed. In fact he has gone on record as saying that, in his view, 'the man (Peckinpah) was sick'.

Gordon's literary relationship with Venables prospered later in the decade with the launch of the first of their *Hazell* books, written under the bizarre nom de plume of P.B Yuill.

'My name is James Hazell and I'm the biggest bastard who ever pushed your bell-button.' Those words essentially encapsulate Hazell's persona: a cocky cockney version of Raymond Chandler's Philip Marlowe or Dashiell Hammet's Sam Spade. The books were well received and in 1978 made an extremely successful transition to the small screen with twenty-two one-hour long episodes, running for two years.

Nicholas Ball starred as Hazell, and there were several in-joke names used in the series. For example, Hazell's lawyer Gordon Gregory worked for 'Venables, Venables, Williams and Gregory'; reference here to the two authors and QPR's chairman at the time, Jim Gregory. One of the villains is named Keith O'Rourke – the surname the same as that of QPR striker John O'Rourke. A former Chelsea player, by the way, he was also at Arsenal. For a short while I was his agent, but that's another story.

The most riotous evening I ever spent with him was at his flat somewhere in Chelsea. The living room was large – you could have described it as a drawing room without being called a snob – and I was there with Marsh and Venables. We had had a long, liquid lunch at Pizza Express, and for some reason found ourselves at Gordon's gaff. The drink continued to flow, and after an hour or three both Rod and Terry left. I stayed with Gordon, and we talked, or more accurately he did, because he possessed a beautiful turn of phrase. I loved his Scottish accent, which reminded me so much of Charlie Cooke and also of those days of watching *The White Heather Club* on the box on New Year's Eve.

He was entertaining, and I probably sounded very young and very naïve to this man of the world, who had seen life at a level that I had never experienced during my feather-bed existence. Someone once told me that Gordon had once been a card-carrying member of the British Communist Party, but I never did manage to suss out his political leanings. Anyway, in my estimation some of the best people were at one time in their lives full-blown Commies.

We spoke, naturally enough, about Chelsea and Ossie and Charlie Cooke. I told him how much I admired Charlie's intellect and what a change it was to meet a professional footballer who was actually excited about literature. I explained that Cooke was a Hemingway man, and he expressed surprise. As glasses were recharged and then recharged again, the conversation deteriorated into that typical limbo land when everything that is said seems on the surface either pithy or witty, before drunkenness itself sets in.

The next thing I know, Gordon is offering me a joint. Not any old joint, but one packed with the Beluga of cannabis resin, and as easy to drag on as a handmade gasper. More chat; probably more nonsense from me. Then suddenly I sort of come round and announce that I had better head home. So I telephoned for a minicab – it was Meadway Radio Cars, based in London NW11 – and waited, still puffing, almost dementedly, on the grass.

What with the booze and the joint, I was by now in 'pretentious moi' territory, saying things to Gordon like: 'Art is like a drug in the sense that perceptions are altered.' Well, my perceptions were being altered, but it had nothing at all to do with art.

By now I couldn't care a sod about anything, so when old Gordon handed me a tin of the stuff to take back with me, I thanked him profusely, and proceeded to light up another joint. Still gassing away, we were, when the cab arrived. There was a big smile on my young face as I held this illegal cigarette in my right hand, which by now had gone out.

The Meadway driver was one of those cockney drivers of the old school: friendly, polite and at the same time talkative. He was also a bloke not worried about ferrying a 'dope fiend' in his car, because as I relit my joint and told him naïvely what I was doing, he didn't bat an eyelid.

During the journey we somehow got on to the subject of football, and when I told him of my relationship with some of the Chelsea players and Peter Osgood in particular, his sleepy-looking eyes lit up. Yes. He was a fan. It was very late and the London traffic was light, but I got the impression my driver was taking me the long way round primarily because he wanted to talk football.

Eventually we arrived in the genteel, quiet serenity that is Hampstead Garden Suburb, and I said farewell to this chatty cabby. Still clutching my elongated joint, I handed him a hefty tip.

Meadway Radio Cars: not a name to conjure with, but it does have one claim to fame. Back in the 1980s, at the height of Maggie Thatcher's 'loads o' money' yuppies, one of the company's founders, a corpulent character lacking in intellect but blessed with a barrow boy's innate sharpness called Harry Shulman (a rough diamond who was more 'rough' than 'diamond'), was – as was very often the case – short of ready money. The reasons for this were numerous, but his main problem was that, amongst other things, he was a gambling addict. He would win and lose vast sums on the tables at the Sportsman Casino on Tottenham Court Road. In fact he once sold the number plate of his way-past-its-sell-by-date Jaguar, YUP1, for over £20,000 just to fuel his habit!

FOURTEEN

EUROPEAN GLORY AND THE ATHENS TRIO

Chelsea's final three league games in 1971 were undistinguished affairs: a 2–1 home win over Coventry City. Then a mere forty-eight hours later, a 1–0 defeat at the hands of Burnley at a sparsely populated Stamford Bridge – the attendance was just 14,356 – and the season was rounded off with a goalless draw at Ipswich. So, come 1 May, and the table saw the Blues in sixth spot, just behind Liverpool on goal average, having suffered nine defeats.

Arsenal finished top of the tree, fifteen points clear of Sexton's boys. They also lifted the FA Cup, collecting their first-ever double. But there were no Champions' League places to be obsessed about in those days, and it is worth noting that Chelsea's points tally was just one shy of third-placed Spurs.

There was a small incident which involved me turning my ankle over in a pothole in Hampstead. This 'nothing event' confirmed to me what I had always thought about the so-called cocky, Jack the lad merchants such as Os, Marsh and Venables.

To the fans on the terraces these were ultra-confident young men, who revelled in showing off. Some people called them 'flash bastards', but I knew this was far from the truth. Anyway, let us get back to my ankle turning: it blew up like a balloon, which necessitated the wearing of a decrepit slipper, and utilising an old hand-me-down walking stick which belonged to my father.

The first time Os saw me walking with a pronounced limp, battered slipper on my right foot and clutching my stick, he gave me the nickname of 'Hoppy'. Walking along the Strand one afternoon towards Fleet Street, he even helped me across the road in the manner of a Good Samaritan assisting some doddery elderly lady. I tried to tell him there was nothing seriously wrong with my foot, but he insisted on doing what he obviously felt was the right thing. I felt somewhat of a fraud, and when I protested, he just smiled and continued to call me 'Hoppy'.

Now, this insignificant event confirmed what I always knew. These guys were brimful of compassion and genuine warmth: their on-stage persona was just a performance in the manner of an actor or a singer. Gordon Williams summed it all up neatly when he said that Terry Venables, for example, was 'a very serious introverted guy – the cheeky cockney chappie was a total act'.

Athens on 19 May 1971 gave the impression of being a much more democratic city than Salonika. Eight months had passed since that edgy and bizarre opening tussle in UEFA's number two tourney, and the Fascist junta continued to run the show in the country that, ironically, gave birth to democracy.

However, the European Cup Winners' Cup Final was a major event in the country's capital, and with all the UEFA big cheeses in attendance plus other dignitaries, the Greek authorities were determined to put on what they considered their 'kinder liberal face'.

The stars of Real Madrid were in a perverse way the perfect opponents for Chelsea. At the time Spain was still being ruled by Fascist dictator, General Franco, who incidentally was himself a fanatical fan of Real. So, despite the glossing-over of the venue and its nasty political overtones and such things as censorship and torture by so many politicians who prided themselves on being democrats, the VIP areas of the stadium were full of self-confessed Fascists. You could say that the game's powerbrokers lacked any semblance of moral gumption.

45,000 supporters were packed into the Karaiskakis Stadium (plus the phalanx of Fascists). The stadium was part of Greek history, having been built as a velodrome for the first modern Olympics in 1896. It was named after a Greek hero, General Georgios Karaiskakis, who helped to defeat the Turks in the revolution of 1821. He was eventually slain not far from the environs of the stadium complex itself.

The Chelsea players knew they would be in for a tough encounter, but as Alan Hudson told me: 'They (Real) were obviously a very good side, but a mere shadow of their pre-decessors. I saw the early '60s version, when they made the European Cup their own personal property. Di Stefano, Puskas, Gento, Kopa and Santamaria: they were a football Hall of Fame.'

Francisco Gento was a dazzling winger who collected 43 caps for Spain and won the European Cup on no less than six occasions with Real Madrid – an unmatched record. But come the Chelsea face-off, he was now three years off forty, a bit on the portly side, and much of his famous oomph and zest had dissipated.

One Real Madrid player more than any other tickled Hudson's fancy: 'Easily their best player was midfielder Pirri, who was beautifully balanced and played the game as I like it played. Chess again. He used his teammates like pawns, working gambits. At the very highest level of a European competition, it really was like playing chess in a top champi-onship: a battle without armour, a war without blood.'

Jose Martinez Sanchez, aka 'Pirri', represented Real Madrid for fifteen years from 1964–1979, winning ten La Liga titles, and the 1966 European Champions' Cup. He gained 41 caps for Spain and after retiring, qualified as a doctor, working for his club's medical staff.

Looking back through the mists of time, Huddy told me that 'Pirri began running the first half – he looked in complete con-trol. But Os put us in front with one of his beauties, and for a very long time it looked as if that would win us the final, but Pirri had other ideas, by pushing on his troops with some masterly football, and with just twenty seconds left, they hit us with an equaliser, Zicco capitalising on a mistake by John Dempsey'.

It has to be remembered that this European showpiece took place some years before the days of penalty shoot-outs and an unhealthy reliance on television money. But even when this is taken into consideration, my mind boggled when I learnt that the UEFA blazers, in their infinite wisdom, had made no plans for a replay!

After a great deal of bureaucratic humming and hawing, it was decided that the rematch should take place two days later at the same venue. This caused problems aplenty, not just for the Chelsea faithful that had made the trip via various packages costing up to £24 (serious folding stuff in '71), but also for players and media people.

One incident, which highlights how times have changed in over forty years, revolves around Chelsea's John Hollins, and was told to me by Alan Hudson. It seems that Hollins was due to be best man at a wedding, and his mother told him he couldn't stay for the replay!

I'll let Hudson take up the story: 'Thursday was ordered as a rest day. Dave Sexton gave instructions that although we needed liquid intake, alcohol was banned. I went off to the market, with drinking the last thing on my mind. I was struggling with an injury to my thigh, and the thought of facing Pirri with a dodgy thigh and a hangover would have been very costly. That long Thursday was solitary and had an almost surreal quality about it because as lunchtime approached, Os, Charlie and Tommy (Baldwin) strolled up to the pool bar at the Athens Hilton, as if on a mission. I cannot in my wildest dreams think of who suggested such an afternoon and why, or can I? Of course I can, it was Osgood, and only because he thought he'd score again. He did!

'It must have been about ninety degrees and there they were downing these tropical punches like they were on an end-of-season-tour or family holiday. Surely they couldn't have forgotten about tomorrow? Here we were, going into the most important match in our lives, and these three were throwing these drinks down them as if tomorrow never came. And had Dave been tipped off, they would have been on the next flight home. I swear when I looked at them I had to check my own head, for they looked like we had won the match the night before and were celebrating.

'Os was wearing a striped shirt that I think he wore after the match the following night, with a pair of Chelsea shorts and sandals. As I left, he raised his glass one last time and said, "Rest your leg, son, don't worry, leave it all to me".

The three mavericks were three completely different characters, but as Hudson has said, 'If you put them together you had a very powerful concoction'.

Alan did actually challenge Peter Osgood about his eccentric pre-match build-up for what was probably Chelsea's most important ever fixture. But he simply sent Hudson back to the hotel with these words: 'Go home and have an early night, son, and leave it to me. I will win us the game.'

In Hudson's own words, 'It was the most frightening confidence, bordering on the ridiculous and arrogance, a sort of blindness, but he had done it time and time again. Absolutely nothing and nobody fazed him.'

And come match number two, Os was true to his word, putting away with aplomb the Blues' second goal, which proved to be the winner. Chelsea's first goal had come from an unlikely source: centre-half John Dempsey, who fired home with a venomous volley. Os' goal was instigated by the battling Baldwin, who passed to the King, and he thundered the ball into the Madrid net.

It was 'squeaky bum time' for Blues fans in the second half, with Fleitas halving the Londoners' advantage with just fifteen minutes left. Then, right on full-time, Bonetti made a save that showed why he bore the nickname of 'The Cat'.

Hudson has christened the threesome 'The Athens Hilton Party', and admitted to me, 'They in fact probably stole the show. They were involved in both the goals that put us on the brink of the club's first-ever European success. They made a mockery of everything surrounding how to prepare for a football match, and they broke every rule in the book along the way. These three players just sat there relaxing with the look of holidaymakers who had earned a long awaited summer holiday. We playboys had now broken new ground in my first two seasons!'

Chelsea's defeat of Real Madrid 2–1 – even a Real side shorn of the class of bygone years – never quite received the accolades that it deserved. But what it did confirm was that if manager Sexton could keep this squad together and somehow manage to instil more consistency as well as that 'it' factor – the ability to prevail when performing badly – then the future at Stamford Bridge looked to be a bright one; one dominated by a constant lifting of trophies. The fact that this never transpired was the fault of men not attempting to understand the human psyche.

It was Groundhog Day down the Fulham Road, as the players drove in triumph past their adoring fans holding aloft their European prize. It didn't quite have that feeling of unadulterated euphoria that so dominated the post-FA Cup-winning revels, but it still was something to behold.

By now the 1960s' atmosphere, which had continued to pervade the early years of the '70s, was changing; not markedly at first, but as the 1971–72 season approached, life in Britain was starting to have a starker look about it, as class confrontation and strikes reappeared on the landscape with ever-increasing frequency and seriousness.

In many ways, Chelsea's season mirrored that of the fortunes of the country: so many what ifs: so many let-downs. One point from the first four First Division encounters of the new campaign was a paltry return for such a talented squad.

In Europe, their opening game in the Cup Winners' Cup was easy-peasy in its truest sense, as Os smashed all the net-finding records with a hat-trick in the first leg of the tie with Luxembourg outfit Jeunesse Hautcharage in an 8–0 canter. And then in the second leg, he bagged five in Chelsea's all-time European record score, which stands to this day, of 13–0.

I watched this travesty of a football match against the amateurs from the Duchy (who included in their line-up a guy with one arm, and another wearing spectacles) from the old stand up in the stars that made the protagonists on the park resemble Subbuteo figures. I sat there in the company of Os' sister Mandy, herself a footballer of outstanding ability, bewildered by what I was witnessing on the pitch: these amateurs from the land of the radio station (208 on the medium wave) that enlivened so many teenagers' lives in the 1950s and early '60s were in all honesty of pub-team class.

Frankly, the lifting of the Luxembourg Cup by Hautcharage was a miracle in itself. The club was based in a picturesque village of some 700 people, and participated in the country's third tier. The 4–1 extra-time victory over one of the Duchy's football superpowers, Jeunesse Esch, was pure David defeating Goliath, and the owners of a local brewery were so overjoyed by this unprecedented success that it offered free beer to the village for three days! Their own dinky home ground was far too small to host the first leg, having a capacity of no more than a 1,000 or so. As such, it was decided to move the game to the national stadium in the capital and 13,000 spectators paid through the turnstiles to witness what was in effect lambs to the slaughter.

Next up were Åtvidabergs of Sweden. Despite being several classes above the bakers and candlestick makers of Luxembourg, a comfortable passage to round three was predicted. But the inconsistency that had dogged Sexton's charges since day one of the season continued unabated.

A 0–0 score line in Sweden was a dour affair, but Ossie and co were expected to up the ante at the Bridge in the second game. That they failed to do so was down to their profligacy in front of goal, highlighted by John Hollins' failure to convert from the penalty spot. The final score was 1–1, with Hudson notching for the Blues, but the Cup holders went out to an outfit of part-timers, on the away goals rule. The 25,000 fans went home shaking their heads in disbelief. Was this new era of glory about to implode?

The answer was no with a capital N, for 'Chopper' Harris and his men, no doubt chastened by the Åtvidabergs experience and the subsequent criticism of their performance, buckled down and proceeded to produce the goods, resulting in an 11-game unbeaten run in all competitions. Yes, the Blues were back on track.

The victories included a memorable 3–2 home win over Spurs in the first leg of the League Cup semi-final three days before Christmas, but a 1–0 reverse at Derby on New Year's Day was a blip, and the first day of 1972 saw them in a mid-table position of tenth.

The decisive second leg of the semi-final with Spurs on 5 January was a stormy affair, with Chelsea scraping into the final 5–4 on aggregate, thanks to goals from Hudson and a Hollins spot-kick.

According to Hudson: 'Os had a running battle with Mike England all night.'

However, seven days before the final with Stoke, they suffered an embarrassing 3–2 FA Cup fifth round defeat at Second Division Orient, despite at one stage leading 2–0, Osgood and Webb on target.

Then to the League Cup Final itself at Wembley Stadium on Saturday 4 March, which in so many respects was the precursor to the break-up of that flamboyant Blues side that so encapsulated the spirit of the age. There was, however, an aspect of the pre-final build-up that did much to enhance the Kings of King's Road's rock 'n' roll credentials, and what better way to do this than with a top-five hit record. Welcome to 'Blue is the Colour', produced by the 'Teenage Rage' of the 1950s, Larry Page. The man who, back in '64, had paid for my slap-up feast at the Pickwick Club. Talk about life going round and round in never-ending circles!

'Blue is the Colour' was released on 26 February 1972 on Penny Farthing Records. In March, it reached number five in the charts, and the Chelsea team members who made the record under Page's direction appeared on BBC TV's flagship show, *Top of The Pops*.

'We appeared just the once on *Top of The Pops*,' Alan Hudson told me. 'I think if we'd won the final against Stoke, the record would have made number one. After the show we joined up with Babs and a couple of the other Pan's People at Alexander's in Chelsea – it was a great night.'

'What did you get for being part of such a successful pop disc?' I asked.

'Just a tax bill!' quipped the former Chelsea midfielder. 'One thing in particular I remember about the recording was that as we approached the studios, I noticed that The Bee Gees were leaving. And when we reached the main door they were walking towards us, having just finished their recording.

They looked at us, and we looked at them. It was almost surreal. Anyway, their record was not a hit, but ours was massive, which just goes to show what can happen. I also remember what I was wearing that day, it was a white cashmere polo neck sweater from Cecil Gee.

'These days the record is played before each and every home game, but I receive nothing for that.'

Hudson also started to make friends in the rock music world, most notably with Frank Allen of The Searchers, which brings me to my own brief 'association' with the hit 1960s group. In 1964, I had a meeting with their manager Les Ackerley – our company was about to launch some Searchers pennants. He immediately struck me as the archetypal Northern showbiz promoter of the time, blunt and to the point. He chain-smoked and consumed a new cocktail that supposedly contained monkey glands; a drink that was meant to keep you looking more youthful. Well, judging from Les' looks, it had failed miserably.

As for Frank Allen, he had replaced bass guitarist Tony Jackson in their line-up in 1964, and was soon involved in the smash-hit 'When You Walk in the Room', a record notable for the first use of the electric twelve-string guitar.

Another rock star to befriend Hudson was a true icon – The Who's Keith Moon. Hudson and Allen would often spend their evenings in Moon's company at the La Chasse club in Soho. I saw Moon and his mates live more than once in 1964, and they were sensational – what a noise! What a racket! No wonder I am a tinnitus sufferer these days!

'Blue is the Colour' has true cult status, and has been covered by various singers in a host of different countries. In what was then Czechoslovakia, Frantisek Ringo Cech came out with a version called 'Zelena je trava' (Green is The Grass), which became a popular football anthem in that country

In 1972 the Danish Olympic team used the tune as their anthem, 'Rod-hvide farver' (Red and White Colours). Six years later, the ditty was re-recorded as 'White is the Colour' for the Vancouver Whitecaps soccer team, and sold enough copies to become a minor Canadian hit.

One version which never appealed to ardent Chelsea fans was the one used by the Tory Party for their successful General Election campaign in 1979. The late Tony Banks, ardent Chelsea fan and Labour MP and minster was one such objector. Here the words were changed to, 'Blue is the Colour, Maggie is her name; we're all together' etc.

Speaking of the late and lamented Tony Banks, who died in 2006 aged sixty-three, one player from the Kings of King's Road era to become close to the Labour politician in the 1990s was Alan Hudson. Banks helped Alan launch his highly acclaimed autobiography, *The Working Man's Ballet*, at a reception at the House of Commons. As Huddy said of the former MP for Newham North West: 'Tony was a real one-off, and a real fan of the club.'

Hudson more than hinted to me that number one would have been theirs for the taking, if the boys had clinched their third pot in as many years. And certainly, it was a major upset when the ageing Stoke outfit prevailed 2–1, with thirty-five-year-old George Eastham claiming the winner after Ossie had brought Chelsea back level, following Terry Conroy's opener.

Some twenty-six years later, Peter Osgood gave me his impressions of the final. 'They had some real gems in their line-up. You know, any side with the likes of Gordon Banks, George Eastham and Peter Dobing had to be respected. I suppose you could say in boxing terms we deserved to win on points. But they got the vital goal when Peter Bonetti blocked Jimmy Greenhoff's shot only for George Eastham to follow up and score from about a yard.'

The final fifteen minutes saw a non-stop siege of the Stoke goal, but Banks was in inspired form. For Stoke, it was their first major trophy in 109 years. As for the Blues, to quote Bob Dylan's 1965 classic song, you could say 'It's all over now, Baby Blue'.

'We did enough to win three Cup Finals,' Hudson pointed out.

In First Division terms the season ended with just the one victory from the last six games, and the final position of seventh represented something of a backward step.

FIFTEEN

AUSTERITY AND THE BIG BREAK UP

Industrial action was the curse of Great Britain during the early years of the 1970s. Despite general improvements in living standards, it was essentially a period of what was termed 'stagflation', and a return to a massive rise in unemployment. By 1973, inflation was a staggering 20 per cent.

At the 1971 Annual Conference of the National Union of Mineworkers, it was decided to ask for a 43 per cent pay rise, at a time when the Tory Government of beleaguered Prime Minister Edward Heath was willing to offer a figure of between 7 and 8 per cent. In late '71, the miners voted to take industrial action if their pay demands were not met in full.

So, on 5 January 1972, the NUM Executive Committee rejected out-of-hand a small pay increase put on the table by the National Coal Board, who then just two days later withdrew all pay offers. On 9 January, miners from all over Great Britain came out on strike.

On 9 February a state of emergency was declared, and three days later, the three-day working week was introduced, coupled with a programme of daily power-cuts: Heath's leadership of the country lasted a mere three years and 259 days, but it was packed with crisis after crisis. All the optimism that had been engendered during the 1960s had dissolved. And in so many ways, Chelsea FC was the perfect microcosm of this.

Soon after the Stoke disappointment, one of the club's three prime showmen was on his way when Charlie Cooke signed for Crystal Palace for £85,000. There was a touch of pure irony when he later re-signed for the Blues in 1974, the same year that saw both Hudson and Osgood depart.

Their league form was patchy, with a final placing of twelfth being the club's worst top-flight ranking since the relegation season of 1961–62. They again displayed their pedigree in knockout situations, by reaching the FA Cup quarter-finals, losing to Arsenal 2–1 at Highbury after a 1–1 draw at the Bridge. In the League Cup the team went one better, bowing out to Norwich City at the semi-final stage.

Ossie did collect one particular accolade during this season, when his goal against Arsenal in their first FA Cup meeting was voted goal of the season.

On a personal level, my phone was not chirping merrily as it once did, and even when Vince Powell called me about using some footballers in a new TV comedy series he had planned, he asked for not just Ossie, but 'a few more, to include players from other clubs'.

I told him I could get a couple of QPR players (Don Givens and Phil Parkes) plus Charlie Cooke and Os, and Vince seemed happy enough. But it just wasn't the same. Life was constantly changing, and the 1960s hedonists were no longer of much interest to either the media or the public at large. Dealing with power cuts and the cost of living had driven the fun out of life. Again to quote Dylan: 'A Hard Rain's A-Gonna Fall.'

By now Rodney Marsh had mooched off from QPR to Manchester City for £200,000, so it came as no surprise when he phoned me to terminate our business relationship. He was probably right: for me, a player had to be based in London. Having to swan up to Manchester on a regular basis was never on for me, particularly as by now our Star Posters operation was buzzing with new lines.

These 'new lines' sold by the bucket, but this gave me no pleasure at all, for gone were the bohemian and rebellious designs and posters of stars like John Lennon and Jimi Hendrix and Frank Zappa, to be replaced by David Cassidy and Donny Osmond, yuck!

I was also now mired in a series of personal crises, and my life seemed to be caught in a rut of producing rubbish that was popular. I tried to break out by putting pen to paper and producing articles for several more intelligent but poorly-paid journals, but this failed to change my mood.

At Stamford Bridge, the celebs were still in situ, but to say that the mood was not good would be an understatement. Os' relationship with boss Sexton, which had often verged on fragile in the past, was now seemingly at an all-time low, and Hudson was also having regular run-ins with the manager.

Season 1973–74: knocked out of the FA Cup in round three by QPR (1–0 in a replay) and dismissed from the League Cup at the first hurdle by Stoke, again 1–0. And in the league, they ended the campaign in seventeenth spot, just five points clear of second-from-bottom relegated Manchester United.

For Ossie there was one shining light: his recall to the England team on 14 November 1973 for the confrontation with Italy. It was his Wembley international debut, and as he told me some twenty-six years later, it was a game that remained high on his list of 'Great Matches'.

'I really turned it on that evening. The Italy coach said after the game that I was the most talented player on the park.

'Even Don Revie, never my number one fan, who took over from Alf (Ramsey) a year later as national boss was ecstatic about my all-round display. Everything to do with the Italy game was tinged with irony. It was my England Wembley debut, and at the same time, my final game for my country. It was also Sir Alf's last match in charge as England boss in this country. It was also Bobby Moore's 108th and last international.

'The fact that Don Revie eulogised all over the shop about me makes me smile even to this day.'

Another little fact about the encounter was that Italy's 86th minute winner in their 1–0 victory was put away by a future England manager. Yes, you've guessed it – one Fabio Capello!

Then in January 1974, all the underlying tensions that existed between Peter Osgood and Alan Hudson on one side and Dave Sexton on the other simmered ever more violently, and subsequently boiled over in the manner of a saucepan of milk left unattended on the cooker. The big break up was

imminent: the Kings of King's Road, as exciting and as exu-
berant a bunch of players that had ever been seen at the
Bridge were slowly but surely decamping and going their
separate ways.

Hudson has told me of his friendship with Eddie
McCreadie, who these days lives in the Southern States of
America. Eddie has real heart, and knowing how much Alan
had suffered following the road accident in December 1997
in which he so nearly lost his life, and knowing that subsequently his friend had had to endure no less than seventy
further operations, the Scotsman invited him out to his house
across the pond. 'He and his wife really looked after me,'
Alan told me.

And it was following a drinking session with his 'best mate'
that the ongoing schism with Sexton turned separation into
divorce. The following day, the manager confronted Alan,
accusing him of smelling of booze; essentially telling him in
no uncertain terms that the midfielder's alcohol consumption
was one of the main reasons why Chelsea were dropping
points. In a real 'all for one, and one for all' gesture, Ossie
spoke up in Hudson's defence, stating that he had been the
team's best player all season.

A few days later more 'words' were exchanged, this
time even more acrimonious than before, and the upshot
was that both players were placed on the transfer list, with
Sexton insisting that he had been trying to get Hudson out
of the club for a very long time, which was an odd response
considering that the manager turned down the midfielder's
previous transfer requests and had stated that 'you would
leave this club over my dead body'.

As Hudson wrote recently: 'I once bumped into tennis star
Tom Okker – 'The Flying Dutchman' – in Alexander's. He'd
obviously had more than just a couple of Heinekens, I say
that Dave (Sexton) wouldn't have liked it, knowing that Tom
had been out relaxing, having a wonderful meal on the night
before a big match on the Centre Court at Wimbledon. No,
you must be tucked up with your following day's instructions
in your hands.'